Ethics, Leadership, and the Bottom Line

D1364811

Ethics, Leadership, and the Bottom Line

CHARLES A. NELSON
&
ROBERT D. CAVEY
Editors

NORTH RIVER PRESS
CROTON-ON-HUDSON,
NEW YORK

PUBLIC LIBRARY, PLAINFIELD, N.J.

174.4
E+37

© 1991 by Charles A. Nelson and Robert D. Cavey. All
rights reserved. Except for review purposes, no part of this
work may be reproduced or transmitted in any form or by any
means, electronic or mechanical, including photocopy,
recording, or any information retrieval system, without the
written permission of the publisher.
For copyright and permission information for each article,
see the first page of each article.

Library of Congress Cataloging-in-Publication Data

Ethics, leadership, and the bottom line
    Charles A. Nelson & Robert D. Cavey, editors.
        p.   cm.
    Includes bibliographical references and index.
    ISBN 0-88427-081-5
    1. Business ethics. I. Nelson, Charles A. II. Cavey, Robert D.,
1952– .
HF5387.E85   1990
174'.4—dc20   90-14161
                                                                CIP

Manufactured in the United States of America

North River Press
Box 309
Croton-on-Hudson, NY 10520

3 9510 2000 2664 2

CONTENTS

CHAPTER 3:

Corporate Codes of Ethics:
Are They Effective?
What Should They Contain?

CHAPTER 4:

Are Good Ethics Good Business?

CHAPTER 8:

What Difference Does Leadership Make?

The Authors

WALTER ADAMS *is Distinguished University Professor and Past President, Michigan State University*

PAUL ASQUITH *is a visiting associate professor at the Sloan School of Management at the Massachusetts Institute of Technology*

BERNARD AVISHAI *is an associate editor of the* Harvard Business Review

ARCHIE J. BAHM *is Professor of Philosophy Emeritus at the University of New Mexico*

RICHARD BEHAR *writes for* Time *Magazine*

RUSSELL P. BOISJOLY *is Associate Dean of the School of Business, Fairfield University, Connecticut*

JAMES W. BROCK *is Professor of Economics, Miami University, Ohio*

YALE BROZEN *is Professor of Business Economics, Graduate School of Business, University of Chicago*

JIMMY CARTER *was 39th President of the United States, 1977–1981*

WINSTON S. CHURCHILL *(1874–1965) was British Prime Minister, 1940–1945 and 1951–1955*

ELLEN FOSTER CURTIS *is Associate Professor of Management, University of Lowell, Massachusetts*

RICHARD G. DARMAN *is Director of the Office of Management and Budget, Executive Office of the President, Washington D.C.*

EDWIN J. DELATTRE *is Olin Resident Scholar in Applied Ethics and Professor of Education at Boston University*

PETER DRUCKER, *writer and consultant, is Clarke Professor of Social Sciences, Claremont Graduate School, California*

AMITAI ETZIONI *is Visiting Professor at the Harvard Business School and University Professor at George Washington University*

LAWRENCE G. FOSTER *is Corporate Vice President of Public Relations, Johnson & Johnson*

BENJAMIN FRANKLIN *(1706–1790) was an American diplomat, author, scientist and inventor*

MILTON FRIEDMAN *is Senior Research Fellow at the Hoover Institution on War, Revolution and Peace*

BRETT DUVAL FROMSON *writes for* Fortune

HERBERT HOOVER *(1874–1964) was Secretary of Commerce in the Coolidge Administration and President of the United States, 1929–1933*

LARUE T. HOSMER *is Professor of Policy and Control at the Graduate School of Business Administration of the University of Michigan*

ROBERT JOHNSON *writes for* The Wall Street Journal

HERBERT JOHNSTON *was Professor in the Department of Philosophy, University of Notre Dame*

IRVING KRISTOL *is Senior Fellow at the American Enterprise Institute*

EUGENE MELLICAN *is Chairperson of the Philosophy Department, University of Lowell, Massachusetts*

DAVID W. MULLINS, JR., *is a Governor of the Federal Reserve Board*

NATHANIEL C. NASH *writes for* The New York Times

MARY ELLEN OLIVERIO *is Professor of Accounting, Graduate School of Business, Pace University, New York*

FRANKLIN D. ROOSEVELT *(1882–1945) was 32nd President of the United States, 1933–1945*

LINCOLN STEFFENS *(1866–1936) was an American author and journalist*

BENJAMIN J. STEIN *writes for* Barron's

HERBERT STEIN, *former Chairman of the President's Council of Economic Advisers, is an American Enterprise Institute Fellow*

JAMES STERNGOLD *writes for* The New York Times
ALEXIS DE TOCQUEVILLE *(1805–1859) was a French statesman and author*
ALFRED NORTH WHITEHEAD *(1861–1947) was an English philosopher and mathematician*
OLIVER F. WILLIAMS *is a Catholic priest and a member of the faculty of the Department of Management at the University of Notre Dame*
ERIC D. WOLFF *is now an employee of the United States Department of Justice*

Preface

Business leaders find themselves today in the devilish position of coming into their greatest global influence at a time when there is no widely accepted agreement on how properly to link business power and responsibility. While the Soviet Union and most of Eastern Europe are displaying an unprecedented eagerness to learn how to function in a market economy, and socialist regimes in other parts of the world are abandoning state-regulated economies in favor of private enterprise, at home in the United States the savings and loan scandals, the excesses of the merger and breakup schemes and other such business activity have led many observers to doubt the ability of corporations to function responsibly in the absence of heavy regulation.

Nevertheless, the prospect of increased government controls generates little of the enthusiasm that has accompanied such efforts in the past. We now know from experience that regulation carries with it inevitable evils—bureaucratic insensitivity, indifference to changing business conditions, and, not least, a weakening of the sense of moral responsibility on the part of those regulated, since there is always someone else to blame for failure. So the question remains whether business leaders can develop sufficient moral responsibility for the consequences of their decisions to forestall a return to increased regulation as the only acceptable—however flawed—response.

Although ethics in business has long been a subject of discussion in the United States, no tradition of business ethics has gained general unchallenged acceptance. Such ideas and convic-

tions about ethics in business as are current today are nevertheless rooted in America's past experience and traditional principles. But these cannot be reduced to simple and unambiguous
propositions to provide a firm moral rudder. How, then, can
executives avoid identifying their personal interests too closely
with those of the corporation? And how can they sustain a concern for the public interest when it appears to conflict with the
bottom-line requirements of the business?

There is also a deeper problem. We are no longer confident of
our ability to work out an ethics of business because we are
apparently, as a people, less confident about our elementary
ideas of right and wrong. Walter Lippmann described this issue a
generation ago as "the crisis within the Western society":

> When Sartre, following Nietzsche, says that "God is dead," the
> critical point is . . . that "if I have done away with God the
> Father, someone is needed to invent values, . . . and value is
> nothing but the meaning you choose" . . . If what is good, what
> is right, what is true is only what the individual "chooses" to
> "invent," then we are outside the traditions of civility.

Despite the prevailing skepticism, we are inclined to the belief
that ethical questions can be penetrated by an informed mind
free of doctrinairism. Our guiding maxim is drawn from Alfred
North Whitehead's essay on "Foresight," which serves as a pro-
logue to the book:

> A great society is a society in which its men of business think
> greatly of their functions.

The present anthology reflects our effort to draw upon the past
to shed light on the future for the benefit of those executives who
take an interest in the larger significance of their professional
activities.

We believe that the ethical issues that business leaders confront
—or should confront—are often complex, frequently disquieting,
and worthy of the same closely reasoned attention that one
expects from a competent engineer or financial analyst. As several of our authors suggest, the continuing search for the rational

foundations underlying ethical practices in business deserves the attention of our best minds.

Charles A. Nelson
Robert D. Cavey

Ethics, Leadership, and the
Bottom Line

ALFRED NORTH WHITEHEAD

A Great Society is a Society in Which Its Men of Business Think Greatly of Their Functions

. . . The recent shortening of the time-span between notable changes in social customs is very obvious, if we examine history. . . . If we compare the technologies of civilizations west of Mesopotamia at the epochs 100 A.D., the culmination of the Roman Empire, and 1400 A.D., the close of the Middle Ages, we find practically no advance in technology. There was some gain in metallurgy, some elaboration of clockwork, the recent invention of gun powder with its influence all in the future, some advance in the art of navigation, also with its influence in the future. If we compare 1400 A.D., with 1700 A.D., there is a great advance; gunpowder, and printing, and navigation, and the technique of commerce, had produced their effect. But even then, the analogy between life in the eighteenth century and life in the great period of ancient Rome was singularly close, so that the peculiar relevance of Latin literature was felt vividly. In the fifty years between 1780 and 1830, a number of inventions came with a rush into effective operation. The age of steam power and of machinery was introduced. But for two generations, from 1830 to

Excerpted from *Adventures of Ideas* by Alfred North Whitehead. Harmonsworth, Middlesex, England: Penguin (Pelican Books), 1933.

1890, there was a singular uniformity in the principles of technology which were regulating the structure of society and the usages of business.

The conclusion to be drawn from this survey is a momentous one. Our sociological theories, our political philosophy, our practical maxims of business, our political economy, and our doctrines of education, are derived from an unbroken tradition of great thinkers and of practical examples, from the age of Plato in the fifth century before Christ to the end of the last century. The whole of this tradition is warped by the vicious assumption that each generation will substantially live amid the conditions governing the lives of its fathers and will transmit those conditions to mould with equal force the lives of its children. We are living in the first period of human history for which this assumption is false.

Of course in the past, there were great catastrophes: for example, plagues, floods, barbarian invasions. But, if such catastrophes were warded off, there was a stable, well-known condition of civilized life. This assumption subtly pervades the premises of political economy, and has permitted it to confine attention to a simplified edition of human nature. It is at the basis of our conception of the reliable business man, who has mastered a technique and never looks beyond his contracted horizon. It colours our political philosophy and our educational theory, with their overwhelming emphasis on past experience. The note of recurrence dominates the wisdom of the past, and still persists in many forms even where explicitly the fallacy of its modern application is admitted. The point is that in the past the time-span of important change was considerably longer than that of a single human life. Thus mankind was trained to adapt itself to fixed conditions.

Today this time-span is considerably shorter than that of human life, and accordingly our training must prepare individuals to face a novelty of conditions. But there can be no preparation for the unknown. It is at this point that we recur to the immediate topic, Foresight. We require such an understanding of the present conditions, as may give us some grasp of the novelty which is about to produce a measurable influence on the immediate future. Yet the doctrine, that routine is dominant in any society that is not collapsing, must never be lost sight of. Thus the grounds, in human nature and in the successful satisfaction of purpose, these grounds for the current routine must be understood; and at the same time the sorts of novelty just entering into social effectiveness have got to be weighed against the old routine. In this way the type of modification and the type of persistence exhibited in the immediate future may be foreseen.

It is now time to give some illustrations of assertions already made. Consider our main conclusions that our traditional doctrines of sociology, of political philosophy, of the practical conduct of large business, and of political economy are largely warped and vitiated by the implicit assumption of a stable unchanging social system. With this assumption it is comparatively safe to base reasoning upon a simplified edition of human nature. For well-known stimuli working under well-known conditions produce well-known reactions. It is safe then to assume that human nature, for the purpose in hand, is adequately described in terms of some of the major reactions to some of the major stimuli. For example, we can all remember our old friend, the economic man.

The beauty of the economic man was that we knew exactly what he was after. Whatever his wants were, he knew them and his neighbours knew them. His wants were those developed in a well-defined social system. His father and grandfather had the same wants, and satisfied them in the same way. So whenever there was a shortage, everyone—including the economic man himself—knew what was short, and knew the way to satisfy the consumer. In fact, the consumer knew what he wanted to consume. This was the demand. The producer knew how to produce the required articles, hence the supply. The men who got the goods onto the spot first, at the cheapest price, made their fortunes; the other producers were eliminated. This was healthy competition. This is beautifully simple and with proper elaboration is obviously true. It expresses the dominant truth exactly so far as there are stable well-tried conditions. But when we are concerned with a social system which in important ways is changing, this simplified conception of human relations requires severe qualification.

It is, of course, common knowledge that the whole trend of political economy during the last thirty or forty years has been away from these artificial simplifications. Such sharp-cut notions as 'the economic man', 'supply and demand', 'competition', are now in process of dilution by a close study of the actual reactions of various populations to the stimuli which are relevant to modern commerce. This exactly illustrates the main thesis. The older political economy reigned supreme for about a hundred years from the time of Adam Smith, because in its main assumptions it did apply to the general circumstances of life as led, then and for innumerable centuries in the past. These circumstances were then already passing away. But it still remained a dominant truth that in commercial relations men were dominated by well-conditioned reactions to completely familiar stimuli.

In the present age, the element of novelty which life affords is too prominent to be omitted from our calculations. A deeper knowledge of the varieties of human nature is required to determine the reaction, in its character and its strength, to those elements of novelty which each decade of years introduces into social life. The possibility of this deeper knowledge constitutes the Foresight under discussion.

. . . We are faced with a fluid, shifting situation in the immediate future. Rigid maxims, a rule-of-thumb routine, and cast-iron particular doctrines will spell ruin. The business of the future must be controlled by a somewhat different type of men to that of previous centuries. The type is already changing, and has already changed so far as the leaders are concerned. The Business Schools of Universities are concerned with spreading this newer type throughout the nations by aiming at the production of the requisite mentality.

I will conclude this chapter by a sketch of the Business Mind of the future. In the first place it is fundamental that there be a power of conforming to routine, of supervising routine, of constructing routine, and of understanding routine both as to its internal structure and as to its external purposes. Such a power is the bedrock of all practical efficiency. But for the production of the requisite Foresight, something more is wanted. This extra endowment can only be described as a philosophic power of understanding the complex flux of the varieties of human societies: for instance, the habit of noting varieties of demands on life, of serious purposes, of frivolous amusements. Such instinctive grasp of the relevant features of social currents is of supreme importance. For example, the time-span of various types of social behaviour is of the essence of their effect on policy. A widespread type of religious interest, with its consequent modes of behaviour, has a dominant life of about a hundred years, while a fashion of dress survives any time between three months and three years. Methods of agriculture change slowly. But the scientific world seems to be on the verge of far-reaching biological discoveries. The assumption of slow changes in agriculture must therefore be scanned vigilantly. This example of time-spans can be generalized. The quantitative aspect of social changes is of the essence of business relations. Thus the habit of transforming observation of qualitative changes into quantitative estimates should be a characteristic of business mentality.

I have said enough to show that the modern commercial mentality requires many elements of discipline, scientific and sociological. But the great fact remains that details of relevant knowledge cannot be foreseen. Thus even for mere success, and apart from any question of intrinsic quality of life, an unspecialized aptitude for eliciting generalizations from particulars and for seeing the divergent illustration of generalities in diverse circumstances is required. Such a reflective power is essentially a philosophic habit: it is the survey of society from the standpoint of generality. This habit of general thought, undaunted by novelty, is the gift of philosophy, in the widest sense of that term.

But the motive of success is not enough. It produces a short-sighted world which destroys the sources of its own prosperity. The cycles of trade depression which afflict the world warn us that business relations are infected through and through with the disease of short-sighted motives. The robber barons did not conduce to the prosperity of Europe in the Middle Ages, though some of them died prosperously in their beds. Their example is a warning to our civilization. Also we must not fall into the fallacy of thinking of the business world in abstraction from the rest of the community. The business world is one main part of the very community which is the subject-matter of our study. The behaviour of the community is largely dominated by the business mind. A great society is a society in which its men of business think greatly of their functions. Low thoughts mean low behaviour, and after a brief orgy of exploitation low behaviour means a descending standard of life. The general greatness of the community, qualitatively as well as quantitatively, is the first condition for steady prosperity, buoyant, self-sustained, and commanding credit.

CHAPTER ONE

Why Worry about Ethics?

Commentary

American business has long been driven by the idea of progress, by the notion that "there is no limit," as Churchill once observed, "to the benefits which human beings may bestow upon one another by the highest exertion of their diligence and skill." Through business organization, we have harnessed our wealth, skills, technology, and energy to create, manage, and distribute new wealth in ever growing quantities with ever greater efficiency. But does that idea still fuel the American imagination?

President Carter and Richard Darman rarely agree on issues of consequence. It is therefore startling to find that, though they spoke on the question more than a decade apart, their answers seem to be identical: the idea of progress is undergoing a crisis of confidence in America. In 1979, President Carter remarked:

> We've always had a faith that the days of our children would be better than our own. Our people are losing that faith.

And as a result:

> In a Nation that was proud of hard work, strong families, close knit communities, and our faith in God, too many of us now tend to worship self-indulgence and consumption.

By 1990, Richard Darman was, if anything, more critical:

> Our current impatience is that of the consumer not the builder, the self-indulgent not the pioneer.

And the risk is that:

> A society whose would-be Masters of the Universe are not forward-looking pioneers, but rather, morally-bankrupt hustlers will itself neither master the universe nor even invent dreams worth living.

In both Carter and Darman, one is troubled to find that the connection between the generations is weakening in America, a process that is undermining the moral fiber of our national life and eroding the productivity of American business. And by underscoring the connection between business and our great national goals, they raise the discussion of business ethics to an unusual level of importance.

But from a purely practical business viewpoint, one could nevertheless wonder what concrete difference it makes, or more specifically, whether there is a sufficiently direct link between the moral condition of the nation and the requisites of successful business management to warrant the attention of senior executives.

The Challenger disaster case study with which the chapter concludes suggests that there is such a linkage, and that ignoring it is as bad for business as it is for the country. What is clear is that the Challenger disaster did not have to happen. Rather, it happened because of a series of specific decisions that were driven by the concrete intentions of the responsible executives and officials. The challenge for business leaders of the future is to decide what moral or ethical ideas deserve to inform the business enterprise on which the material security of future generations will unavoidably depend.

JIMMY CARTER

A Crisis of Confidence

. . . Ten days ago I had planned to speak to you again about a very important subject—energy. For the fifth time I would have described the urgency of the problem and laid out a series of legislative recommendations to the Congress. But as I was preparing to speak, I began to ask myself the same question that I now know has been troubling many of you. Why have we not been able to get together as a nation to resolve our serious energy problem?

It's clear that the true problems of our Nation are much deeper —deeper than gasoline lines or energy shortages, deeper even than inflation or recession. And I realize more than ever that as President I need your help. So, I decided to reach out and to listen to the voices of America.

I invited to Camp David people from almost every segment of our society —business and labor, teachers and preachers. Governors, mayors and private citizens. And then I left Camp David to listen to other Americans, men and women like you. It has been an extraordinary 10 days, and I want to share with you what I've heard.

First of all, I got a lot of personal advice. Let me quote a few of the typical comments that I wrote down.

This from a southern Governor: "Mr. President you are not leading this Nation—you're just managing the Government."

"You don't see the people enough any more."

"Some of your Cabinet members don't seem loyal. There is not enough discipline among your disciples."

"Don't talk to us about politics or the mechanics of government, but about an understanding of our common good."

Excerpted from "Crisis of Confidence," an address by President Jimmy Carter nationally televised from Camp David, Maryland, July 15, 1979.

"Mr. President, we're in trouble. Talk to us about blood and sweat and tears."

"If you lead, Mr. President, we will follow."

Many people talked about themselves and about the condition of our Nation. This from a young woman in Pennsylvania: "I feel so far from government. I feel like ordinary people are excluded from political power."

And this from a young Chicano: "Some of us have suffered from recession all our lives."

"Some people have wasted energy, but others haven't had anything to waste."

And this from a religious leader: "No material shortage can touch the important things like God's love for us or our love for one another."

And I like this one particularly from a black woman who happens to be the mayor of a small Mississippi town: "The big shots are not the only ones who are important. Remember, you can't sell anything on Wall Street unless someone digs it up somewhere else first."

This kind of summarized a lot of other statements: "Mr. President, we are confronted with a moral and a spiritual crisis."

Several of our discussions were on energy and I have a notebook full of comments and advice. I'll read just a few.

"We can't go on consuming 40 percent more energy than we produce. When we import oil we are also importing inflation plus unemployment."

"We've got to use what we have. The Middle East has only 5 percent of the world's energy, but the United States has 24 percent."

And this is one of the most vivid statements: "Our neck is stretched over the fence and OPEC has the knife."

"There will be other cartels and other shortages. American wisdom and courage right now can set a path to follow in the future."

This was a good one: "Be bold, Mr. President. We may make mistakes, but we are ready to experiment."

And this one from a labor leader got to the heart of it: "The real issue is freedom. We must deal with the energy problem on a war footing."

And the last that I'll read: "When we enter the moral equivalent of war, Mr. President, don't issue us BB guns."

These 10 days confirmed my belief in the decency and the strength and the wisdom of the American people, but it also bore out some of my longstanding concerns about our Nation's underlying problems.

I know, of course, being President, that government actions and legislation can be very important. That is why I've worked hard to put my campaign promises into law—and I have to admit, with just mixed success. But after listening to the American people I have been reminded again that all the legislation in the world can't fix what's wrong with America. So, I want to speak to you first tonight about a subject even more serious than energy or inflation. I want to talk to you right now about a fundamental threat to American democracy.

I do not mean our political and civil liberties. They will endure. And I do not refer to the outward strength of America, a nation that is at peace tonight everywhere in the world, with unmatched economic power and military might.

The threat is nearly invisible in ordinary ways. It is a crisis of confidence. It is a crisis that strikes at the very heart and soul and spirit of our national will. We can see this crisis in the growing doubt about the meaning of our own lives and in the loss of a unity of purpose for our Nation.

The erosion of our confidence in the future is threatening to destroy the social and the political fabric of America.

The confidence that we have always had as a people is not simply some romantic dream or a proverb in a dusty book that we read just on the Fourth of July. It is the idea we founded our Nation on and has guided our development as a people. Confidence in the future has supported everything else—public institutions and private enterprise, our own families, and the very Constitution of the United States. Confidence has defined our course and has served as a link between generations. We've always believed in something called *progress*. We've always had a faith that the days of our children would be better than our own.

Our people are losing that faith, not only in government itself, but in the ability as citizens to serve as the ultimate rulers and shapers of our democracy. As a people we know our past and we are proud of it. Our progress has been part of the living history of America, even the world. We always believed that we were part of a great movement of humanity itself called democracy, involved in the search for freedom and that belief has always strengthened us in our purpose. But just as we are losing our confidence in the future, we are also beginning to close the door on our past.

In a Nation that was proud of hard work, strong families, close knit communities, and our faith in God, too many of us now tend to worship self-indulgence and consumption. Human identity is no longer defined by what one does, but by what one owns. But we've discovered that owning things and consuming things does not satisfy our longing for meaning. We've learned that piling up material goods cannot fill the emptiness of lives which have no confidence or purpose.

The symptoms of this crisis of the American spirit are all around us. For the first time in the history of our country the majority of our people believe that the next 5 years will be worse than the past 5 years. Two-thirds of our people do not even vote. The productivity of American workers is actually dropping and the willingness of Americans to save for the future has fallen below that of all other people in the Western world.

As you know, there is a growing disrespect for government and for churches and for schools, the news media, and other institutions. This is not a message of happiness or reassurance, but it is the truth and it is a warning.

These changes did not happen overnight. They've come upon us gradually over the last generation, years that were filled with shocks and tragedy.

We were sure that ours was a nation of the ballot, not the bullet, until the murders of John Kennedy and Robert Kennedy and Martin Luther King Jr. We were taught that our armies were always invincible and our causes were always just, only to suffer the agony of Vietnam. We respected the Presidency as a place of honor until the shock of Watergate.

We remember when the phrase "sound as a dollar," was an expression of absolute dependability, until 10 years of inflation began to shrink our dollars and our savings. We believed that our

Nation's resources were limitless until 1973 when we had to face a growing dependence on foreign oil.

These wounds are still very deep. They have never been healed.

Looking for a way out of this crisis, our people have turned to the Federal Government and found it isolated from the mainstream of our Nation's life. Washington, D.C., has become an island. The gap between our citizens and our government has never been so wide. The people are looking for honest answers, not easy answers; clear leadership, not false claims and evasiveness and politics as usual.

What you see too often in Washington and elsewhere around the country is a system of government that seems incapable of action. You see a Congress twisted and pulled in every direction by hundreds of well-financed and powerful special interests.

You see every extreme position defended to the last vote, almost to the last breath by one unyielding group or another. You often see a balanced and a fair approach that demands sacrifice, a little sacrifice from everyone, abandoned like an orphan without support and without friends.

Often you see paralysis and stagnation and drift. You don't like it, and neither do I. What can we do?

First of all, we must face the truth and then we can change our course. We simply must have faith in each other, faith in our ability to govern ourselves and faith in the future of this Nation.

Restoring that faith and that confidence to America is now the most important task we face. It is a true challenge of this generation of Americans.

One of the visitors to Camp David last week put it this way: "We've got to stop crying and start sweating, stop talking and start walking, stop cursing and start praying. The strength we need will not come from the White House, but from every house in America."

We know the strength of America. We are strong. We can regain our unity. We can regain our confidence. We are the heirs of generations who survived threats much more powerful and awesome than those that challenge us now. Our fathers and mothers were strong men and women who shaped a new society during the Great Depression, who fought world wars and who carved out a new charter of peace for the world.

We ourselves are the same Americans who just 10 years ago put a man on the moon. We are the generation that dedicated our society to the pursuit of human rights and equality. And we are the generation that will win the war on the energy problem and in that process rebuild the unity and confidence of America.

We are at a turning point in our history. There are two paths to choose. One is a path I warned about tonight, the path that leads to fragmentation and self-interest. Down that road lies a mistaken idea of freedom, the right to grasp for ourselves some advantage over others. That path would be one of constant conflict between narrow interests ending in chaos and immobility. It is a certain route to failure.

All the traditions of our past, all the lessons of our heritage, all the promises of our future point to another path, the path of common purpose and the restoration of American values. That path leads to true freedom for our Nation and ourselves. We can take the first steps down that path as we begin to solve our energy problem.

Energy will be the immediate test of our ability to unite this Nation and it can also be the standard around which we rally. On the battlefield of energy we can win for our Nation a new confidence, and we can seize control again of our common destiny . . .

The energy crisis is real. It is worldwide. It is a clear and present danger to our Nation. These are facts and we simply must face them.

What I have to say to you now about energy is simple and vitally important.

Point one: I am tonight setting a clear goal for the energy policy of the United States. Beginning this moment, this Nation will never use more foreign oil than we did in 1977—never.

Point two: To ensure that we meet these targets, I will use my Presidential authority to set import quotas.

Point three: To give us energy security, I am asking for the most massive peacetime commitment of funds and resources in our Nation's history to develop America's own alternative sources of fuel—from coal, from oil shale, from plant products for gasohol, from unconventional gas, from the Sun.

Point four: I'm asking Congress to mandate, to require as a

matter of law, that our Nation's utility companies cut their massive use of oil by 50 percent within the next decade.

Point five: I will urge Congress to create an energy Mobilization Board which, like the War Production Board in World War II, will have the responsibility and authority to cut through the redtape.

Point six: I am proposing a bold conservation program to involve every State, county and city and every average American in our energy battle. This effort will permit you to build conservation into your home and your lives at a cost you can afford.

I ask Congress to give me authority for mandatory conservation and for standby gasoline rationing. To further conserve energy, I'm proposing tonight an extra $10 billion over the next decade to strengthen our public transportation systems. And I'm asking you for your good and for your Nation's security to take no unnecessary trips, to use car pools or public transportation whenever you can, to park your car one extra day per week, to obey the speed limit and to set your thermostats to save fuel. Every act of energy conservation like this is more than just common sense—I tell you it is an act of patriotism.

Our Nation must be fair to the poorest among us, so we will increase aid to needy Americans to cope with rising energy prices. We often think of conservation only in terms of sacrifice. In fact, it is the most painless and immediate way of rebuilding our Nation's strength. Every gallon of oil each one of us saves is a new form of production. It gives us more freedom, more confidence, that much more control over our own lives.

So the solution of our energy crisis can also help us to conquer the crisis of the spirit in our country. It can rekindle our sense of unity, our confidence in the future and give our Nation and all of us individually a new sense of purpose.

RICHARD G. DARMAN

Now-Now-Ism

The deficit can be a colossally boring subject. Recently, it has shrunk somewhat as a percent of Gross National Product. It is moving down toward $150 billion and, if the Budget Agreement is fully implemented, on toward 100. But that has only made it more tedious. No longer can a President joke that "the deficit is big enough to take care of itself." Indeed, no longer is the deficit quite big enough to command sustained public attention.

The deficit is, of course, still a problem. Federal debt keeps moving on up—toward $3 trillion. That rising debt should not be ignored. In the spirit of avoiding tedium, however, let me look toward more interesting issues that underlie the deficit—and reach beyond it . . .

"Now-now-ism" is a short-hand label for our collective short-sightedness, our obsession with the here and now, our reluctance adequately to address the future.

America has long been an impatient culture. That is part of our distinctive strength. But it is one thing to be impatient about such forward-looking challenges as opening new frontiers. It is something entirely different to be impatient about consuming the fruit of overplowed ground. Our current impatience is that of the consumer not the builder, the self-indulgent not the pioneer. It borders dangerously on imprudence.

In our public policy—as, to some degree, in our private behavior —we consume today as if there were no tomorrow. We attend too little to the issues of investment necessary to make tomorrow brighter.

Like the spoiled '50's child in the recently-revived commercial, we seem on the verge of a collective Now-now scream: "I want my

Excerpted from "Beyond the Deficit Problem: 'Now-Now-Ism' and 'The New Balance'," an address by Richard G. Darman, Director of the Office of Management and Budget, before the National Press Club, Washington, D.C., July 20, 1989.

Maypo; I want it NOWWWWWWW! " But while the Maypo syndrome may be great for breakfast, and good for television advertising, cultural Now-now-ism is a formula for trouble.

The deficit is but one more symptom of our Now-now-ism. Many think of it as a *cause of problems.* But it is also a *symptom: a kind of silent Now-now scream.* It is the mathematical representation of our wish to buy now, pay later—or, more accurately, buy now and let others pay later.

The wish is understandable. Like the decision to accumulate debt, it is not necessarily bad. The test is whether current expenditure satisfactorily increases future benefit and future capacity to pay. Unfortunately, much of ours does not:

- In 1960, *interest payments* were only 7.5% of the budget. Now we are scheduled to pay 15% of the coming year's federal budget—almost $180 billion—for interest on our mounting public debt. That buys the future nothing. And it buys the present nothing more than the ability to keep its borrowing game going. (This 15% does not include the interest the government owes to its own trust funds. We aren't paying for that; we just write it down on paper.)
- In 1960, *transfer payments* to individuals were about a quarter of the budget. Now they comprise about half the budget (another 50%)—for Social Security, Medicare, means-tested entitlements, Veterans compensation, federal retirement programs, etc. While this radical shift in the pattern of public expenditure may seem morally attractive as a matter of current equity, it does little for the future. Indeed, the related trust funds that pretend to hold "surpluses" for future beneficiaries in fact hold hundreds of billions of dollars in unfunded IOUs. These are a little surprise for the workers of tomorrow left by the consumers of today.
- Our so-called investment in *housing programs* seems to have been mis-managed, at best. In some cases, it appears to have done a better job of transferring wealth to developers and middlemen than to intended beneficiaries.
- Our rapidly rising investment in *drug-abuse control* has yet to show satisfactory results. Spending for next year will be 150% of what it was for 1988. Yet, there is a widespread sense that we are still treating symptoms, not addressing underlying causes.
- Our public investment in applied civilian R&D has been declin-

ing as a share of GNP. In total *civilian R&D,* measured as a
percent of GNP—once an area of unequivocal U.S. advantage
—we are losing our lead to Japan.

- Our investment in *education* is tilted heavily toward the status
  quo: an atrophied system, demonstratably below the standard
  necessary to keep America number one. Our comparative test
  scores should be seen as both troubling and embarrassing. In an
  earlier period, more concerned about the future, such scores
  would have elicited howls of outrage . . .

Further:

- Our *corporate tax system* is biased toward the accumulation of
  debt over equity. Some of our most creative and energetic private sector talents are motivated to invent paper transactions
  that merely reward financial manipulators, rather than expand
  private productive capacity. And in a world of fast-moving
  deals, institutions responsible for longer-term investment feel
  obliged to chase near-term financial plays.
- Individuals are encouraged toward *current consumption* at the
  expense of saving and longer-term gain.
- And the culture generally seems to go for the *short-term "play."*
  Some people, who are apparently confident, trust in the motto:
  "You can have it all." Others, apparently less sure, seem to live
  by the dictum: "Take the money and run."

But worse, *our culture seems to tolerate all this rather blithely.*
We are rightly outraged at the breakdown of individual morality
when it shows itself starkly—as in "wilding" in the park. It is
uncivilized. But civilization is not measured merely by the presence or absence of physical brutality. It is measured also by the
capacity to build—to create for the future, to bridge construc-
tively across generations. Our Now-now culture acts as if it were
willing to let that capacity degenerate.

Collectively, we are engaged in a massive *Backward Robin
Hood* transaction—robbing the future to give to the present. This
Backward Robin Hood game operates on a scale that should be
able to move the likes of "Robin HUD" below the fold. In its
private form, it may be understood as short-sighted selfishness—
the entrepreneurial spirit gone a bit awry. In the public domain,

3

however, this self-indulgent theft from the future borders on *public policy wilding*. Still, it is not of much evident interest.

I do not mean this indictment to be too broad. From time to time, we have been able to show a clear interest in the future. For the past three decades, there has been one pre-eminent symbol of public policy commitment to the future: the space program. Today, of course, is the twentieth anniversary of its proudest moment: "one small step for man, one giant leap for mankind." And today, I am proud to say, President Bush is not only celebrating that moment, but also calling on us to expand our horizons with exciting new space missions for the benefit of generations yet to come.

Stepping back a bit from this celebratory moment, however, let us look at what has happened in recent years to our culture's attitude toward space. That, too, has been an unattractive *symptom of Now-now-ism* . . .

When President Kennedy first spoke of exploring the stars, he was not obsessed with the claims of the present. His near-term target—man on the moon—was a decade away, beyond his own tenure. Of his larger vision he said, "All of this will not be finished in . . . the first one thousand days . . . nor even perhaps in our lifetime on this planet. But let us begin."

In the '70s, Tom Wolfe's bestseller celebrated *The Right Stuff* of the space pioneers. It resonated with an admiring public. By the early '80s, however, the public seemed to have lost its enchantment with space and the future. Wolfe's bestseller audience turned to *The Bonfire of the Vanities.* In it, a new "Master of the Universe" was found: Sherman McCoy—an '80s-style bond salesman, found on his hands and knees on the marble floor of his Park Avenue cooperative, wrestling unsuccessfully with a reluctant dachshund, whose alleged need for a walk was to provide the excuse for a quick liaison with the would-be Master's mistress. Let me note the obvious: A society whose would-be Masters of the Universe are not forward-looking pioneers, but rather, morally bankrupt hustlers will itself neither master the universe nor even invent dreams worth living . . .

In a democracy, the future is at a disadvantage relative to the present: its voters are not here to represent themselves. They are dependent upon the values of those who are here—our collective sense of moral obligation to the future.

Indeed, *the heart of the Now-now problem is a problem of values.* The deficit is, in a sense, an expression of *contempt for the burden of debt that is left to the future.* That burden is now an average of *$45,000—and rising—for every American family of four.* It's like a second mortgage—but without the house.

The deficit can be brought under control, however. It is now moving in the right direction. The Bipartisan Budget Agreement was a constructive, though modest, first step. With good will and responsible leadership, a more substantial multi-year deficit reduction package could also be agreed to this year. It should and could meet the Gramm-Rudman-Hollings deficit targets, while also improving the budget process and strengthening measures to restore fiscal discipline. This would be the right thing to do. Of course, that does not mean that it will be done. But if the political system cannot rise to its responsibility in a calm and orderly manner, it will ultimately have to do so in the context of crisis. In the end, the system is bound to respond.

But *though the deficit may be brought under control, problems that stem from Now-now values extend far beyond the deficit.* They are pervasive. Merely balancing the budget will not suffice to get at these problems:

- A balanced budget would still leave us with rising debt unless we also get straight the way we account for increasing unfunded obligations to trust funds. The *accounting issues* go beyond conventional "balance." They raise the issue of whether we wish to be *honest with ourselves* about our future obligations.
- A balanced budget *per se* would not shift the distribution of federal expenditure toward investment in the future unless we also restrain rapidly growing transfer payments. *The composition of the budget matters. Inescapably, it reflects a value choice in its distribution of costs and benefits to the present vs. the future.*
- Beyond budgetary issues, the HUD-type scandals present issues of *managerial values.* With or without a balanced budget, such scandals may proliferate unless expenditures are subject to both improved control systems and people committed to integrity—

in the endless quest to keep near-term greed within socially acceptable bounds.

- The *drug problem will not be solved by budgets alone at any likely level of expenditure.* Legal economic incentives cannot compete with the short-term psychological high that drug-abuse provides or with the economic rewards that illegal drug trafficking can offer. Yet, civilization must protect itself. We do not wish to become either a drug haven or a police state. So there has to be attention to the inner voice, the values, that tell people not to succumb to drugs' obvious near-term temptations—*the voice that can speak for long-term consequences.* A culture that in so many ways emphasizes the here and now is bound to have a hard time changing that inner voice, the internal balance between today and the future. *But the larger culture will have to show greater respect for the future if it is to be credible in asking young Americans to do so.*

- Similarly, *the education problem will not be solved unless there is a cultural change—a cultural reawakening.* I don't mean something esoteric. I mean a broad and basic awakening that finds these symptoms of short-sightedness to be wrong: decisions by students to drop out of school prematurely; decisions by many educational administrators to underinvest in technology; decisions by some parents and caretakers to underattend to homework; decisions by a host of American employers to undervalue advanced quantitative training; decisions by the community at large to underinvest in the length of the school year; and decisions by television programmers—a major American educational force—to underinvest in substantive content. If this *pervasive cultural shortsightedness* is not changed, it is naive to expect that America's educational system will meet its most basic challenges: keeping America competitive, transmitting America's strengths and capacities across the generations.

- And, as I've suggested before, many of *corporate America's problems* with current and future competitiveness will not be solved by changes in economic incentives or the cost of capital alone—important though these be. High discount rates and inherent uncertainties will often put the future at a disadvantage relative to near-term rewards—*unless there is a value judgment that gives special weight to the future.*

As a general matter, we will mislead ourselves if we believe that fixing the fiscal deficit alone will solve many of our more basic problems. It will help with some. It may be a precondition for addressing others. But *unless we see it as a symptom of a more basic problem—Now-now-ism, a problem of cultural values that must also be addressed*—we will miss a chance to secure America's historic place and mission . . .

Historically, America has been fundamentally—indeed, quintessentially—a future-oriented society: educating, hard-working, saving, unwilling to accept conventional limits, risk-taking, pioneering, building. If we have strayed a bit from this American cultural tradition, we need only look within ourselves to reawaken it.

The current historical context could hardly be more favorable for a reawakening of appreciation for distinctively *American values.* A Soviet leader has captured public imagination by borrowing two fundamentally *American* concepts: restructuring ("peristroika") and openness ("glasnost"). Chinese students parade with statues of liberty. The Japanese have risen to power with a post-war politico-economic system that was, in no small measure, borrowed from *America.* Europe, at last, is moving toward what *America* has pioneered: a single, open, continental market. And today, specifically, the world recalls that heroic triumph of *American ingenuity and commitment, American courage and grace:* the journey of Apollo. It would be a ridiculous irony if we ourselves did not realize that we, *first and foremost,* can build on traditional *American* strengths.

But what of our Now-now-ism? Again: in some measure, impatience has long been an American characteristic. The question is one of *balance.* In recent years, we have tipped too much toward the present.

Yet, a reawakening may now be under way. As must be evident, I like to look at signs from popular culture. And some of the signs give reason for encouragement.

Consider, for example, a bit of the entertainment culture close to many of our homes. A few years ago, the most popular youth movie was *Ferris Bueller's Day Off.* Ferris was a forward-looking kid in only a limited sense. He was brilliant at plans to play hookey from school—entertaining, but hardly constructive. Now, the three most popular movies are more positive morality plays, wrapped in healthy romance. *Indiana Jones' Last Crusade* is a quest that binds two generations in search of the holy grail. *Batman* has returned to rid the world of Gotham's greed. And in the very heart of America, *A Field of Dreams* is built out of a barely self-sustaining farm in response to a guiding voice: "If you build it, he will come." Lost generations are reborn, future generations are inspired, in a seamless game of catch that stretches across the generations. One senses the spirit being renewed.

Now back for a moment to the Budget: one way or another it will be brought under control. *We will find our way to accountant's balance. But what I am trying to suggest is that the New Balance demands more of us.*

The American dream is not meant to be filtered through green eyeshades. Nor is the human spirit meant to crawl on the floor like a dachshund. It is meant to rise up with wings like eagles. Ours *is* a seamless game of catch across the generations. If we do no more than make the farm break even, we will break the magical connection with the future. *It is only if we build, that we'll see the field of dreams.*

RUSSELL P. BOISJOLY, ELLEN FOSTER CURTIS, EUGENE MELLICAN

Roger Boisjoly and the Challenger Disaster

. . . On January 28, 1986, the space shuttle Challenger exploded 73 seconds into its flight, killing the seven astronauts aboard. As the nation mourned the tragic loss of the crew members, the Rogers Commission was formed to investigate the causes of the disaster. The Commission concluded that the explosion occurred due to seal failure in one of the solid rocket booster joints. Testi-

Excerpted from "Roger Boisjoly and the Challenger Disaster: The Ethical Dimensions" by Russell P. Boisjoly, Ellen Foster Curtis and Eugene Mellican. *Journal of Business Ethics,* No. 8 (1989), pp. 217–225, 229. © 1989 Kluwer Academic Publishers. Reprinted by permission of Kluwer Academic Publishers.

mony given by Roger Boisjoly, Senior Scientist and acknowledged rocket seal expert, indicated that top management at
NASA and Morton Thiokol had been aware of problems with the
O-ring seals, but agreed to launch against the recommendation of
Boisjoly and other engineers. Boisjoly had alerted management to
problems with the O-rings as early as January, 1985, yet several
shuttle launches prior to the Challenger had been approved without correcting the hazards . . .

. . . On January 24, 1985, Roger Boisjoly, Senior Scientist at
Morton Thiokol, watched the launch of Flight 51-C of the space
shuttle program. He was at Cape Canaveral to inspect the solid
rocket boosters from Flight 51-C following their recovery in the
Atlantic Ocean and to conduct a training session at Kennedy
Space Center (KSC) on the proper methods of inspecting the
booster joints. While watching the launch, he noted that the temperature that day was much cooler than recorded at other
launches, but was still much warmer than the 18 degree temperature encountered three days earlier when he arrived in Or-
lando . . .

. . . When he inspected the solid rocket boosters several days
later, Boisjoly discovered evidence that the primary O-ring seals
on two field joints had been compromised by hot combustion
gases (i.e., hot gas blow-by had occurred) which had also eroded
part of the primary O-ring. This was the first time that a primary
seal on a field joint had been penetrated. When he discovered the
large amount of blackened grease between the primary and secondary seals, his concern heightened. The blackened grease was
discovered over 80 degree and 110 degree arcs, respectively, on
two of the seals, with the larger arc indicating greater hot gas
blow-by. Post-flight calculations indicated that the ambient temperature of the field joints at launch time was 53 degrees. This
evidence, coupled with his recollection of the low temperature
the day of the launch and the citrus crop damage caused by the
cold spell, led to his conclusion that the severe hot gas blow-by
may have been caused by, and related to, low temperature. After
reporting these findings to his superiors, Boisjoly presented them
to engineers and management at NASA's Marshall Space Flight
Center (MSFC). As a result of his presentation at MSFC, Roger
Boisjoly was asked to participate in the Flight Readiness Review

(FRR) on February 12, 1985 for Flight 51-E which was scheduled for launch in April, 1985. This FRR represents the first association of low temperature with blow-by on a field joint, a condition that was considered an "acceptable risk" by Larry Mulloy, NASA's Manager for the Booster Project, and other NASA officials. . . .

. . . The tough questioning he received at the February 12th FRR convinced Boisjoly of the need for further evidence linking low temperature and hot gas blow-by. He worked closely with Arnie Thompson, Supervisor of Rocket Motor Cases, who conducted subscale laboratory tests in March, 1985, to further test the effects of temperature on O-ring resiliency. The bench tests that were performed provided powerful evidence to support Boisjoly's and Thompson's theory: Low temperatures greatly and adversely affected the ability of O-rings to create a seal on solid rocket booster joints. If the temperature was too low (and they did not know what the threshold temperature would be), it was possible that neither the primary or secondary O-rings would seal!

One month later the post-flight inspection of Flight 51-B revealed that the primary seal of a booster nozzle joint did not make contact during its two minute flight. If this damage had occurred in a field joint, the secondary O-ring may have failed to seal, causing the loss of the flight. As a result, Boisjoly and his colleagues became increasingly concerned about shuttle safety. This evidence from the inspection of Flight 51-B was presented at the FRR for Flight 51-F on July 1, 1985; the key engineers and managers at NASA and Morton Thiokol were now aware of the critical O-ring problems and the influence of low temperature on the performance of the joint seals.

During July, 1985, Boisjoly and his associates voiced their desire to devote more effort and resources to solving the problems of O-ring erosion. In his activity reports dated July 22 and 29, 1985, Boisjoly expressed considerable frustration with the lack of progress in this area, despite the fact that a Seal Erosion Task Force had been informally appointed on July 19th. Finally, Boisjoly wrote the following memo, labelled "Company Private", to R. K. (Bob) Lund, Vice President of Engineering for Morton

Thiokol, to express the extreme urgency of his concerns. Here are some excerpts from that memo:

> This letter is written to insure that management is fully aware of the seriousness of the current O-ring erosion problem . . . The mistakenly accepted position on the joint problem was to fly without fear of failure . . . is now drastically changed as a result of the SRM 16A nozzle joint erosion which eroded a secondary O-ring with the primary O-ring never sealing. If the same scenario should occur in a field joint (and it could), then it is a jump ball as to the success or failure of the joint . . . The result would be a catastrophe of the highest order—loss of human life . . .
>
> It is my honest and real fear that if we do not take immediate action to dedicate a team to solve the problem, with the field joint having the number one priority, then we stand in jeopardy of losing a flight along with all the launch pad facilities (Boisjoly, July, 1985a).

On August 20, 1985, R. K. Lund formally announced the formation of the Seal Erosion Task Team. The team consisted of only five full-time engineers from the 2500 employed by Morton Thiokol on the Space Shuttle Program. The events of the next five months would demonstrate that management had not provided the resources necessary to carry out the enormous task of solving the seal erosion problem . . .

. . . At 10 a.m. on January 27, 1986, Arnie Thompson received a phone call from Boyd Brinton, Thiokol's Manager of Project Engineering at MSFC, relaying the concerns of NASA's Larry Wear, also at MSFC, about the 18 degree temperature forecast for the launch of Flight 51-L, the Challenger, scheduled for the next day. This phone call precipitated a series of meetings within Morton Thiokol, at the Marshall Space Flight Center, and at the Kennedy Space Center that culminated in a three-way telecon involving three teams of engineers and managers, that began at 8:15 p.m. E.S.T.

Joe Kilminster, Vice President, Space Booster Programs, of Morton Thiokol began the telecon by turning the presentation of the engineering charts over to Roger Boisjoly and Arnie Thompson. They presented thirteen charts which resulted in a recommendation against the launch of the Challenger. Boisjoly demonstrated their concerns with the performance of the O-rings in the field joints during the initial phases of Challenger's flight with charts showing the effects of primary O-ring erosion, and its timing, on the ability to maintain a reliable secondary seal. The tremendous pressure and release of power from the rocket boosters create rotation in the joint such that the metal moves away from the O-rings so that they cannot maintain contact with the metal surfaces. If, at the same time, erosion occurs in the primary O-ring for any reason, then there is a reduced probability of maintaining a secondary seal. It is highly probable that as the ambient temperature drops, the primary O-ring will not seat, that there will be hot gas blow-by and erosion of the primary O-ring; and that a catastrophe will occur when the secondary O-ring fails to seal.

Bob Lund presented the final chart that included the Morton Thiokol recommendations that the ambient temperature including wind must be such that the seal temperature would be greater than 53 degrees to proceed with the launch. Since the overnight low was predicted to be 18 degrees, Bob Lund recommended against launch on January 28, 1986 or until the seal temperature exceeded 53 degrees.

NASA's Larry Mulloy bypassed Bob Lund and directly asked Joe Kilminster for his reaction. Kilminster stated that he supported the position of his engineers and he would not recommend launch below 53 degrees.

George Hardy, Deputy Director of Science and Engineering at MSFC, said he was "appalled at that recommendation", according to Allan McDonald's testimony before the Rogers Commission. Nevertheless, Hardy would not recommend to launch if the contractor was against it. After Hardy's reaction, Stanley Reinartz, Manager of Shuttle Project Office at MSFC, objected by pointing out that the solid rocket motors were qualified to operate between 40 and 90 degrees Fahrenheit.

Larry Mulloy, citing the data from Flight 61-A which indicated to him that temperature was not a factor, strenuously objected to Morton Thiokol's recommendation. He suggested that Thiokol was attempting to establish new Launch Commit Criteria at 53 degrees and that they couldn't do that the night before a launch. In exasperation Mulloy asked, "My God, Thiokol, when do you want me to launch? Next April?" (McConnell, 1987). Although other NASA officials also objected to the association of temperature with O-ring erosion and hot gas blow-by, Roger Boisjoly was able to hold his ground and demonstrate with the use of his charts and pictures that there was indeed a relationship: The lower the temperature the higher the probability of erosion and blow-by and the greater the likelihood of an accident. Finally, Joe Kilminster asked for a five minute caucus off-net.

According to Boisjoly's testimony before the Rogers Commission, Jerry Mason, Senior Vice President of Wasatch Operations, began the caucus by saying that "a management decision was necessary". Sensing that an attempt would be made to overturn the no-launch decision, Boisjoly and Thompson attempted to re-review the material previously presented to NASA for the executives in the room. Thompson took a pad of paper and tried to sketch out the problem with the joint, while Boisjoly laid out the photos of the compromised joints from Flights 51-C and 61-A. When they became convinced that no one was listening, they ceased their efforts. As Boisjoly would later testify, "There was not one positive pro-launch statement ever made by anybody" (Report of the Presidential Commission, 1986, IV, p. 792, hereafter abbreviated as R.C.).

According to Boisjoly, after he and Thompson made their last attempts to stop the launch, Jerry Mason asked rhetorically, "Am I the only one who wants to fly?" Mason turned to Bob Lund and asked him to "take off his engineering hat and put on his management hat" . The four managers held a brief discussion and voted unanimously to recommend Challenger's launch . . .

. . . Aside from the four senior Morton Thiokol executives present at the teleconference, all others were excluded from the final decision. The process represented a radical shift from previous NASA policy. Until that moment, the burden of proof had always been on the engineers to prove beyond a doubt that it was safe to launch. NASA, with their objections to the original Thiokol recommendation against the launch, and Mason, with his request for a "management decision", shifted the burden of proof in the opposite direction. Morton Thiokol was expected to prove that launching Challenger would not be safe (R.C., IV, p. 793) . . .

On January 28, 1986, a reluctant Roger Boisjoly watched the launch of the Challenger. As the vehicle cleared the tower, Bob Ebeling whispered, "we've just dodged a bullet." (The engineers who opposed the launch assumed that O-ring failure would result in an explosion almost immediately after engine ignition.) To continue in Boisjoly's words, "At approximately T+60 seconds Bob told me he had just completed a prayer of thanks to the Lord for a successful launch. Just thirteen seconds later we both saw the horror of the destruction as the vehicle exploded" (Boisjoly, 1987) . . .

. . . [W]hy [were] the concerns raised by the Morton Thiokol engineers about the effects of cold weather on the O-rings during the teleconference the night before the launch . . . not passed up from Level III to Levels II or I in the preflight review process[?] The NASA launch procedure clearly demands that decisions and objections methodically follow a prescribed path up all levels. Yet, Lawrence Mulloy, operating at Level III as the Solid Rocket Booster Project Manager at MSFC, did not transmit the Morton Thiokol concerns upward (through his immediate superior, Stanley Reinartz) to Level II. When asked by Chairman Rogers to explain why, Mr. Mulloy testified:

> At that time, and I still consider today, that was a Level III issue, Level III being a SRB element or an external tank element or Space Shuttle main engine element or an Orbiter. There was no violation of Launch Commit Criteria. There was no waiver required in my judgment at that time and still today (R.C., I, p. 98).

In examining this response in terms of shifting responsibility onto the review process itself, there are two things that are particularly striking in Mr. Mulloy's statement. The first is his emphasis that this was a "Level III issue." In a formal sense, Mr. Mulloy is correct. However, those on Level III also had the authority—and, one would think, especially in this instance given the heated discussion on the effects of cold on the O-rings, the motivation—to pass objections and concerns on to Levels II and I. But here the second important point in Mr. Mulloy's testimony comes into play when he states, "there was no violation of Launch Commit Criteria." In other words, since there was no

Launch Commit Criteria for joint temperature, concerns about joint temperature did not officially fall under the purview of the review process. Therefore, the ultimate justification for Mr. Mulloy's position rests on the formal process itself. He was just following the rules by staying within the already established scope of the review process. . . .

Certainly, there can be no more vivid example than the shuttle program to verify that, in fact, "an emphasis on management systems can, in itself, serve to separate the people engaged in the program from the real world of hardware." Time and time again the lack of communication that lay at the heart of the Rogers Commission finding that "there was a serious flaw in the decision making process leading up to the launch of flight 51-L" (R.C., I, p. 104) was explained by the NASA officials or managers at Morton Thiokol with such statements as, "that is not my reporting channel," or "he is not in the launch decision chain," or "I didn't meet with Mr. Boisjoly, I met with Don Ketner, who is the task team leader" (R.C., IV, p. 821, testimony of Mr. Lund). Even those managers who had direct responsibility for line engineers and workmen depended on formalized memo writing procedures for communication to the point that some "never talked to them directly" (Feynman, 1988, p. 33).

Within the atmosphere of such an ambiguity of responsibility, when a life threatening conflict arose within the management system and individuals (such as Roger Boisjoly and his engineering associates at Morton Thiokol) tried to reassert the full weight of their individual judgments and attendant responsibilities, the very purpose of the flight readiness review process, i.e., to arrive at the "technical" truth of the situation, which includes the recognition of the uncertainties involved as much as the findings, became subverted into an adversary confrontation in which "adversary" truth, with its suppression of uncertainties, became operative (Wilmotte, 1970).

What is particularly significant in this radical transformation of the review process, in which the Morton Thiokol engineers were forced into "the position of having to prove that it was unsafe instead of the other way around" (R.C., IV, p. 822; see also p. 793), is that what made the suppression of technical uncertainties possible is precisely that mode of thinking which, in being challenged by independent professional judgments, gave rise to the adversarial setting in the first place: groupthink. No more accurate description for what transpired the night before the launch of the Challenger can be given than the definition of groupthink as:

> . . . a mode of thinking that people engage in when they are deeply involved in a cohesive in-group, when the members' strivings for unanimity override their motivation to realistically appraise alternative courses of action. . . . Groupthink refers to the deterioration of mental efficiency, reality testing, and moral judgment that results from in-group pressures (Janis, 1972, p. 9).

From this perspective, the full import of Mr. Mason's telling Mr. Lund to "take off his engineering hat and put on his management hat" is revealed. He did not want another technical, reality-based judgment of an independent professional engineer. As he had already implied when he opened the caucus by stating "a management decision was necessary," he wanted a group decision, specifically one that would, in the words of the Rogers Commission, "accommodate a major customer" (R.C., I, p. 104). With a group decision the objections of the engineers could be mitigated, the risks shared, fears allayed, and the attendant responsibility diffused. . . .

Note

A contrasting interpretation of the meeting the night before the launch, given by Howard Schwartz, is that NASA began to view itself as the ideal organization that did not make mistakes. According to Schwartz, "The organization ideal is an image of perfection. It is, so to speak, an idea of God. God does not make mistakes. Having adopted the idea of NASA as the organization ideal it follows that the individual will believe that, if NASA has made a decision, that decision will be correct" (Schwartz, 1987).

In his testimony before the Rogers Commission, Roger Boisjoly indicated the extent to which NASA procedure had changed: "This was a meeting (the night before the launch) where the determination was to launch, and it was up to us to prove beyond the shadow of a doubt that it was not safe to do so. This is the total reverse to what the position usually is in a preflight conversation or a flight readiness review" (Bois-joly, 1986).

As Schwartz indicates: "If it was a human decision, engineering standards of risk should prevail in determining whether it is safe to launch. On the other hand, if the decision was a NASA decision, it is simply safe to launch, since NASA does not make mistakes" (Schwartz, 1987).

CHAPTER TWO

Can Ethics Be Taught?

Commentary

The previous chapter offers plenty of evidence that there is reason to worry about the state of ethics in our American society. And in government and business, there are more tales of misbehavior rolling off the presses than one likes to count.

If there is reason to worry, then one must ask: what can be done about it? Can anything be done about it? And that leads us straight to the question: can ethics be taught? The readings in this chapter are addressed primarily to what the schools can do. In the following chapter, we are reminded that the corporation too is an educational institution and thus faces the same question.

Can ethics be taught? It is one of the great persisting questions in Western thought. In Plato's dialogue *Meno,* the opening words set the stage for two thousand years of argument:

Can you tell me, Socrates, whether virtue is acquired by teaching or by practice; or if neither by teaching nor practice, then whether it comes to man by nature, or in what other way?

When Socrates replies that he doesn't even know what virtue is, much less how it is acquired, the dialogue is off and running. The selections that make up this chapter reveal that the conversation is still going on, and that there is no agreement about the answers. It is not even evident that much progress has been made in developing the terms of the argument. Another way to describe the history of the idea is to say that the Greeks, though they certainly did not succeed in settling the question, did manage to ask it in an enduring fashion.

How are our colleges and business schools confronting this issue? Can business ethics be taught in the classroom? Why do some schools choose not to try? Can courses in ethics overcome shortcomings in family teachings and examples beginning in infancy? Is it possible to know what is the right thing to do, and then choose not to do it? If so, can teaching help students to decide to *do* what is right as well as to *know* what is right? Can ethics be taught rationally like chemistry or accounting, or is everyone equally entitled to his or her own opinion when it comes to matters of right and wrong?

The selections in this chapter address these questions from widely differing points of view. Archie J. Bahm, in surveying the working hypotheses of a number of the new, specialized centers set up for the study of ethics, reports that they attempt to teach courses in applied ethics "without the teacher or student knowing (or even caring) what are the ultimate bases for moral appeals, or without understanding the nature of intrinsic values. . . ." He voices his skepticism that effective teaching of ethics can take place in such a barren environment.

LaRue T. Hosmer poses the question: why is it that so many schools of business administration do not offer a course in business ethics? He reports the results of his conversations with his teaching colleagues and uncovers what he believes to be the underlying reservations.

Edwin J. Delattre looks at the methods chosen by the schools that *do* attempt to teach ethics, and finds fault with one of the most common approaches—that of analyzing so-called "dilemmas." He believes that failures to respond ethically are not so much due to inept reasoning about dilemmas, but rather to "moral indifference, disregard for other people, weakness of will, and bad or self-indulgent habits of life." He extols the value of practice in achieving ethical conduct and shows how schools can provide the opportunities for such practice and the examples to inspire the best response.

Herbert Johnston claims that there is such a thing as a science of morals, and that it can be taught. But such a general treatment is not enough, and specific teaching of business ethics is necessary because many students "seem totally unaware of the existence of moral problems in business life." He acknowledges, as does Delattre, that *knowing* is not sufficient. In the absence of a moral sensibility, a conviction of the will, knowledge will not be translated into action.

The underlying problem in teaching ethics is two-fold—knowing what to teach, and knowing how to move the learner from knowledge of what is good action to acting in accordance with that knowledge. As Aristotle says in the *Nicomachean Ethics,*

> . . . It is well said, then, that it is by doing just acts that the just man is produced, and by doing temperate acts the temperate man; without doing these no one would have even a prospect of becoming good.
>
> But most people do not do these, but take refuge in theory and think they are being philosophers and will become good in this way, behaving somewhat like patients who listen attentively to their doctors, but do none of the things they are ordered to do. As the latter will not be made well in body by such a course of treatment, the former will not be made well in soul by such a course of philosophy. (Book II, Chapter 4)

ARCHIE J. BAHM

Teaching Ethics Without Ethics to Teach

. . . In our world of cultural changes, where beliefs about the ultimate bases for ethical knowledge have become unsettled, we know from whence we have come but lack a clear conception of where we are going. Returning from a Boston conference recently, I sat next to a college student also working as an insurance adjuster. Becoming aware of my interests, he volunteered: "Older people often wonder what youth today have as a purpose in life. You may ask me." I asked. He replied: "I don't have any, except to earn enough to serve my basic needs." Commitments to a purpose in one's life imply basic values serving as foundations or judgment. How many generations are being suspended between our previous consensus and any future consensus not yet in sight? How can we teach ethics in an age when people lack confidence that reliable foundations for ethical beliefs exist?

Now Daniel Callahan writes about 'The Rebirth of Ethics' . . .

> Whatever the reasons . . . educators, professional organizations, and even the federal government are rushing about at a furious rate to revive an almost-dead interest in moral problems. . . . It is as if the American people, particularly the well-educated, are profoundly attracted to moral problems and yet, at the same time, exceedingly skeptical that they can be dealt with in a rational fashion.

and that "there would be little profit in attempting to work out some systematic response to moral problems". He quotes one respondant as saying "There are no answers to ethical questions, so it's not worth spending time on".

Excerpted from "Teaching Ethics Without Ethics to Teach" by Archie J. Bahm. *Journal of Business Ethics,* No. 1 (1982), pp. 44–47. © 1982 Kluwer Academic Publishers. Reprinted by permission of Kluwer Academic Publishers.

Where, then, is "the rebirth"? "Close to 1000 courses in medical ethics or bioethics are taught at the undergraduate level. The interest in applied ethics has spread . . . into schools of business, law, journalism, and most other professional fields." In addition to new courses, we have new professors, chairs, departments, and institutes or centers, and a flourish of new articles, textbooks, curricula, conferences, and societies. Two new associations of applied ethicists have sprung up during the past year: the Society for the Study of Professional Ethics and the Society for the Study of Business Ethics.

Perhaps most significant of all is the establishment of several new centers or institutes funded to organize and facilitate interests in promoting applied ethics. What are these institutes? How do they represent (both as products of and reenforcers of) our mainstrain attitude? The following five are selected as exemplary.

1. The Hastings Center, or the Institute of Society, Ethics and the Life Sciences, Hastings-on-Hudson, established in 1969, had a half-million budget already in 1973. It has become perhaps the most influential institute through its conferences, workshops, fellowships, internships, books, articles, and the *Hastings Center Report,* six times a year.

Its director, Daniel Callahan, explains:

> Our own institute has from the very first been concerned with the foundations of ethics. . . . It is central to our work. At the same time, I really do not think it possible, either philosophically or psychologically, to attempt to settle fundamental questions of ethical theory and value theory before tackling immediate moral dilemmas. (Letter dated April 29, 1975.)

2. The Human Dimensions Center, or Center for the Study of the Human Dimensions of Science and Technology, Rensselaer Institute of Technology, Troy, is involved in a three-year National Project on Philosophy and Engineering Ethics and in major efforts in journalistic, computer, and nursing ethics. It is directed by Robert J. Baum, who edits an informative quarterly newsletter, *Business and Professional Ethics.* Baum is one of the most active and influential scholars in applied ethics, and has served as Program Manager for the National Science Founda-

tion's EVHIST program and is active in American Association for the Advancement of Science committees and its Workshop on Professional Ethics.

Baum teaches ethics, being "concerned with distinguishing good moral decisions from bad ones". But he does so somewhat indirectly by focusing on the nature of arguments because "a judgment concerning the goodness or badness of a decision normally must be supported by an argument". But he offers little hope of success,

> insofar as only a few of the literally infinite number of possible arguments really provide any significant support for their conclusions. . . . It cannot be emphasized too strongly that this book in and of itself can provide little if any assistance to persons wishing to develop the basic skills of analyzing and evaluating ethical arguments.

Even the basic concern is unclear:

> Although it would certainly be useful at this point to provide a precise definition of the term 'moral decision', it is unfortunately impossible to do this, since there are a number of different definitions of the term, most of which are incompatible with the others.

Dictionaries do not help, since "we are simply led in circles without ever gaining a clear understanding of the basic concept of moral decision".

3. The Center for Business Ethics, Bentley College, Waltham, "was established to provide a nonpartisan forum for the exchange of ideas on business ethics . . . and to foster greater awareness and understanding of moral conflicts from various perspectives". It has sponsored three annual national conferences on business ethics, participated in by prominent national leaders in government, business and professional fields. These are ably summarized, and photographed, in the annual *Business Ethics Report.*

Its director, W. Michael Hoffman, says: "Perhaps more than at any other time in the history of our nation we find ourselves in a moral crisis". One of his conference speakers, Boston University

Philosophy Professor Alisdair MacIntyre, expressed the mainstream attitude:

> With reasoned argument, Alisdair MacIntyre explained why the
> problems of business ethics are insoluble in the modern world.
> . . . our pluralistic society has no common ground with which to
> attack moral questions . . . when we come to concrete moral
> questions we do not know how to weigh one claim against the
> other.

4. The Center for the Study of Ethics in the Professions, Illinois Institute of Technology, Chicago, was established in 1976, "to encourage scholarship dealing with ethical and social issues inherent in the practice of the professions". It has prepared a *Bibliography on Engineering Ethics,* sponsored a series of interdisciplinary workshops, developed special courses in professional ethics, and published case studies in occasional papers.

Vivien Weil teaches a course in 'Moral Issues in Engineering' and insists that "there really can be systematic, reasonable thinking about moral judgments". But experience has taught her to emphasize case studies.

> I've eliminated the hunk on moral theory because students didn't
> see how it connected, and it was hard. We try to avoid being
> abstract now. . . . Teachers should read books on moral theory
> so their heads are clear and they can work through questions that
> arise, but there's no particular need for the students to read them.

5. The Center for the Study of Values, University of Delaware, Newark, was established in 1977 to "encourage interaction among academics, members of the professions, and members of the general public" and to "function as an arena where men and women may wrestle with ethical problems that arise in contemporary society". It has sponsored a distinguished lecture series, including one on 'Ethical Theory in the Last Quarter of the Twentieth Century', honoring four American ethicists. It has sponsored conferences on 'Ethical Issues in Economics' (1977–78), 'Ethical Issues in Education' (1978–79), and 'Ethics in Government' (1979–80). Norman L. Bowie, Director of the Center,

also serves as the American Philosophical Association's National-Endowment-for-the Humanities-sponsored business ethics curriculum development project.

When I asked Bowie, "What is your theory of the nature of intrinsic value?" he replied: "I do not have a carefully worked out theory on the matter of intrinsic value. . . . The Center welcomes philosophers of varying traditions within value theory and provides an opportunity to apply their respective theories to contemporary problems." (Letter dated July 17, 1977.) When his *Ethical Theory and Business* (coedited with Tom L. Beauchamp, Prentice-Hall, Englewood Cliffs, 1979) appeared, only the first chapter dealt with ethical theories and only two kinds, the teleological (utilitarian) and deontological, were considered. "When we consider the adequacy of these traditional theories . . . , no one theory seems to be free of serious objections. Also, no one theory provides a complete answer to the question, 'What ought I to do?' . . . there are good reasons why such a demand is impossible to satisfy."

All five of these centers engage in teaching ethics, applied ethics, and in assisting others to teach applied ethics courses. Yet all appear to agree that courses in applied ethics can be taught without the teacher or student knowing (or even caring) what are the ultimate bases for moral appeals, or without understanding the nature of intrinsic values and of rightness and wrongness. Are they not trying to "teach ethics without having ethics to teach"? None claims that students should expect to find definite answers. But all seek and accept foundation money.

My study of these and other centers of applied ethics has generated a thesis about American culture: a new mainstream attitude regarding ethical knowledge prevails among American intellectuals, professionals, business and political leaders, and scientists and educators. It has been developing for several decades. What is new about it is that this changed attitude has now become stabilized and a substantial contributor to the attitudes of more and more persons, including children being inducted into it as a part of their cultural inheritance. Its two main characteristics are:

1. Practical ethical problems are becoming more complex and

more urgent, so more effort should be devoted to dealing with them.

2. Ethical theory, or knowledge of the ultimate bases for moral appeals inherent in human nature, of the nature of intrinsic values, and of the nature of rightness and wrongness, is not necessary in making such effort.

Many reasons contribute to why such knowledge is believed not necessary:

1. Pluralistic presuppositions pervading Western civilization incline us to accepting many differing views. A history of ethics or an introductory course in ethics reveals many different ethical theories, each with its own advantages and disadvantages. A person remains uninformed ethically until he understands several such theories. To teach one of these while excluding others is feared as indoctrination.

2. U.S. Constitutional guarantees of freedom of opinion require us to respect each individual's rights to his own explanation of ethical ultimates as long as his acts do not harm others. To wade through the peculiarities, complexities, inadequacies, and falsities of the views of each of several persons trying to cooperate in solving a practical problem would add enormous difficulties to those inherent in the problem itself. Attention to them can be not only a waste of time but can dredge up fundamental disagreements preventing cooperative solution altogether.

3. The truth about value ultimates cannot yet be found by looking for them. Some day we may know; but today disputes among professional philosophers persist without expectation that they will be settled soon. Each of several alternative theories has recognizable merits, but no theory is yet available having all such merits.

4. People usually believe that they know what is right and wrong in particular situations even when they cannot explain why. Hence knowledge of ethical theory is not necessary for solving ethical problems.

5. Persons enjoying freedom from earlier ethical systems, whether prescriptive or explanatory, have little interest in adopting another one just because it has changed, possibly up-dated, presuppositions. If the onerous task of tracing the rightness and wrongness of particular decisions to their ultimate theoretical

foundations is unnecessary, then we not only can but should avoid it and get on with more urgent matters.

If my thesis is correct, then shall we compliment our centers for correctly sensing and expressing our mainstream attitude regarding ethical knowledge? Or does lack of serious concern for such knowledge constitute a deficiency in American culture that needs to be overcome? Callahan proclaims "the rebirth of ethics." He should know because he is a major participant in this rebirth: increasing concern for solving practical ethical problems and federal (and other) funding for organized efforts. But I do not discern a rebirth of interest in soundly grounding solutions to problems in demonstrably reliable foundational principles. Are we experiencing a rebirth of 'teaching ethics' without a rebirth of 'ethics to teach'?

LARUE T. HOSMER

Why a Majority of Our Business Schools Do Not Offer a Course in Business Ethics

. . . Why do close to 60% of the colleges and universities that replied to a scholarly inquiry on the teaching of ethics in business not offer courses, either elective or required, on the ethical problems of management? . . .

I teach at a school of business administration. . . . We do not offer a course on business ethics, and a proposal for such a course was rejected eight years ago by the Curriculum Committee. I believe that a proposal for an elective course in this area would be rejected today. Let me report on the results of conversations and discussions I have had with other faculty concerning this rejection over the past eight years. This is not research; it is specula-

Excerpted from "The Other 338: Why a Majority of Our Schools of Business Administration Do Not Offer a Course in Business Ethics" by LaRue T. Hosmer. *Journal of Business Ethics,* No. 4 (1985), pp. 17–22. © 1985 Kluwer Academic Publishers. Reprinted by permission of Kluwer Academic Publishers.

tion, but it is speculation on a critically important area of business management and management training. There appear to be three major reasons for the rejection of a course on business ethics at this and other universities:

1. There is a lack of understanding about the nature of ethics in management

Ethical issues—they are seldom termed 'dilemmas' by people who reject the need for a course on business ethics—are seen as dichotomous, with a 'yes' choice and a 'no' choice, and with very explicit financial benefits and social costs associated with each of the two alternatives. Should we dispose of this toxic waste in leaking 55 gallon drums, or not? Should we make this blatantly untrue statement in our advertising, or not? Should we pay a $1,000 bribe to this purchasing agent, or not? These acts are prima facie wrong and, unless we can discover some unusual circumstances inevitably associated with each, such as the employment of large numbers of displaced workers or the development of an exceedingly effective anti-cancer drug, we must reject them quickly. However, these simple contrasts have no resemblance to what most of us have in mind when we think of ethical problems in business.

The ethical problem in business is the conflict, or at the least the possibility of that conflict, between the economic performance of an organization, measured by revenues, costs and profits, and the social performance of that organization, stated in terms of obligations to other persons both within the organization and within the society. The nature of these obligations is, of course, open to interpretation, but most people would agree that they include requirements to prevent environmental deterioration, to maintain competitive markets, and to produce useful and safe products and services. The problem is that these obligations are costly, both for organizations evaluated by financial standards and for managers subject to financial controls. The chemical company that discharges hazardous wastes into a waterway will be more profitable than an equivalent firm that invests in proper disposal equipment. The sales manager who pays a small bribe to a purchasing agent will have a better record, and receive

higher commissions, than another person who refuses to coun-
tenance illegal payments. The design engineer who agrees to
sharply reduce material costs will be more appreciated, and more
likely to be promoted, than another who emphasizes product
quality and consumer safety. There is, or should be, a balance
between economic performance and social responsibility. The
purpose of a course on business ethics is firstly to examine that
balance, identifying the components in the decision, and then to
develop logical means of reasoning that will help in determining
the proper or 'right' balance among those components.

Determination of the proper balance between economic performance and social responsibility for an organization is not a simple choice between dichotomous alternatives, each with a clearly
identified outcome and each with a known probability of occurrence. Instead, there are multiple alternatives, each representing
mixed benefits and harms, each having an uncertain chance of
occurrence, and each with personal as well as organizational implications . . .

People who view ethical issues as simple dichotomous choices
between known alternatives believe that personal moral standards are adequate for the decision. That is why we hear so often
that, "You can't teach moral standards; by the time our students
get to the senior class in college, or the 2nd year of a graduate
M.B.A. program, their moral standards are set, by their parents,
their church, their associations, etc." My response is that I do
not want to teach moral standards; I want to teach a method of
moral reasoning through complex ethical issues so that the students can apply the moral standards they have. Of course, I will
not be displeased if, as a result of looking at complex ethical
issues and the obvious group injustices and personal wrongs that
derive from some managerial decisions, the students' moral sensi-
tivities have been increased and their moral standards have been
reinforced, but that will be a consequence and not the objective of
the course in business ethics.

People who view ethical issues in business as simple dichotomous choices, and who consequently believe that personal moral
standards are adequate for those choices, often express the basic
moral question in management as "Shall we take the right action?" Others, who think that ethical issues in business are com-

plex and extended decisions between multiple alternatives with mixed outcomes and uncertain probabilities, would state the same basic moral question of management as "What is the right action to take?" There is a world of difference between those two personal challenges, and the second requires instruction in moral reasoning to resolve.

2. There is an obvious reliance upon the concept of Pareto Optimality in economics

Economics has often been described as the basic discipline of business, and many of the current business functions (finance, production and marketing) and techniques (financial accounting, managerial accounting and operations research) are increasingly based upon the microeconomic paradigm. It might seem difficult to relate the debits and credits of financial accounting to microeconomics, but information is viewed as an input factor of the firm, along with capital, labor and material, and is 'priced' in much the same way, through a factor market.

A central concept of economic theory is that the price relationships of the product markets (for consumer goods and services) and of the factor markets (for capital, labor, material and, currently, information) can be used to optimally satisfy consumer wants/needs *provided* the managers of the producing firms act to maximize profits. A firm is maximizing profits when it is producing the most wanted products with the most available resources, so that if all managers would follow a decision rule to profit maximize, the society could reach a state of equilibrium termed Pareto Optimality. At this equilibrium, as is well known, the scarce resources of society are being used so efficiently that no member of the society can be made better off without harming some other member. Economic theory recognizes the possible injustices in this utilitarian result, and a political process is added to the economic system to distribute the benefits and allocate the costs democratically.

Pareto Optimality, combined with a political system to ensure democratically-determined justice in the distribution of benefits and the allocation of costs, is a difficult paradigm to oppose. It forms the unstated basis of Milton Friedman's famous article

'The Social Responsibility of Business Is To Increase Its Profits', and is an accepted tenet of economic thought. Technical arguments—that it is difficult for a firm to compute the external costs of environmental pollution so that they may be added to the internal cost of the product, for example—and pragmatic objections—that many markets are not truly competitive, but are dominated by large corporations—are not viewed as major issues by most economists. The standard reply is that the external or social costs of production can be approximated, particularly with the data processing capability of modern computers, and that non-competitive markets can be made price competitive by public policy changes to reduce company size and eliminate entry barriers.

Theoretic arguments against the economic paradigm are much more effective than the technical or pragmatic objections, but they have not been widely publicized. The theoretic arguments are that there are assumptions in economic theory about both the nature of human beings and the worth of human beings that are simply not tenable. On the nature of human beings, it is necessary in the economic model to accept that members of society are able to selfishly maximize their personal utilities for goods and services in the product markets and their personal receipts of wages, interest payments and rents in the factor markets at the same time as they are generously distributing social benefits and allocating social costs through democratic decisions in the political system. This complete reversal of roles that must occur instantaneously as the individual moves between the economic system and the political system does not seem wholly realistic.

The assumptions about the worth of human beings also appear to be undefensible. Everyone in the economic system must be treated as a means and not as an end in themselves. Customers for goods and services are people who maximize material satisfactions as a means of determining product demand curves. Owners of land, capital and labor are people who maximize financial revenues as a means of determining factor supply curves. Company managers are people who maximize corporate profits for the shareholders as a means of determining market supply and factor demand. No one acts as an independent human being, pursuing their own goals of self-development and self-actualization, and no one acts as a moral human being, treating others with consideration and respect.

The economic reliance upon the concept of Pareto Optimality may decline as the untenable assumptions become recognized, but at present this attitude or belief serves as a major barrier to instruction in the ethics of management at many schools of business administration.

3. There is an objection to management ethics on the grounds that the study is 'unscientific'

The last argument that I have heard expressed against courses in business ethics is that the topic is, by its nature, non-empirical and consequently non-scientific. The few people who make this argument are willing to admit that ethical decisions in business are complex, with multiple alternatives, mixed outcomes and uncertain probabilities, so that the personal moral standards of the students are often not adequate to resolve ethical dilemmas, and they are prepared to reject the comforting concept of Pareto Optimality in economics, but they are not ready to accept moral reasoning and ethical analysis as a full academic discipline. It is alleged that business decisions are, or should be, based upon objective thought processes, and that ethical analysis has to be subjective, and therefore has no place in the business curriculum. In prior years there was little that could be said against this view, except to admit that the 'two cultures' were alive and well, or at least that one of those cultures was fully represented at many schools of business administration.

Now, there is a more convincing response. Many of the recent writings on the overall direction or general management of large corporations have emphasized the need for an orientation toward values rather than towards profits. Both Pascale and Athos and Peters and Waterman, two of the books in this stream of literature that have appeared on the best selling list of the New York Times, have positioned 'shared values' as central to the management of successful firms, surrounded by the subordinate concepts of 'strategy', 'structure', 'systems', 'skills', 'staff' and 'style'. If shared values are important in management, and the objective evidence of Japanese industrial performance over the past ten years seems to indicate that they are, then it is necessary for business managers to be able to work with values, and determine not only what they are but what they should be. The determination of what values should be is the province of 'unscientific' and 'subjective' ethical analysis. I think that most of us will admit the shortcomings of our field of study and confess that there is no scientific or objective means of determining what is right and just and proper and, for modern business organizations, what is likely to bring about the personal commitment of large numbers of people. The lack of a scientific basis does not make the topic unimportant. Employees at all levels want to be able to devote their efforts to a cause that is right and just and worthy, but someone has to decide upon that cause . . .

What can be done? I believe that persons active in the study of moral standards and social responsibilities for business organization have to explain the complexity of ethical decisions, the assumptions of economic theory, and the importance of shared values [to] our colleagues in other disciplines. This can be done by seminars and workshops at schools of business administration, and through articles submitted to the professional journals in marketing, finance, organizational theory, etc. The essence of these seminars, workshops and articles would be "Here are important ethical problems that are not tractable to your usual forms of analysis; what should be done about them?" In the past, we have often spoken about the need to sensitize business students to the presence of ethical problems in management; I am suggesting the prior need to sensitize business faculty to the importance of those problems.

EDWIN J. DELATTRE

Who Can Have a Dilemma, Anyway?

I have chosen this as my central question because one major response to the problems of dishonorable conduct in business is to increase the study of ethics in business schools and undergraduate programs. The study of ethics is often taken, in turn, to consist primarily of the study of quandaries—cases that are supposed to be dilemmas. The same path is being followed by corporations and by governmental agencies. I doubt the wisdom and effectiveness of this approach.

Last week, for example, I worked with the governmental officials of a major resort city on the East Coast. They are concerned for honorable and trustworthy performance in government, and they sometimes study putative dilemmas. One of the situations they invited me to discuss is included in a set of case studies prepared by the International City Management Association, and it runs as follows:

> You are an assistant city manager in a mid-American city where you have worked for several years. You become a candidate and accept an offer to become city manager of a city in Alaska; you also receive their check for moving expenses. However, you then learn that your wife is pregnant, decide that you do not want to leave your family and friends, interview for and accept a job as city manager of a local community. You then call the mayor in Alaska, inform him that because of your wife's pregnancy, you have decided not to come, promise to return the check, and remind him that you gave him no acceptance in writing.

The question is what you should have done when faced with the "dilemma" of your acceptance of the offer in Alaska and your desire to change plans when your wife became pregnant.

Adapted from a speech given by Edwin J. Delattre at the School of Management, University of California at Los Angeles, 1987. Printed by permission of the author.

Now, as this hypothetical case is cast, is it a moral dilemma? Of course not. A moral dilemma is, by definition, a choice between two mutually exclusive courses of action, each of which has serious arguments on its side to being morally right. In this case, we have not a dilemma, but a tension between duty and desire, not between two *prima facie* obligatory courses of action. The case might be made into a dilemma if the facts were changed —say, you and your wife have had great difficulty conceiving, your wife's health is frail, she needs to be near the doctors you have worked with for several years, and so on. It wouldn't be a very hard dilemma, and the main question it would raise is why you didn't tell this to the Alaskans in the beginning. But as the case stands, none of these facts obtains.

To see that the case as offered poses no dilemma, put yourself in the place of the Alaska mayor. What would you say as mayor if you received the call described from a man who had accepted your offer to be city manager? My response would be to say I was glad to learn of his wishes, ask him to return the check, and say goodbye. I would then tell my colleagues that we had misjudged the man, that he was either remarkably immature or dishonorable or both, and that we were most fortunate to learn it early. Immature? Yes, because he cannot even plan his personal life to accommodate perfectly normal events and changes (he and his wife know where babies come from, after all), let alone plan the future of a city. Dishonorable? Yes, because he breaks his commitments when they interfere with his transient desires. Perhaps worse, he has told me implicitly that his word counts for nothing unless he gives it in writing. If you want to appreciate how dishonorable this is, imagine breaking a promise to one of your children and then justifying your betrayal by reminding the child that you did not make the promise in writing. Would you be willing for your son or daughter to grow up to be the kind of person who imitates such behavior?

Clearly, the problem with the case is that it illegitimately elevates a tension between duty and desire to the status of a dilemma. But even if what were posed as a problem for reflection were a genuine dilemma, the exercise would still miss the point about most of the elements of moral life.

Moral life is, after all, not one hard decision about duty after another; days are not "one damn thing after another," not one dilemma after another. If they were, everybody would go crazy in a week. Further, who *can* have a moral dilemma? In order to be torn between two arguably right but mutually exclusive actions, a person must already care what is right, care to discover what is right, care to do what is right or obligatory. Nobody can have a moral dilemma without already caring very much to be morally decent and honorable. For this reason, I doubt that the study of dilemmas can encourage decency; instead, such study presupposes it. For people who do not already care to be decent, "dilemmas" are only word games. All of us know people who are very good at such games and whose intellectual skill at diagnosing the elements of moral issues has absolutely no effect on their behavior in practice, except when they are concerned to maintain appearances.

Relatively few of our normal moral failings and failures are, I think, attributable to inept reasoning about dilemmas. Many more arise from moral indifference, disregard for other people, weakness of will, and bad or self-indulgent habits of life. If it were otherwise, then every philosopher who is good at moral reasoning, and every student of ethics, would be an admirable person. But as all of us in academe know, this is simply not the case.

I infer these things not just from the logic of discourse in ethics, but also from experience of moral strength and weakness exhibited in history and by people I work with in many different walks of life. Some of the work that matters most to me is with those who bear the public trust such as law enforcement personnel . . .

. . . I know [a police sergeant] who was on stakeout in an alley and found a paper bag in the trash with $9,000 in it. He didn't face some crisis about whether to take the money and run; he simply turned it in. The next morning, an old man came into the precinct crying that he had thrown out his life savings rather than the garbage. He described the bag, the money, and so on, and it was returned to him. He then asked whether the officer who had turned in the money was in the station, and was directed to the sergeant in question. The man went to his desk, emptied the bag onto it, counted the money, returned it to the bag, and said to the cop, "You son of a bitch, it's a good thing it's all here."

I asked the sergeant what he would do if he found such a bag again. His response: "I'd turn it in just like last time, only I wouldn't expect anybody to say thank you." No dilemma, no strain of real temptation, because he already cares about his own decency and about the people he is charged to protect and to serve . . .

Whether in law enforcement or business or government, the point is the same. A person who has a chance to profit by inside trading is not faced with a dilemma but with a chance to become a crook for profit. A federal agency that decides to launch a shuttle when people on the ground know it is dreadfully dangerous to do so at low temperature—and others in positions of decision-making authority know they know—is not faced with a dilemma. It is faced with a problem of personnel who are insufficiently serious about the lives of others. I do not see how the study of dilemmas can address the question of habits of decency and moral seriousness at all, and so I do not see the basic problems of personal and institutional weakness and corruption as problems of decision making, problems to be treated by the study of quandary ethics . . .

. . . It seems to me that neither business nor business education can do much about the moral maturation of genuinely ruthless people; in fact, I doubt that there is any remedy except to weed them out when they are identified—remove them from positions whose powers are susceptible to abuse. But what of those who are not ruthless? Who are these people? I think the category pretty much encompasses the rest of us: all of us vulnerable to one sort of temptation or another; victimized at times by inordinate self-love; weakness of will; thoughtlessness; occasionally, to be sure, inept reasoning; and sometimes, on the other side of the coin, moral excess: self-righteousness, presumption of the infallibility of our conscience, zealotry. How can education and business look to considerations of character, decency, self-knowledge, and trustworthy judgment in us? And what are realistic levels of expectation?

I suppose the first caveat about expectations is that in a contingent world of fallible human beings, there are no unconditional guarantees. If the study of ethics does not guarantee character, neither does good upbringing, as the heartache of many parents testifies. Neither does profound opportunity to live and work with moral exemplars, or as they are now so crudely called, "role models." The opportunities in this regard, for instance, of Alcibiades and Judas were spectacular, but neither achieved rock-bottom decency or trustworthiness.

Still, I think that most of the people I trust and rely on learned the Golden Rule in childhood and saw it practiced by adults who loved them. Most of the people I know who deserve to hold their positions of profound trust in education, government, law enforcement, the military services, and business have benefited from the companionship of good men and women as colleagues, friends, supervisors, teachers, and mentors. I find that such people are strongly influenced by asking themselves, "Would I find this course of action justifiable if I were on the other end of the stick?" and, "Would I deserve the respect and affection of my family and friends if I did what I am considering?" I think that these questions have greater power in mature adult lives than such questions as, "Is this what I studied in Ethics 101?" Many of the best businessmen and women I know give these questions greater specificity by asking whether they would find an action justifiable from the point of view of every type of stakeholder—customer, shareholder, employee, supplier, and member of the local community. What this shows is that they both know how to apply the Golden Rule in practice and that they care enough to do so. Then, and only then, can they *perceive* the really difficult and demanding *moral* questions that arise from conflict of stakeholder interests, let alone deliberate conscientiously about them . . .

. . . [W]hat *can* we do in education and in business to encourage decency—to refine moral sensibilities—and to cultivate intellectual rigor—to refine capacity for good reasoning in more or less difficult moral cases?

. . . I know of no substitutes for practice. Daily, purposeful, attentive practice. Practice in active conduct, practice in study. These are the only means I know for the refinement of intellect and moral sensibility. In my judgment, it is best for such practice

to begin in childhood, but whether or not it does, formal education ought to be designed on the same principle—lots of practice
in the conduct of life and the conduct of study. This is the activity of building reliable habits of mind, heart, and body and of
increasing self-knowledge.

Practice at what, specifically? Practice at behaving decently
and practice at thinking well. These might be called learning
integrity by practice. Why?

Most of the students I talk to have not much of an idea what
"integrity" means. They say "honesty" or "sincerity." They do
not know that integrity means wholeness, that having integrity is
to a person or an institution what being homogenized is to milk.
Homogenized milk is one thing through and through; so is a
person of integrity—not one person in a corporate boardroom or
a sales office and another in the bedroom of his or her children.
Human decency cuts all the way through a life of integrity; it is
not a matter of episode or activation and deactivation. Moral
sensibility and the decency it motivates cut all the way through a
life if they cut in any significant way; intellectual rigor applies
everywhere if it applies anywhere. A life of integrity is not
schizophrenic, and thus practice at decent behavior and rigorous
thought applies throughout.

For this reason, it seems to me that, in education, if our purposes are to refine sensibility and improve thinking, then we
should not make of ethics an isolated domain of inquiry in the
curriculum. Such isolation of ethics may be fine if our purpose is
to train and educate philosophers. But here our purposes are
different from that. Neither can we wisely treat the curriculum as
the only educational element in our school; in my account of
integrity, the broader domain of student life is relevant. The same
points seem to me to apply in business corporations. That is,
their programs of orientation, their working conditions, their policies and practices, the behavior of their leaders, are all elements
of life that count, and all of these are means by which institutional respect for decency can be exhibited and expectations
made explicit.

. . . To the extent that the purpose of education is self-knowledge, we should provide opportunity, as by such studies, for students to come to know us—and themselves—as we are. They will

not thereby become invulnerable to wrongdoing and evil, but they may become less likely to be deceived by either one.

Finally, I think that the capacity to resent ill treatment and unfairness to ourselves runs very deep in most of us. And so, I think that we can advance respect for the Golden Rule by building on that capacity. Take, for example, a passage from Martin Luther King's "Letter from Birmingham Jail."

In the Letter, King responds to critics who have urged him to stay away, urged him to wait, urged him to avoid even nonviolent confrontation. He declines the invitation and responds by appealing to 340 years of discrimination and injustice toward black people in America. And he explains that human endurance and willingness to wait passively "run over . . . when you suddenly find your tongue twisted and your speech stammering as you seek to explain to your six year old daughter why she can't go to the public amusement park that has just been advertised on television, and see tears welling up in her eyes when she is told that Funtown is closed to colored children, and see ominous clouds of inferiority beginning to form in her little mental sky. . . ."

How are we to help students and employees to see that here the fact of injustice causes such needless heartache and that the fact of needless heartache is intolerable? This much is certain: the best of their sensibilities and intelligence cannot be cultivated without exposure to powerful materials. Thus, we must, given limits of time, choose for their studies, their investment of time, materials that are worthy of *their* best efforts and ours, materials like King's Letter.

These seem to me to be basic considerations in our concern for decent and honorable conduct in business and education. I have no doubt that we will sometimes be disappointed by failures, but I am equally confident that if we neglect the broad context of moral life that I have tried to sketch, we will advance little more than cleverness at word games. We must call up sustained practice at more serious things if we hope to contribute to the ability —and it is an ability—even to have a dilemma, let alone to face it. Because to reach that level at all, we have to nurture or sustain individual conscience that has humility but not an on-off switch.

HERBERT JOHNSTON

The Case for Teaching Business Ethics

. . . Can morality in business be taught to students in a formal course, or is it rather something that can be expected to develop from a general study of liberal and humanizing subjects, or even to be picked up as a set of professional attitudes in the course of business practice itself? Professor Ben Miller in *Toward a Philosophy of Business Education* asserts that "formal courses designed to explore the whole question of morality in business are utterly essential." Professor Ernest M. Fisher, of Columbia University, considers that broad training rather than courses in exclusively business areas will best contribute to the student's moral education. On the other hand, James M. Shipton, manager of General Electric's Advanced Business Courses Service at Crotonville, New York, maintains that little is known about how to teach business ethics, and that it is something that is absorbed by osmosis over a long period of time.

This article will support the first possibility, that of Professor Miller, outlined above. Perhaps some of the differences of opinion arise from confusion between the moral and the intellectual results to be expected from a formal course in ethics. Can one reasonably hope that such a course, or any classroom course, will "completely transform a potential executive's ethical code"? If this question asks whether a course in ethics can directly change an unjust man into a just man, a dishonest man into an honest one, the answer is, of course, no. For these are moral virtues, perfections of various human appetites and especially of the will, enabling men to *do* what is right in the sense of good. A classroom course is devoted, directly, to the development of an intellectual virtue, a perfection of human cognitive powers and espe-

Excerpted from "Ethics in Business Education" by Herbert Johnston in *Business and Liberal Arts,* John J. Clark & Blaise J. Opulente, eds. New York: St. John's University Press, 1962. Reprinted by permission of the Estate of Herbert Johnston. All rights reserved.

cially of the intellect, enabling men to *know* what is right in the sense of true. The one simply is not the other. Whether moral virtue can be taught will depend on one's definition of teaching; but it certainly cannot be taught in the sense that an intellectual discipline can be taught, for it is not a matter of knowing but of doing; and moral vice, in spite of Socrates, is more than a matter of ignorance.

Yet ignorance rather than sheer malice may lie behind the performance of many materially immoral actions, and there is much evidence that it frequently does, perhaps especially in the tortuous and difficult paths of contemporary business practice. It is true that for a student who is already cynically determined to pursue money and status by any means whatever, a course in ethics is nothing more than a requirement to be fulfilled for graduation. But most students are willing to learn how to live well because they want to live well, and for them a course in ethics can be really though remotely practical, and of genuine help for their moral lives. Ethics is only remotely practical because it is a science in the Aristotelian sense of the word, and its conclusions are in general rather than in particular terms. They have to do with a type or species of act, such as lying or respecting another's rights, rather than with this action done here and now, such as saying this rather than that, or bribing this competitor's employee to get specific confidential information. Instruction in ethics leads to general moral knowledge, whereas human actions are individual and even unique, done in the midst of concrete and sometimes agonizing circumstances. Each person, each moral agent, must reason as prudently as he can and finally reach his own judgment, his own act of conscience, about what he should do. In this reasoning he must take variable circumstances into account, and this is why his task is often so difficult. Yet in this task he must also start somewhere, for he cannot apply general moral knowledge to the existing circumstances unless he first has the general moral knowledge. The aim of a course in ethics is to put this knowledge on as scientific a basis as possible, to make the student something of a professional moralist in somewhat the same sense that a course in accounting is designed to make the student something of a professional accountant. Ethics is not prudence; it is only remotely and not immediately practical; but it is practical.

All this says something for a course in ethics, but not yet for a specific course in business ethics. If the businessman is a man among other men, why not give him a course in general ethics and let him apply the conclusions there reached to business situations? For two reasons. The first is that most students need instruction to enable them to recognize the moral implications of most business situations, to see that there is a problem and what kind of problem it is. The second is that they also need instruction in how to tackle this or that kind of problem, how to relate it to more general moral knowledge, how to come to a reasonable, prudential judgment in a problem that may resemble those that they will face in the future. The case for business ethics is the same as the case for legal ethics and medical ethics; it is that the problems concerned are too highly specialized for their handling to be left to the student's untutored efforts.

In preparing students to handle particular business situations, then, we face this twofold difficulty. Many of them seem totally unaware of the existence of moral problems in business life. Perhaps this attitude springs largely from the atmosphere of the world they live in, an atmosphere that does not encourage the discovery of such problems in such a setting. Whatever the reason, the view of economic life as part of a larger moral life is all too rare, and the view of economic life as a world of its own with its own rules of conduct is all too common. The first part of our job, then, is to convince students—and convince them through intellectual evidence, not merely persuade them through rhetorical exhortation—that moral problems exist as an integral part of business situations.

The second part of our job arises from the fact that, even after problems are recognized, they must be attacked; and some instruction in methods of attack is, for practical purposes, indispensable. The usual college instruction in moral theology or in ethics does not do more than touch this vast area that is of such importance to future men of business. It is simply not enough to remind students that moral problems exist in business life, and to urge them to apply moral principles to the solution of those problems. They may well ask: "What are the moral principles that apply to this particular problem, and are there other moral principles that apply to other problems? And just how do you go about applying a moral principle to a problem of this sort?" We do not teach students pure mathematics and then tell them to go ahead and keep accounts with it; we teach them accounting. It is true that mathematics underlies accounting, and that general theory must come before practice and particular application. It is also true that general ethics underlies business ethics, and that an indispensable minimum must be taught before the more specialized considerations of business ethics will be intelligible. But general ethics alone is not enough to prepare students either to recognize or to deal with the moral problems to be met in business life. They can be so prepared by being asked to handle repeated and varied examples, by being led to see again and again the relation between general moral principles and the moral aspects of particular business situations.

This involves bringing students to see that the *same* question has economic, psychological, legal, moral, and usually other dimensions. When they face a particular problem, they face *one* problem with several aspects, one more example of the recurring question of the one and the many. They ordinarily find no particular difficulty in looking at and dealing with this single problem from its many points of view: they can see it as economic, as legal, as psychological, perhaps as historical, and they quite expect to take all of these and other points of view into account in dealing with it in a practical way. They see it as a single problem with more than one dimension, and often do a pretty good job of coordinating the various kinds of knowledge that are needed to attack what is still one problem. The aim of a course in business ethics is to get students to see these same business problems in their moral dimension as well.

When, for example, a college graduate is offered a sales position involving a month's training period, may he accept the training even though he is uncertain whether he wants to stay with the company or even in that occupation? Are there any circumstances in which he may take the training and then leave the company? In this case there are involved the rights and obligations attaching to the use of speech, and, more particularly, the nature and scope of an implied contract, especially as applying to employment. This constitutes a series of related moral problems, already too specialized to be tackled with much hope of success on the basis of a general ethics course alone. Again, may a person in a position of trust use confidential information to his own advantage, supposing that he would thereby harm no one else? Must expense accounts be literally true in every detail, or may they be padded to make up for the inconvenience of being away from home or to supplement a small salary? Should an insurance salesman (counselor?) unload as much as he can persuade the client to buy, or as much as he thinks the client needs, or as much as the client thinks he needs? Should a seller point out faults in what he is offering for sale, for example, the poor location of a piece of real estate? Would it make any difference whether he was selling to a professional or to a private person? And so on, indefinitely. By dealing with such cases, by handling example after example, students will become convinced that moral problems do exist within business situations, and will gain some experience in relating these questions to the moral principles involved, thus approaching a reasonable solution.

Another aspect of the task of preparing students for business life arises from the fact that they will be actively participating in the operation of various economic institutions. In order both to guide their own conduct intelligently and to influence these institutions for good, however slightly at first, they must have some basis for judgment better than their personal interests and prejudices. Just how free, for example, should free enterprise be? What is its ultimate purpose? What are the moral problems involved in monopoly or in oligopoly? Should employees share in the policy decisions of management? Should they share in profits? What about the industry council plan, "right-to-work" laws, political activity on the part of labor unions? What is the place of government in the economic order? These are large questions. The answers given to them at any particular period will greatly influence all our lives. And the answers given to them at any particular period will depend on what the preponderant convictions on these questions are at that time. Both as citizens and as businessmen, students should have an introduction to the moral as well as the other aspects of these problems before they leave school, and these are problems that a general ethics course alone does not ordinarily touch.

To sum up: Our task as teachers of business students is to make them conscious of the existence of moral problems *within* business situations, to provide them scientifically with the moral principles to apply to those problems, and to give them as much practice as possible in making such applications. All three of these aims can be combined; indeed, each of them can best be achieved in combination with the others . . .

CHAPTER THREE

Corporate Codes of Ethics: Are They Effective? What Should They Contain?

Commentary

In September, 1982, a cunning criminal inserted cyanide crystals in some Tylenol capsules, causing the death of seven persons in the Chicago area. In Lawrence Foster's account of Johnson & Johnson's response to this devastating event, he describes the effect of the company's long-standing credo on the behavior of top executives and other employees. The example suggests that where a code (or "credo" as Johnson & Johnson calls it) has a long history in the company, and where it has been inspired and constantly adhered to by the top leadership, it can have a powerful influence on conduct in a time of acute crisis.

While it cannot be assumed that in all cases adherence to ethical standards guarantees good financial results, in this instance the evidence is impressive. In his account, written in 1983, Foster reports the remarkable fact that "five months after the tragedy struck, Tylenol had recaptured nearly 70% of the market it had previously held." Market recovery continued strong until February, 1986, when a young woman died after taking two cyanide-contaminated Tylenol capsules from a box purchased in Bronxville, New York. At this point the company concluded that the triple-sealed package developed as a result of the first event was vulnerable and discontinued the use of capsules in all its products. Johnson & Johnson then launched a campaign to get users to switch to caplet or tablet forms of the popular drug. This effort resulted in an even faster recovery of market share than had occurred in 1983.

The impact of a strong commitment to a corporate code of conduct may also be seen in the examples of Cummins Engine Company, discussed in the next chapter, and J. C. Penney, described in Chapter Eight.

The Conference Board in New York houses a large collection of codes of ethics obtained in the course of a survey of its member companies. Some indication of the status of these codes and the sensitivity surrounding them may be gleaned from the fact that the Conference Board felt it necessary to reassure the corporations surveyed that the materials collected would be available only to member companies, and for that reason the editors of this book were denied access to the collection. In our subsequent efforts to obtain copies directly from a small number of companies, some did not reply, and the president of one well-known manufacturer responded, "I am sorry we cannot provide this information to you, as it is our policy not to share data of this nature outside our company." We hazard the guess that in another ten years or so, such a response will seem as quaint and inappropriate as would the refusal of a publicly owned company to provide a copy of its most recent audited financial statement.

In contrast, the five companies whose codes we cite here have no hesitation in sharing this information with the public. There is an element of corporate pride involved, as a study of the documents clearly reveals.

BankAmerica publishes a 34-page booklet entitled "Working at BankAmerica." These pages contain quite specific information about Standards of Conduct under three rubrics: The Work Environment, Protecting Our Integrity and Legal Requirements. We reproduce here virtually the entire text of the first section. The section entitled "Protecting Our Integrity" deals with conflict of interest, recordkeeping, expense accounts, accepting or giving gifts, payments and preferential treatment, insider trading, political activities, and other such matters. The section on Legal Requirements covers the Anti-Kickback Act of 1986, the Comprehensive Crime Control Act of 1984, financial accounting and reporting requirements, and examples of standards of conduct.

The Equitable Financial Companies publishes an eight-page booklet entitled "Policy Statement on Ethics." It has four parts: Business Practices, Honesty, Fairness and Obeying the Law, Conflicts of Interest, Care of Assets, and Reporting Violations. We reproduce here the first part.

The Code of Conduct of AT&T is contained in a 17-page booklet entitled "A Personal Responsibility." The code is organized under the following headings: Nondiscrimination, Personal Conduct, Privacy of Communications, Safeguarding Communications Services, Conflict of Interest, Inside Information and Investment in Securities, Proprietary Information, Copyrighted Works, Computer Systems, Espionage and Sabotage, Company Records, Company Property, Company Funds, Fair Competition and Antitrust Law, Federal Government Business and Classified Information, US Foreign Corrupt Practices Act, Export Control Laws, Foreign Economic Boycotts, Political Activity/Contributions, and Fidelity Bond Coverage. We reproduce here the sections entitled Privacy of Communications, Conflict of Interest, Fair Competition and Antitrust Law, and US Foreign Corrupt Practices Act.

Du Pont publishes an 11-page booklet entitled "Du Pont Business Conduct Guide" and a four-page statement of "Business Ethics Policy." The latter "consolidates in one document all policies with respect to Business Ethics and Conflict of Interest for E. I. du Pont de Nemours and Company and its subsidiaries in which it has a majority interest or for which it has operating responsibility," and we reproduce it in full.

IBM's "Business Conduct Guidelines" is contained in a 42-page booklet organized under four main headings: You and Your Job in IBM, Conducting IBM's Business, On Your Own Time, and You, IBM and Competition Law. We publish excerpts from each of these sections.

Copies of the full texts of the five codes quoted in this chapter may be obtained from the respective corporate headquarters.

LAWRENCE G. FOSTER

The Johnson & Johnson Credo
and the Tylenol Crisis

For some time now, corporate planning groups have included crisis management as an important part of preparing to operate in a variety of future business environments. Such planning often involves creating a crisis management center and a disaster plan that includes detailed responses to worst-case scenarios.

No crisis management plan would have been sufficient in the face of the Tylenol poisonings because not even the best of managers could have planned for a tragedy of that proportion. Fortunately, Johnson & Johnson had a 40-year-old corporate business philosophy to turn to. That philosophy established the company's priorities and defined its responsibilities to its constituencies. Although such a philosophy is not unique to Johnson & Johnson, it served us immeasurably in responding to and managing the greatest crisis ever to confront our business.

The Tylenol tragedy was without precedent. In the fall of 1982, an unknown criminal poisoned pain relief capsules with cyanide and seven people in the Chicago area died. Overnight, Tylenol toppled from its preeminent position as the nation's leading analgesic product. Many marketing experts predicted that it never would recover.

Johnson & Johnson and its affiliate, McNeil Consumer Products Company, the manufacturers of Tylenol, dealt with the crisis head-on. Out of this devastation they began rebuilding the business step by step. By early 1983, five months after the tragedy struck, Tylenol had recaptured nearly 70 percent of the market it previously held.

The decisions that brought Johnson & Johnson and McNeil

From "The Johnson & Johnson Credo and the Tylenol Crisis" by Lawrence G. Foster. *New Jersey Bell Journal,* Vol. VI, No. 1, Spring 1983. Reprinted by permission.

through the crisis, and paved the way for the remarkable turn-around, will be discussed and debated by business people long into the future. And while there are many elements of the Tylenol experience that have not been defined clearly, one aspect of the tragedy that can be put into proper perspective concerns the methods that Johnson & Johnson used to deal with a crisis of this magnitude.

"There probably are as many emergency plans worked out and ready to go within the Johnson & Johnson organization as there are in any other company that tries to prepare for unforeseen emergencies," David R. Clare, president of Johnson & Johnson and chairman of its Executive Committee commented. "But the events surrounding the Tylenol crisis were so atypical that we found ourselves improvising every step of the way.

"I doubt that even now we could devise a plan of action to deal with all aspects of the Tylenol situation. Events happened so quickly and so unpredictably that it would be impossible to antic-ipate the critical decisions that had to be made.

"Crisis planning did not see us through this tragedy nearly as much as the sound business management philosophy that is em-bodied in our credo. It was the credo that prompted the decisions that enabled us to make the right early decisions that eventually led to the comeback phase."

Crisis Planning and Sound Business Management

The credo to which Mr. Clare refers is a simple, four stanza document written in the mid-1940s by the late Robert Wood Johnson, the company's leader for some 50 years. Mr. Johnson was a maverick when it came to the philosophy of running a business. He saw business as having responsibilities to society that went far beyond the usual sales and profit incentives. To this end, he defined his company's responsibility to four constituen-cies: consumers and medical professionals using its products, em-ployees, the communities where its people work and live and, finally, its stockholders.

Mr. Johnson felt deeply that unless business recognized these responsibilities it could not be successful in the long run. He thought that paying attention to these priorities would be not only moral, but profitable as well. For nearly 40 years, succeeding

Our Credo

We believe our first responsibility is to the doctors, nurses and patients, to mothers and all others who use our products and services. In meeting their needs everything we do must be of high quality. We must constantly strive to reduce our costs in order to maintain reasonable prices. Customers' orders must be serviced promptly and accurately. Our suppliers and distributors must have an opportunity to make a fair profit.

We are responsible to our employees, the men and women who work with us throughout the world. Everyone must be considered as an individual. We must respect their dignity and recognize their merit. They must have a sense of security in their jobs. Compensation must be fair and adequate, and working conditions clean, orderly and safe. Employees must feel free to make suggestions and complaints. There must be equal opportunity for employment, development and advancement for those qualified. We must provide competent management, and their actions must be just and ethical.

We are responsible to the communities in which we live and work and to the world community as well. We must be good citizens— support good works and charities and bear our fair share of taxes. We must encourage civic improvements and better health and education. We must maintain in good order the property we are privileged to use, protecting the environment and natural resources.

Our final responsibility is to our stockholders. Business must make a sound profit. We must experiment with new ideas. Research must be carried on, innovative programs developed and mistakes paid for. New equipment must be purchased, new facilities provided and new products launched. Reserves must be created to provide for adverse times. When we operate according to these principles, the stockholders should realize a fair return.

Johnson & Johnson

managements at Johnson & Johnson have successfully adhered to the same belief.

As the Tylenol crisis grew by the hour, the company turned to the credo philosophy for guidance and the decisions came rapidly. The public and the medical community were alerted immediately. The Food and Drug Administration authorities were notified. Production was halted. Complete cooperation was given to the news media. Tylenol capsules were withdrawn from the national marketplace.

Appearing before the Associated Press Managing Editors meeting in San Diego several weeks later, chairman of the board and CEO James E. Burke said: "It was a demonstration without parallel of government and business working with the news media to help protect the public." One dramatic result of that cooperation was that two bottles of Tylenol capsules containing cyanide were recovered before they could claim more victims.

The first critical decision, made immediately by the public relations staff with total support from management, was to cooperate fully with the news media. The press, radio and television, were key to warning the public of the danger.

Tylenol quickly captured the nation's attention. Queries from the press on the Tylenol story exceeded 2,500. Two news clipping services generated in excess of 125,000 clippings. One of them said the Tylenol story had resulted in the widest domestic coverage of any story since the assassination of President John F. Kennedy. Associated Press and United Press International gave it second place as the impact story of 1982; only coverage of the nation's economy ranked higher. The television and radio coverage was staggering.

When the company held a 30-city press conference via satellite to announce the Tylenol comeback and introduce the new triple-safety-sealed packaging, news media gave the story wide coverage. Then the public responded positively by buying the product in its new tamper-resistant packaging. Given all the facts, the public was eminently fair in its assessment of what had happened.

Editorials and columns in hundreds of newspapers have commented favorably on the company's performance. Some said a new level of corporate responsibility had been achieved, while others suggested that a gap had been bridged between the news media and public relations in business. Jerry Knight wrote in the *Washington Post:* "Johnson & Johnson has effectively demonstrated how a major business ought to handle a disaster."

Later we realized that no meeting had been called to make the first critical decision: to be open with the press and put the consumer interest first. "Every one of us knew what we had to do," Mr. Burke commented. "There was no need to meet. We had the credo philosophy to guide us."

The Social Consequences of Business

Back in the mid-1940s when Mr. Johnson pioneered his approach to running a business, he placed strong emphasis on corporate responsibility, a little-used term at that time. About corporate responsibility, he wrote:

"The evidence on this point is clear . . . Institutions, both public and private, exist because the people want them, believe in them, or at least are willing to tolerate them. The day has passed when business was a private matter—if it ever really was. In a business society, every act of business has social consequences and may arouse public interest. Every time business hires, builds, sells or buys, it is acting for the . . . people as well as for itself, and it must be prepared to accept full responsibility."

Mr. Johnson's conviction that paying attention to social responsibilities would be beneficial to the business proved valid in the Tylenol situation: the early actions taken by Johnson & Johnson to protect the public produced very positive results. Essentially, the credo forms the bedrock of Johnson & Johnson's corporate culture and, as such, has influenced the company's operations, policies and decisions.

While Mr. Johnson was alive, he personally saw to it that the intent of the credo was carried out. Following his death in 1968, ways were explored to keep that philosophy in the forefront of management decisions. In the spring of 1972, we decided to make the credo the theme of that year's annual report to stockholders and to conduct dinner meetings for management employees to reinforce the company's awareness of and belief in its business philosophy. More than 4,000 employees attended the credo meetings led by chairman Philip B. Hofmann.

Three years later the company faced a critical decision concerning the location of its new world headquarters. Chairman Richard B. Sellars said that the credo's emphasis on responsibility to the community was at the core of the decision to remain in New Brunswick and deal with its urban problems rather than move to a more pastoral setting in a smaller community.

In 1975, Mr. Burke, who was then president, proposed and led credo challenge meetings that included every member of top management from the worldwide Johnson & Johnson family of companies. Both the philosophy and the wording of the credo were vigorously debated. Its phrasing was changed somewhat to modernize the language; the substance of the document withstood the test. Credo indoctrination and challenge meetings are now part of the orientation for new management employees.

Implementing the Credo Philosophy
In reflecting on the implementation of decisions made during the crisis, Mr. Clare said: "Many within the organization felt that our ability to deal quickly with the Tylenol emergency was a reaffirmation of the advantages of our decentralized form of management." For more than 90 years Johnson & Johnson has prided itself on its decentralized philosophy of managing a world health care business, which includes more than 150 companies in 60 countries. One of the benefits of decentralization is the ability to generate quick decision making and to delegate authority to manageable groups of people.

Much of the crisis management, as well as the careful planning that went into the comeback phase, was delegated to the McNeil company under the direction of its chairman, David D. Collins and its president, Joseph R. Chiesa. Virtually every employee in McNeil participated in the Tylenol experience. Meanwhile, other decisions were made at the corporate level, where board chairman Burke headed the seven-member strategy committee.

People throughout the Johnson & Johnson organizations are acutely aware that the victims and their families suffered the most as a result of the senseless poisonings. But out of the tragedy there were some positive results to which the company could point. Mr. Burke referred to them in this way:

"Two things are clear to us. The first is that the value system, as articulated in the credo, now permeates the company in a way that could not have been possible without the crisis. The credo was tested—and it worked. Further, we learned that the reputation of the corporation, which has been carefully built for over 90 years, provided a reservoir of good will among the public, the people in the regulatory agencies, and the media, which was of incalculable value in helping to restore the brand."

Johnson & Johnson's reaffirmation of its credo philosophy accounted for its ability to respond to one of the most devastating incidents in American corporate history. Despite the enormity of the Tylenol tragedy, the corporation's image as a socially conscious business remains undiminished.

Excerpts from Corporate Codes:
  BankAmerica Corporation
  The Equitable Financial Companies
  AT&T
  Du Pont
  IBM Corporation

BANKAMERICA CORPORATION

Excerpt from "Working at BankAmerica" August 1989

Standards of Conduct: The Work Environment

"The organization has always been very much like a large family, in the relationship between members of the staff. People often comment on what they call the 'spirit' of the institution. It is in reality the friendly interest expressed in the service of our customers."

—*A.P. Giannini*

EQUAL EMPLOYMENT OPPORTUNITY

BankAmerica strives to make employment decisions on the basis of equal employment opportunity. We believe it makes good business sense to practice equal employment opportunity and to recognize diversity, in part because the result is a workforce that reflects the diverse backgrounds of the communities we serve . . .

EMPLOYEE STATUS

Your employment with BankAmerica has no specified length, and either you or the company may end it at any time, with or without notice or cause. In addition, under federal law, officers of Bank of America NT&SA and its subsidiaries are subject to the at pleasure dismissal provisions of the National Bank Act. (BankAmer-

Reprinted by permission

ica encourages salaried employees to give at least two weeks' notice. If you decide to leave the company, failure to give such notice can disrupt the unit's ability to meet its objectives. Therefore, failure to give such notice may impact your eligibility for rehire.)

WORK HOURS

All employees are expected to know the work hours of their unit and to comply with established minimum work hours. In most locations, full-time employees—non-exempt and exempt—work a minimum of an eight-hour day and are expected to begin work at a specified time. You should confirm your work hours with your manager.

Non-exempt employees, which includes employees classified as hourly, must be paid overtime when they work beyond a specified number of hours. This means actual hours worked and does not include paid time off, such as vacations, holidays, or paid sick days. *Exempt employees* who are salaried are not eligible for overtime pay.

If you are a non-exempt employee, you are expected to routinely record your work time on a time sheet or other company approved time record, each day. This is to satisfy requirements of both state and federal laws enacted for your protection. You need to complete this record accurately, truthfully, and on time. Time worked is all the time actually spent on the job. All of your time spent doing work for the company must be recorded, and rest periods are considered work time. Time worked does not include lunch breaks or time off for medical appointments, dental appointments, jury duty, or personal business or errands.

Non-exempt employees may be required to work overtime or extra hours for staffing or other business reasons.

In addition, exempt employees are expected to work the number of hours needed to get the job done, including longer or varied hours as necessary.

JOB PERFORMANCE

The Performance Planning, Coaching, and Evaluation (PPC&E) guideline is important to each employee. It can let you know what is expected of you, periodically tell you how well you are doing, and measure your final results. If you have questions about your PPC&E objectives or your performance, talk with your manager. You must satisfactorily meet performance expectations.

ATTENDANCE GUIDELINES

Good attendance and punctuality are vital for efficient customer service and effective operation of the company. Your unit may have specific attendance or punctuality guidelines; check with your manager. You may not be excessively absent or late for any reason.

If you are unable to come to work or will be late for any reason, including for medical reasons, you are expected to promptly notify your manager.

Your manager may request a doctor's statement for any absence due to illness. In all cases, you are required to submit a doctor's statement if your medical absence is for 8 or more calendar days. In addition, you may be required to be examined by a doctor of the company's choice. If you do not submit medical evidence acceptable to the company, the absence may be considered as unauthorized. You may not have unauthorized absences.

Short periods of time off for personal reasons may be granted by your manager with or without pay, subject to applicable attendance guidelines . . .

LEAVE OF ABSENCE

A leave of absence is authorized time off without pay that exceeds fourteen calendar days, and requires prior approval. Leaves may be granted—subject to business needs—for child care, military duty, educational purposes, or other personal reasons.

Reinstatement guidelines, and your obligation to give notice of your intent to return from a leave of absence, differ depending on the type of leave granted to you. Before taking a leave, you should discuss these guidelines—which are noted on the reverse side of the *Leave of Absence Agreement* (EXEC-42)—with your manager.

DRESS STANDARDS

You are expected to dress appropriately for the type of work you do and with regard for appropriate standards of the marketplace. Since standards may vary by unit or location, you should consult your manager for what is appropriate for your work unit and follow those standards.

SAFETY

BankAmerica seeks to provide a safe and healthful work environment for all employees, and maintains programs designed to prevent occupational injuries. The success of the safety program depends upon the personal commitment of each employee. You should correct or report to management in an appropriate manner any unsafe conditions you encounter, and are required to comply with safety procedures established by the company or your unit.

TREATMENT OF EMPLOYEES

Our policy is that the workplace should be free of harassment. Harassment includes such things as:

- *Verbal harassment* (e.g., derogatory comments, jokes, slurs, abusive language);
- *Physical harassment* (e.g., unwanted physical contact, assault);
- *Visual harassment* (e.g., derogatory posters, cartoons or drawings); or
- *Sexual harassment* (e.g., an unwanted or unwelcomed sexual advance that is verbal, physical, or creates an offensive or hostile working environment).

Do not tolerate such treatment. It is up to you to promptly notify management or go directly to Personnel Relations if you feel you are being harassed.

You may not be discriminated or retaliated against for reporting what you believe to be unlawful harassment. You should promptly notify your manager *or* a Personnel Relations representative if you believe you, or others, are being harassed or discriminated or retaliated against. (You do *not* have to speak first with a manager you believe is treating you improperly. You also may raise such matters through the Let's Talk program.)

Where evidence of harassment or unlawful discrimination or retaliation is found, disciplinary action up to and including termination may result.

SMOKING IN THE WORKPLACE

In all locations, employees must not smoke while serving customers or while working in areas visible to the public during normal business hours. Smoking also is prohibited in areas where equipment, records, or supplies—including cleaning fluids, or other flammable liquids—would be exposed to hazard from fire, ashes, or smoke; and where combustible fumes can collect—such as in garage, maintenance, and storage areas—and all other areas where smoking would create a safety hazard.

In addition, smoking is prohibited in libraries, medical facilities, elevators, stairwells, copy rooms, and any areas where smoking is prohibited by local ordinance.

In other workplace areas, unless smoking is prohibited by local ordinance, a reasonable accommodation is expected to be made between the non-smoker and the smoker in BankAmerica buildings and facilities. When the preference of the non-smoker and the smoker conflict, and a reasonable accommodation is not possible, non-smokers will be given preference and smoking may be prohibited in that work area. In cases where smoking is prohibited in the work area, efforts may be made to accommodate smoking, depending on the facility. Management reserves the right to prohibit smoking in any workplace or facility.

ALCOHOL AND DRUGS IN THE WORKPLACE

BankAmerica strives to provide its employees a safe workplace that is free of the problems associated with the use and abuse of controlled substances, as well as provide a safe business location for its customers and clients. The use of controlled substances is inconsistent with the behavior expected of employees. It also subjects the company to unacceptable risks of workplace accidents, errors, or other failures that would undermine the company's ability to operate effectively and efficiently. Therefore, to maintain a drug free workplace, the presence or use of controlled substances or unauthorized alcohol on company premises will *not* be tolerated.

Controlled substances for purposes of this policy include drugs that are not legally obtainable, as well as drugs that are legally obtainable but are used for illegal purposes. Also included are the controlled substances listed in the federal Controlled Substance Act, 21 U.S.C. Section 812, including, but not limited to, marijuana, cocaine (including "crack" and other cocaine derivatives), morphine, heroin, amphetamines, and barbiturates, as well as those substances controlled under state or local laws. Controlled substances used with a valid prescription are not included.

The sale, purchase, transfer, manufacture, distribution, dispensation, use, or possession of controlled substances as defined here, by anyone on company premises or other work sites where employees may be assigned, or conducting company business, is strictly prohibited. Also prohibited is the use, sale, purchase, possession, transfer, dispensation, manufacture, and distribution of illegal drugs on non-working time if it affects an employee's safety on the job or ability to perform his or her job, or interferes with the job performance or safety of others, or if this activity would affect the reputation of the company with the general public or threaten its integrity.

If the use of any drug, including alcohol, affects your job performance or safety, or interferes with the job performance or safety of others—including while driving a company vehicle or while driving on company business, as with other provisions of this booklet, BankAmerica may take disciplinary action, including dismissal. Also, when physician-directed drugs adversely affect an employee's job performance or safety, or the job performance or safety of others, it may be in the best interest of the employee, co-workers, or the company that time off or other job arrangements be made, if possible. However, the company reserves the right to take other action.

The company also does not allow unauthorized use or presence of alcoholic beverages on company premises. The use or presence of alcoholic beverages on company premises may be approved by management *only* for the entertainment of customers, special business-related events, or on other occasions approved by senior management.

To help assure a safe work environment, free of drugs and alcohol, BankAmerica reserves the right to take appropriate action. By way of example, BankAmerica may inspect, search, or maintain surveillance . . .

(Personal property includes, but is not limited to, purses, packages, briefcases, and the contents of an employee's pockets.)

If you are convicted of controlled substance-related violations in the workplace under local, state or federal law, or you plead guilty or nolo contendere to such charges, you must inform the company within five days of such conviction or plea. Additionally, if you are working on a federal contract, the company is required by the Drug Free Workplace Act to notify the contracting agency within ten working days after receiving notice of such conviction, and your abiding by the company's policy on drugs in the workplace is a federally mandated condition of employment . . .

FALSE OR MISLEADING REMARKS

You must not make false or misleading remarks about company suppliers, customers, competitors, or other employees. You also should not make false statements about the financial condition of the company.

PRICING ARRANGEMENTS

Any activities that violate, or appear to violate, antitrust laws must be avoided. This includes discussing prices with competitors or making arrangements with them that affect prices, services, or other competitive policies and practices.

Obtain guidance from legal counsel before engaging in any action or conversation that could have antitrust implications.

MEMBERSHIPS IN PRIVATE CLUBS AND ORGANIZATIONS

Special circumstances may require the use of facilities other than our offices for conducting business. When an employee's job duties include regular business entertainment, the company may provide for the use of certain private clubs and organizations.

- The company will not maintain a membership, or reimburse business expenses, in any club or organization that discriminates on the basis of race, color, religion, sex, age, national origin, handicap, or veteran status.
- Business-related expenses incurred as part of job duties will be approved, if they are reasonable, properly authorized, and in accordance with the company's expense policies, guidelines, and procedures.

Country Club Memberships

The company may provide membership in certain country clubs in order to allow authorized officers to entertain key customers and prospective customers. These memberships are reserved for the authorized use of company officers who, because of the nature of their position, are responsible for promoting business relationships with key members in the communities served.

- Country club membership must be approved by the Managing Committee Member responsible for the employee's division or unit. Reimbursement of fees, dues, and other business expenses will be treated in accordance with the company's expense policies, guidelines, and procedures.
- *The company owns the membership.* If the officer who was assigned to the country club membership retires, transfers, or leaves the company, the company may, at its discretion: sell the membership back to the club, reassign the membership, or offer to sell the membership to the officer.
- The company reserves the right to suspend or cancel an officer's use of any country club membership that it provides, or to can-

cel, transfer, or surrender a country club membership at any time.

Luncheon Clubs

Where it is common to conduct business and entertain business guests at a luncheon club, the company may provide a luncheon club membership. These memberships are reserved for the authorized use of company officers who, because of the nature of their position, have a business need for such a club.

- Luncheon club memberships must be approved by the Managing Committee Member responsible for the employee's division or unit, or the Member's designee.
- All membership-related expenses will be treated in accordance with the company's expense policies, guidelines, and procedures.
- The company reserves the right to suspend or cancel an officer's use of any luncheon club membership that it provides, or to cancel, transfer, or surrender a luncheon club membership at any time.

Service Organizations

Although employees may participate in service organizations—such as Lions, Kiwanis, and Rotary Clubs—it is not the company's normal practice to reimburse membership dues. However, business expenses may be reimbursed, in accordance with expense policies, guidelines, and procedures.

Athletic, Health, and Fitness Clubs

The company ordinarily does not reimburse employees for memberships in clubs designed primarily to promote personal health and fitness, and lacking in formal dining and business entertainment facilities—for example, health spas, body building, and certain racquetball and tennis clubs.

DEVELOPMENT OF PRODUCTS OR SERVICES WHILE EMPLOYED AT BANKAMERICA

You are obligated to disclose promptly in writing to your manager all improvements or inventions (whether or not patentable, copyrightable or otherwise protectable) made during the course of, or relating to, your duties, whether made during normal working hours or any other time. Any such improvements or inventions are the exclusive property of BankAmerica.

THE EQUITABLE FINANCIAL COMPANIES

Excerpt from "Policy Statement on Ethics" December 1988

POLICY STATEMENT ON ETHICS

This Policy Statement on Ethics is for all employees, registered representatives, and agents of The Equitable Financial Companies [The Companies]. It is a guide to ethical practices in working with clients, suppliers, the public, and each other. Your company or business unit may have additional guidelines, and federal and state laws and regulations may also apply to the work you do. But statements of policy, laws, and regulations cannot cover every ethical question that may arise. Your own personal integrity and good judgment are the best guides to ethical and responsible conduct.

BUSINESS PRACTICES: HONESTY, FAIRNESS, AND OBEYING THE LAW

Earn Client's Trust

The Equitable's reputation for integrity is tested every day by the way you treat clients. Honesty, fairness, and keeping commitments must be hallmarks of the way you do business.

Reprinted by permission

- Sell products on their merits. Describe them truthfully and without exaggeration, pointing out their benefits but also making clear their risks and costs.
- Explain contracts, products, services, and investment opportunities clearly. Clients should not be surprised by finding provisions or conditions about which they were not informed.
- Ensure that commitments are honored and that all your clients receive the highest quality service that you can provide.

Present The Equitable
Financial Companies Truthfully

Communications with the public should reinforce a sense of trust in The Companies. Whether statements are channeled through the mass media or made in private conversation, "Honesty is the best policy."

- Portray The Companies accurately. Public statements should be sufficiently candid, clear, and complete so that they neither mislead nor lend themselves to misinterpretation. These criteria apply to all communications about The Companies, including advertisements, reports to clients, sales literature, speeches, and responses to inquiries.

Ensure Data Integrity

Financial information, employee files, and other corporate data should meet a single standard: complete integrity. If you have responsibility for any aspect of the recordkeeping process, you share responsibility for upholding this standard.

- Make sure corporate records are scrupulously accurate, are fully documented, and comport with the highest standards of professional practice. Financial data should be complete and current, with all assets, funds, and liabilities fully and properly recorded.

Safeguard Confidential Information

The nature of the business gives many of you access to personal and private information about clients and employees. Maintaining their trust requires that you protect the confidentiality of this information.

- Information about a client's financial circumstances, business plans, health, or family matters is confidential. Disclosure within The Companies should be only on a business need-do-know basis. Disclosure to outsiders, except to comply with legal requirements, is not only unethical but in some cases may be illegal.
- Information in employees' and agents' personnel and benefits records is sensitive and private. Treat it as confidential, disclosing only on a business need-to-know basis. Medical records are never to be disclosed without the individual's written permission, unless necessary to comply with the law.

Obey Laws and Regulations

You have a personal responsibility to become familiar and comply with the laws and regulations related to your job responsibilities. There are probably other laws—not directly related to your job but of general relevance to work situations—of which you should be aware. If you have any questions about what is within the law and what is not, seek advice immediately from your business head.

Specific Laws. Since laws dealing with securities markets and competitive practices have broad applicability in financial services, they are specifically referenced below.

- Securities laws forbid individuals and corporations from profiting from material nonpublic information—information that could influence decisions to buy, sell or hold on to particular securities. Such information may relate to the financial condition of a company, its products, the market for its securities, its investment intentions, or plans for a merger or acquisition. Such information may also include nonpublic information about The Companies' investment intentions. You may not make trades of securities based on material inside information or give such information to others.
- Antitrust and trade regulation laws prohibit actions that restrain competition. You may not, for example, cooperate with competitors to fix or stabilize prices, "divide up" clients or markets, boycott competitors or clients, or otherwise interfere with free competition. You should not even discuss the possibility of

such activities with competitors. These laws also prohibit certain kinds of tie-in sales and other practices that would be unfair to clients.

AT&T

Excerpt from "A Personal Responsibility" 1988

Over the years, privacy of communications has been basic to AT&T's business, not only because it is required by law, but because the public has placed its trust in the integrity of AT&T's people and its service. AT&T customers expect, for example, that their conversations will be kept private.

In recent years, with the ever-increasing volume of data transmission over the network, that trust has taken on a special significance. Today it is the responsibility of every AT&T employee to protect not only the privacy of conversations on the network, but also the flow of information in data form that in the wrong hands could have serious economic or legal consequences for the parties involved.

The basic rules for privacy have not changed. Violating any one of them could tarnish a reputation AT&T has earned over many years. The basic rules are:

—Don't tamper with or intrude upon any transmission, whether by voice, non-voice or data.

—Don't listen to or repeat anyone else's conversation or communication, or permit them to be monitored or recorded except as required in the proper management of the business.

—Don't allow an unauthorized person to have access to any communication transmitted over AT&T facilities. This includes divulging information about who was speaking or what was spo-

Reprinted by permission

ken about, except as authorized by the customer or required in the proper management of the business.

—Don't install or permit installation of any device that will enable someone to listen to, observe, or realize that a communication has occurred, except as authorized by an official service or installation order issued in accordance with Company practices.

—Don't use information from any communication, or even the fact that a communication has occurred, for your personal benefit or for the benefit of others.

—Don't disclose information about customer billing arrangements, or the location of equipment, circuits, trunks, and cables to any unauthorized person.

Contact the AT&T Corporate Security Organization if you believe that the privacy of any communication has been compromised, or if you receive a subpoena, court order, or any other type of request for information from anyone (including law enforcement and other government agencies) concerning any AT&T service.

The fundamental rule is that employees in their business dealings must never be influenced—or even appear to be influenced—by personal interests.

Employees are expected, both on and off the job, to support the Company's efforts to succeed in the worldwide marketplace.

Employees are not permitted to compete with the Company; they may not assist others to compete with the Company, and they may not use their position with the Company, its proprietary information or its relationship with customers for personal gain or benefit.

AT&T's policy concerning suppliers is to award business solely on merit, at the lowest reasonable price, and, wherever practicable, on a competitive basis.

Basic points to keep in mind are:

—Have no relationship, financial or otherwise, with any supplier or competitor that might be construed as a conflict of interest, or that might even appear to impair your judgment on behalf of the Company.

—Never accept or solicit, even indirectly, gifts, loans, "kickbacks", special privileges, services, benefits or unusual hospitality. This does not apply to unsolicited promotional materials of nominal monetary value of a general advertising nature, such as imprinted pencils, memo pads and calendars. Determining when hospitality is "unusual" is a matter of degree. Acceptance of a meal or entertainment in the normal course of business relations is permitted as a matter of courtesy and should be, when practical, on a reciprocal basis. Generally, any extensive hospitality beyond this would be considered unusual. Exceptions to this rule may be appropriate for special events, such as sporting events, or trade shows, where Company business may be conducted. You should report invitations to any such events to your supervisor for concurrence in your acceptance of the invitation.

—Report gifts other than promotional materials of nominal value promptly to your supervisor and then return them to the donor, if possible, or dispose of them in another appropriate manner.

—Do not give inappropriate gifts or provide unusual hospitality to customers or potential customers or their employees that will unfairly influence their purchasing decision. For example, do not give expensive gifts that could be construed as a bribe or a reward for purchasing from AT&T.

—Comply with local, state and federal laws and regulations governing relations between government customers and suppliers. These laws and regulations may prohibit or modify marketing activities used with other customers. Special care must also be exercised with customers that are heavily regulated by the government, e.g., banks, because they may be subject to similar restraints.

—Do not in any way assist competitors. Specifically, do not assist anyone outside the business in the planning, design, manufacture, sale, purchase, installation, or maintenance of any competitors' equipment or services. Do not become involved in activities or businesses that compete with AT&T activities or business. This policy, of course, does not apply to AT&T's partners in joint ventures, or to our competitors when performed under approved Company programs.

—Avoid any outside activity that could adversely affect the independence and objectivity of your judgment, interfere with the timely and effective performance of your duties and responsibilities, or that could discredit the Company or conflict, or appear to conflict, with the Company's best interests. Since each employee's primary obligation is to the Company, any outside activity, such as a second job or self-employment, must be kept totally separate from employment with the Company. Unless expressly authorized by the Company—for example, Junior Achievement —no outside activity should involve the use of Company time, its name or its influence, assets, funds, materials, facilities, or the services of other employees.

—Don't undertake any activity that is aimed at, or that could reasonably have the effect of, retarding the success of the Company in the marketplace. Avoid any actions inconsistent with this commitment to help the Company succeed, such as suggesting that customers or potential customers refrain from dealing with the Company, or deal with a competitor instead of with the Company.

If an actual—or even a potential—conflict of interest develops, it must be reported promptly to supervision. The Law Department and the AT&T Corporate Security Organization may also be consulted.

AT&T's policy is to comply fully with all laws and regulations, domestic and foreign, that apply to it. The U.S. antitrust laws apply to competition within the U.S. and to some international business transactions by U.S. firms. Firms like AT&T that export or do business in other countries must also comply with the applicable antitrust laws of those countries.

The objective of the U.S. antitrust laws is to benefit consumers by promoting vigorous competition. The basic U.S. antitrust statutes are the Sherman, Clayton and Federal Trade Commission Acts.

The Sherman Act prohibits contracts and conspiracies that unreasonably reduce or eliminate competition. These include agreements between competitors to divide markets, establish prices or refuse to deal with others. Employees must avoid:

—Agreements or understandings with competitors that would establish minimum or maximum prices, divide customers or markets, or in any other way lessen competition between AT&T and its competitors.

—Agreements or understandings with competitors concerning how—or whether—to deal with any customer or competitor, or any group of customers or competitors.

Under some circumstances, the Sherman Act also prohibits a company from requiring its customers to buy a product or service they do not want in order to buy one they want, i.e., tying. A company also may not place certain restrictions on resellers of its products or services.

The Sherman Act also covers monopolies and prohibits, among other things, attempts to obtain or retain a monopoly position in a market by using strategies designed to destroy a competitor or to foreclose competition.

The Clayton Act addresses exclusive dealing arrangements, price discrimination, and acquisitions. The Federal Trade Commission Act generally prohibits unfair or deceptive trade practices.

Failure to comply with these laws can have serious consequences. Corporations and individuals accused of violating the Sherman Act, for example, may be indicted on felony charges. Violations may also result in costly damage awards and burdensome injunctive orders.

AT&T's competitive efforts must rely on the merits of its products and services. Employees should concentrate on anticipating and satisfying the needs of our customers, and should not seek to limit the competitive opportunities of our rivals. In order to accomplish this, employees should:

—Never misrepresent the quality, features or availability of AT&T products or services or those of its competitors.

—Never engage in industrial espionage or commercial bribery.

—Never unlawfully interfere with contracts between a competitor and a customer.

—Never buy from suppliers, or hint that we will buy from them, on the condition that they use AT&T products or services.

Antitrust proceedings often involve evidence that is largely circumstantial. Judges, jurors, and agencies interpreting this evidence are likely to be influenced by appearances. Consequently, to minimize AT&T's exposure to civil and criminal penalties, AT&T must avoid not only actively engaging in improper competitive practices, but also inadvertently appearing to engage in improper practices.

For example, employees should avoid careless language that might incorrectly suggest that we are seeking to eliminate our competitors or to foreclose competition. And because price fixing and division of markets is illegal, employees should also not discuss with competitors such things as costs, prices, terms of sale, production levels or capacity, inventories, marketing plans, distribution arrangements or procurement arrangements. However, with Law Department guidance, limited exceptions may be made for competitors who are also AT&T's customers, suppliers, or prospective joint venture partners.

Employees should consult the AT&T Competition Guidelines for more detailed guidance on antitrust matters.

AT&T is also bound by the terms of the Modification of Final Judgement (MFJ), entered on August 24, 1982. In consenting to the MFJ, AT&T has endorsed the public policy objective of creating a fully competitive telecommunications marketplace. AT&T is therefore committed to fair, nondiscriminatory dealings with the divested operating companies. See the AT&T Competition Guidelines for more information about the restrictions imposed by the MFJ.

Furthermore, under the nonstructural safeguards promulgated by the Federal Communications Commission in Computer Inquiry II/III, and under the Communications Act, AT&T may not discriminate in providing basic services under tariff. Specifically, AT&T must never engage in, and must take affirmative steps to prevent, discrimination in the timing of installation and maintenance and in the quality and reliability of its tariffed basic services. This requirement on AT&T applies with respect to all enhanced services providers—whether or not affiliated with AT&T—and their customers, as well as to users of customer premises equipment ("CPE"), whether or not such CPE is purchased from AT&T. Moreover, AT&T is forbidden to make claims that by purchasing AT&T enhanced services, or AT&T CPE, customers will obtain network services of a superior quality or more quickly than if purchased from a non-AT&T vendor.

Finally, employees must adhere strictly to AT&T Document

Retention Guidelines, including those issued in connection with pending litigation.

When questions arise concerning the antitrust laws, the MFJ, or CI II/III, consult the Law Department. On document retention matters, consult your designated Document Retention Coordinator or Company instructions.

AT&T policy is that its employees, joint venture partners, agents, distributors and representatives comply strictly with the U.S. Foreign Corrupt Practices Act. This law prohibits payments or offers of payments of anything of value to foreign officials, political parties, or candidates for foreign political office in order to secure, retain, or direct business. Payments made indirectly through an intermediary, under circumstances indicating a reason to believe that such payments would be passed on for prohibited purposes, are also illegal. Any employee with a question concerning the propriety of any potential payment should contact the International Law Division.

The law also contains significant internal accounting control and recordkeeping requirements that apply to our domestic operations.

Specifically, the law requires that the Company's books and records accurately and fairly reflect all financial transactions in reasonable detail, and that the Company's internal accounting controls provide reasonable assurances that:

—Transactions are carried out in an authorized manner.

—Transactions have been reported and recorded so as to permit correct preparation of financial statements and accurate records of assets.

—Access to assets is in accordance with management's authorization.

—Inventories of assets are taken periodically, and appropriate action is taken to correct discrepancies.

All employees are responsible for following Company procedures, including appropriate schedules of authorization and internal accounting controls, for carrying out and reporting business transactions.

Violations of this law can result in fines and imprisonment, or both, for individual employees, as well as significant penalties against the Company. Any questions on interpreting this law, or on the adequacy of the Company's internal accounting controls, should be referred to the Chief Financial Officer Organization or the International Law Division.

DU PONT

Full Text of Du Pont's Code of Ethics October 1988

The policy was first adopted by the company in October 1975 and was last amended by the Board of Directors on October 26, 1988. It consolidates in one document all policies with respect to Business Ethics and Conflict of Interest for E. I. du Pont de Nemours and Company and its subsidiaries in which it has a majority interest or for which it has operating responsibility.

BUSINESS ETHICS POLICY

It always has been and continues to be the intent of the company that its employees maintain the highest ethical standards in their conduct of company affairs. The following sets forth in summary form for the benefit of all company employees, wherever located, the company's long-standing policy with respect to (1) gifts, favors, entertainment and payments given or received by employees, (2) potential conflicts of interest, and (3) certain other matters.

The essence of this policy is that each employee will conduct the company's business with integrity, in compliance with applicable laws, and in a manner that excludes considerations of personal advantage.

Reprinted by permission

A. PAYMENTS BY THE COMPANY

1. Gifts, favors and entertainment may be given others at company expense only if they meet *all* of the following criteria:

    a. they are consistent with customary business practices,

    b. they are not excessive in value and cannot be construed as a bribe or pay-off,

    c. they are not in contravention of applicable law or ethical standards, and

    d. public disclosure of the facts will embarrass neither the company nor the employee.

2. In connection with sales by the company, commissions, rebates, discounts, credits and allowances should be paid or granted only by the company on whose books the related sale is recorded, and such payments should:

    a. bear a reasonable relationship to the value of goods delivered or services rendered,

    b. be by check or bank transfer to the specific business entity with whom the agreement is made or to whom the original related sales invoice was issued—not to individual officers, employees or agents of such entity or to a related business entity,

    c. be made only in the country of the entity's place of business, and

    d. be supported by documentation that is complete and that clearly defines the nature and purpose of the transaction.

    Agreements for the company to pay commissions, rebates, credits, discounts or allowances should be in writing. When this is not feasible, the payment arrangement should be supported by an explanatory memorandum for file prepared by the approving department and reviewed by Legal Department.

3. In connection with the company's purchases of goods and services, including commissions related thereto, payments

should be made only in the country of the seller's or provider's place of business or in the country in which the product was delivered or service rendered. All such payments shall be consistent with corporate and trade practice.

B. GIFTS RECEIVED

1. Employees shall neither seek nor accept for themselves or others any gifts, favors or entertainment without a legitimate business purpose, nor seek or accept loans (other than conventional loans at market rates from lending institutions) from any person or business organization that does or seeks to do business with, or is a competitor of, the company. In the application of this policy:

   a. Employees may accept for themselves and members of their families common courtesies usually associated with customary business practices.

   b. An especially strict standard is expected with respect to gifts, services, discounts, entertainment or considerations of any kind from suppliers.

   c. It is never permissible to accept a gift in cash or cash equivalents (e.g., stocks or other forms of marketable securities) of any amount.

C. CONFLICTS OF INTEREST

1. Employees should avoid any situation which involves or may involve a conflict between their personal interests and the interests of the company. As in all other facets of their duties, employees dealing with customers, suppliers, contractors, competitors or any person doing or seeking to do business with the company are to act in the best interests of the company to the exclusion of considerations of personal preference or advantage. Each employee shall make prompt and full disclosure in writing to his Department Management of a prospective situation which may involve a conflict of interest. This includes:

a. Ownership by an employee or, to the employee's knowledge, by a member of the employee's family of a significant financial interest* in any outside enterprise which does or seeks to do business with or is a competitor of the company.

b. Serving as a director, officer, partner, consultant, or in a managerial position with, or employment in a technical capacity by, any outside enterprise which does or is seeking to do business with or is a competitor of the company.

c. Acting as a broker, finder, go-between or otherwise for the benefit of a third party in transactions involving or potentially involving the company or its interests.

d. Any other arrangement or circumstance, including family or other personal relationships, which might dissuade the employee from acting in the best interest of the company.

All information disclosed to management as required by this policy shall be treated confidentially, except to the extent necessary to protect the company's interests.

D. INSIDE INFORMATION

1. Employees shall not:

a. Give or release, without proper authority, to anyone not employed by the company, or to another employee who has no need for information, data or information of a confidential nature obtained while in company employment.

b. Use nonpublic information obtained while in company employment (including information about customers, suppliers or competitors) for the personal profit of the employee or anyone else. This includes, but is not lim-

---

* As a minimum standard, a "significant" financial interest is a direct or indirect aggregate interest of an employee and family members of more than:
(a) 1% of any class of the outstanding securities of a firm or corporation,
(b) 10% interest in a partnership or association, or
(c) 5% of the total assets or gross income of such employee.

ited to, taking advantage of such information by (1) trading or providing information for others to trade in securities, (2) acquiring a real estate interest of any kind, including but not limited to plant or office sites or adjacent properties, or (3) acquiring (or acquiring options to obtain) interests in oil and gas leases, royalties, minerals or real property for the purpose of obtaining mineral or royalty interest, or any interest in oil or gas production or profits from the same.

E. POLITICAL CONTRIBUTIONS

1. Employees shall not make any contribution of company funds, property or services to any political party or committee, domestic or foreign, or to any candidate for or holder of any office of any government—national, state, local or foreign. This policy does not preclude (a) the operation of a political action committee under applicable laws, (b) company contributions, where lawful, to support or oppose public referenda or similar ballot issues, or (c) political contributions, where lawful and reviewed in advance by the Executive Committee, or by a committee appointed by the Executive Committee for this purpose.

F. ACCOUNTING STANDARDS AND DOCUMENTATION

1. All accounts and records shall be documented in a manner that:
   a. clearly describes and identifies the true nature of business transactions, assets, liabilities or equity, and
   b. properly and timely classifies and records entries on the books of account in conformity with generally accepted accounting principles.

No record, entry or document shall be false, distorted, misleading, misdirected, deliberately incomplete or suppressed.

Strict adherence to this policy will protect the company and its employees from criticism, litigation or embarrassment that might result from alleged or real conflicts of interest or unethical practices. Employees should report apparent violations of this policy through their line organization or, if they prefer, directly to the company's General Auditor or a member of internal auditing management. The Auditing Division can be contacted by writing the General Auditor in Wilmington, Delaware, or by calling (302) 774-1300. Every effort will be made to protect the identity of the employee, or an employee may elect to report anonymously.

IBM CORPORATION

Excerpt from "Business Conduct Guidelines" June 1988

Personal Conduct

IBM's hard-earned reputation for the highest standards of business conduct is never taken for granted. It rests, not on periodic audits by lawyers and accountants, but on the high measure of mutual trust and responsibility that exists between employees and the company. It's based on you as an individual acting in accordance with IBM's business conduct guidelines.

Ethical behavior on the job essentially comes down to honesty and fairness in dealing with other employees, with customers, suppliers, competitors and the public. It's no exaggeration to say that IBM's integrity and reputation are in your hands.

IBM's basic belief of respect for the individual has led to a strict regard for the privacy and dignity of each employee. However, when IBM management decides that your personal conduct on or off the job adversely affects your performance, that of other employees, or the legitimate interests of the company, it may become a concern to IBM.

Reprinted by permission

Protecting IBM's Assets

IBM has a large variety of assets. Many are of great value to IBM's competitiveness and its success as a business.

They include not only our extremely valuable proprietary information, but also our physical assets. IBM proprietary information includes intellectual property, typically the product of the ideas and hard work of many talented IBM people. It also includes the confidential data entrusted to many employees in connection with their jobs.

Protecting all of these assets is very important. Their loss, theft or misuse jeopardizes the future of IBM.

For this reason, you are personally responsible not only for protecting IBM property entrusted to you, but also for helping to protect the company's assets in general. Here is where your awareness of security procedures can play a critical role. You should be alert to any situations or incidents that could lead to the loss, misuse or theft of company property. And you should report all such situations to the security department or your manager as soon as they come to your attention.

What types of assets should you be concerned about protecting? And what are your responsibilities in this regard?

Proprietary Information

Proprietary information is information that is the property of IBM and is usually classified under the IBM classification system. Such information includes the business, financial, marketing, and service plans associated with products. It also includes personnel information, medical records, and salary data. Other proprietary information includes designs; engineering and manufacturing know-how and processes; IBM business and product plans with outside vendors and a variety of internal data bases; and patent applications and copyrighted material such as software.

Much of this information is called intellectual property, and represents the product of the ideas and efforts of many of your fellow employees. Also, it has required substantial investments by IBM in planning, research and development.

Obviously, if competitors could secure proprietary information such as product design specifications without making the same substantial investment in research and engineering, they would be getting a free ride on IBM's investment. Pricing information and marketing plans are also highly useful to competitors.

The value of this proprietary information is well known to many people in the information industry. Besides competitors, they include industry and security analysts, members of the press, consultants, customers, and other so-called "IBM watchers." Some of these individuals will obtain information any way they can. No matter what the circumstances, IBM alone is entitled to determine who may possess its proprietary information and what use may be made of it, except for specific legal requirements such as the publication of certain reports.

As an IBM employee, you probably have access to information that the company considers proprietary. Given the widespread interest in IBM—and the increasingly competitive nature of the industry—the chances are you probably have contact with someone interested in acquiring information in your possession. So it's very important not to use or disclose proprietary information except as authorized by IBM and to provide adequate safeguards to prevent loss of such information.

Inadvertent Disclosure

The unintentional disclosure of proprietary information can be just as harmful as intentional disclosure.

To avoid unintentional disclosure, never discuss with any unauthorized person information that has not been made public by IBM. This information includes unannounced products, prices, earnings, procurement plans, business volumes and capital requirements. Also included are: confidential product performance data; marketing and service strategies; business plans; and other confidential information. Furthermore, you should not discuss confidential information even with authorized IBM employees if you are in the presence of others who are not authorized—for example, at a trade show reception or in a public area such as an airplane. This also applies to discussions with family members or with friends, who might innocently or inadvertently pass the information on to someone else.

Finally, keep in mind that harmful disclosure may start with the smallest leak of bits of information. Such fragments of information you disclose may be pieced together with fragments from other sources to form a fairly complete picture.

Direct Requests for Information

If someone outside the company asks you questions, either directly or through another person, do not attempt to answer them unless you are certain you are authorized to do so. If you are not authorized, refer the person to the appropriate source within the company. For example, if you are approached by security analysts or investors, you should refer them to your local communications manager or to the Office of the Treasurer. Similarly, unless you have been authorized to talk to reporters, or to anyone else writing about or otherwise covering the company or the industry, direct the person to the information specialist in your communications department. If you do not know what functional area the questioner should be referred to, ask your manager.

Disclosure and Use of Confidential Information

Besides your obligation not to disclose any IBM confidential information to anyone outside the company, you are also required as an employee to use such information only in connection with IBM's business. These obligations apply whether or not you developed the information yourself. And they apply by law in virtually all countries where IBM does business.

Agreement Regarding Confidential Information and Intellectual Property

When you joined IBM, you should have been required to sign an agreement that sets out specific obligations you have as an employee, relating to the treatment of confidential information. Also under the agreement, when you are employed in a managerial, technical, engineering, product planning, programming, scientific or other professional capacity, you assign to IBM the rights to any ideas and inventions that you develop if they are in an area of the company's business. Subject to the laws of each country, this obligation applies no matter where or when—at work or after hours—such intellectual property is created. The existence of this intellectual property must be reported to IBM, and the property must be protected like any other proprietary information of the company. However, if you believe that your idea or invention falls outside the area of IBM's business interests, you may ask IBM for a written disclaimer of ownership.

Copyrightable Material

In most cases, the copyrights in employee generated works of authorship such as manuals and computer programs are automatically owned by IBM through operation of law. In other cases, title to the copyrights is given to IBM by contractual provisions. IBM considers it important to limit the distribution of copyrightable material within IBM to that in which the copyright is owned by or appropriately licensed to IBM. To assure that material not owned by IBM is appropriately licensed, IBM may request a license from you before you will be permitted to place copyrightable material into or on any IBM owned distribution channel, including internal mail and electronic channels such as conferencing disks, VM or PROFS. This license may be requested whether you or IBM actually owns the material. If there is a question of ownership, you should consult your manager before you distribute material in IBM through any distribution channel. Your manager may consult the legal and the intellectual property law departments to determine whether you will be permitted to place the material in the particular distribution channel.

Leaving IBM

If you leave the company for any reason, including retirement, you may not disclose or misuse IBM confidential information. Also, IBM's ownership of intellectual property that you created while you were an IBM employee continues after you leave the company.

Legal Remedies

Regrettably, there have been significant cases in which IBM's intellectual property has been wrongfully taken or misused. In some of these instances, IBM has not limited its response to disciplinary action against offending employees, but has also taken legal action against everyone involved. Also, a number of individuals, including former IBM employees, have been prosecuted for their actions by government authorities and convicted of crimes for their part in stealing information.

IBM will continue to take every step necessary, including legal measures, to protect its assets because of their importance to the company.

Conducting IBM's Business

What business conduct and ethical issues might you encounter in dealing with outside organizations and people? What are the proper ways of handling these issues?

Some General Standards

Today, IBM deals with a growing variety of outside organizations. And more than one kind of relationship often exists between IBM and these organizations at the same time. For example, a firm that is an IBM customer may concurrently be a supplier and an IBM competitor. No matter what type of organization you are dealing with or what its relationship is to IBM, you should always observe the following general standards.

Avoiding Misrepresentation

Never make misrepresentations to anyone. If you believe that the other person may have misunderstood you, promptly correct any misunderstanding. Honesty based on clear communication is integral to ethical behavior. The resulting trustworthiness is essential to sound, lasting relationships.

Refraining From Using IBM's Size Unfairly

IBM has achieved its size through legitimate business success over many years. And there is certainly no need to apologize for it. That said, you should never use the fact of IBM's size to intimidate or threaten another person or organization. In other words, do not throw IBM's weight around in dealing with other companies, organizations or the public.

However, there is nothing wrong with citing legitimate advantages that accrue from our size—as long as such assertions are accurate and free from misleading statements. For example, it is permissible to discuss the advantages that derive from large-scale buying, selling, servicing and manufacturing. Whenever you are discussing any aspects of our size, you should make sure that your statements are accurate and relevant, and not misleading. For example, you may discuss IBM's national service coverage or the broad range of our product offerings as long as such references are accurate and relevant in demonstrating IBM's capability to meet a particular customer's need.

Treating Everyone Fairly

Everyone you do business with is entitled to fair and evenhanded treatment. That should be true no matter what your relationship with an outside organization may be—whether you are buying, selling or representing IBM in any other capacity.

IBM will continue to compete vigorously in bidding for government and commercial business. If circumstances require modified pricing or service terms, the modifications must be specifically approved by the appropriate level of management. Never extend any modified service or contract terms to government or commercial enterprises without prior authorization.

IBM extends appropriate terms to each type of customer. For example, distributors, dealers and end users purchase certain IBM equipment under different terms. However, within each category, IBM endeavors to conduct its business so that all customers who are procuring in similar quantities and under similar business conditions are treated in a similar manner.

You must treat all suppliers fairly. In deciding among competing suppliers, weigh all the facts impartially. You should do so whether you are in a purchasing job, a branch office or any other part of the business—and whether you are buying millions of parts or just a few, contracting for a small repair job or any other service.

Whether or not you are in a position to influence decisions involving the evaluation or selection of suppliers, you must not exert or attempt to exert influence to obtain "special treatment" on behalf of a particular supplier. Even to appear to do so can undermine the integrity of our established procedures. It is essential that suppliers competing for IBM's business have confidence in the integrity of our selection process. That confidence could be jeopardized if former IBM employees competing as suppliers or suppliers' representatives are perceived to have "inside information" or an unfair advantage because of their former IBM job responsibilities. To ensure that there is no unfairness or perception of unfairness under such circumstances, IBM generally will not accept you as a supplier or supplier's representative to your former geographic location for a period of one year after your employment with IBM is ended.

Avoiding Reciprocal Dealing

Seeking reciprocity is contrary to IBM policy and may also be unlawful. In other words, you may not tell a prospective supplier that your decision to purchase its goods or services is conditioned on the supplier's agreement to purchase IBM products or services. To avoid allegations of reciprocal dealing, do not tell a prospective customer that IBM deserves its business because of IBM's purchases from that customer.

This does not mean that an IBM customer is precluded from being an IBM supplier. It simply means that IBM's decision to buy goods and services from a supplier must be made independently from that supplier's decision to purchase IBM products and services.

Reporting Violations of Procurement Laws

IBM employees should make known to appropriate levels of management any allegations that government procurement laws have been violated. This may be done either directly through your manager or through the Open Door or Speak Up programs.

Retribution against employees for reporting such allegations will not be tolerated. Subject to any applicable legal requirements, employee anonymity and confidentiality will be protected.

Fairness in the Field

If you work in a marketing or service activity, IBM asks you to compete not just vigorously and effectively but fairly as well.

Disparagement

It has long been IBM's policy to sell products and services on their merits, not by disparaging competitors, their products or their services. False or misleading statements and innuendos are improper. Don't make comparisons that unfairly cast the competitor in a bad light. Such conduct only invites disrespect from customers and complaints from competitors.

In short, stress the advantages of IBM products and services, and be sure that all comparisons are fair and accurate.

Premature Disclosure

IBM does not disclose unannounced offerings to a prospect or a customer which have not been disclosed to customers generally. There are exceptions. One is when the national interest is involved. Another is when a customer works with IBM under a formal agreement to develop or test new products, programs, services or distribution plans. In addition, IBM will make limited disclosures to provide planning direction to customers.

For these exceptions and other special situations, there are specific procedures to be followed. And for each, appropriate authorization must be obtained.

Selling Against Competitive Orders

If a competitor already has a firm order from a customer for an application, it is IBM practice not to market IBM products or services for that application before it is installed.

What is a "firm order"? Letters of intent, free trials, conditional agreements and similar arrangements usually are not considered firm orders; unconditional contracts are. Generally, if a firm order does not exist, you may sell to that customer. However, this is a complicated subject, and as a result it is often difficult to determine if a firm order actually exists. When a situation is unclear, seek advice from your marketing practices, business practices or legal department.

Multiple Relationships With Other Organizations

Frequently, other organizations have more than one relationship with IBM. For example, a distributor may be both an IBM customer and a competitor. Another organization may be an IBM supplier and customer at the same time. A few organizations may even be suppliers, competitors, distributors, and end users of IBM products. In addition, IBM has relationships with many other types of organizations that continue to emerge in our industry. They include leasing companies, software houses, distributors, dealers, banks and other financial institutions, remarketers, equipment manufacturers, maintenance companies, third-party programmers and many others who compete with, buy from or sell to IBM. In any dealings, it is important that you understand the various relationships involved.

Generally, you should deal with another organization in only one relationship at a time. For example, if you are buying from another company, don't try to sell to it at the same time. That could form the basis for a possible allegation of reciprocal dealing, which, as previously mentioned, should be avoided.

Complementary Third Parties

IBM has various relationships with complementary third parties to facilitate the installation of IBM offerings. These complementary third parties are outside organizations that provide end users with information-handling solutions that use or rely upon an IBM offering.

If your responsibilities bring you into contact with these third parties, you must follow the marketing and services guidelines published by your function that describe the appropriate conduct in dealing with IBM authorized remarketers, IBM authorized assistants and reference organizations. In addition to their complementary offerings, some of these third parties market products that compete with IBM. When such a situation arises, you must exercise caution and follow established guidelines.

Business Contacts With Competitors

Because many companies have multiple relationships with IBM, it is important to recognize when a company you are dealing with, as a supplier or a customer, is also an IBM competitor. Such relationships require extra care. It is inevitable that you, other IBM employees, and competitors will, from time to time, meet, talk, and attend the same industry or association meetings. Many of these contacts are perfectly acceptable as long as established procedures are followed. Acceptable contacts include sales to other companies in our industry; purchases from them; participation in approved joint bids; and attendance at business shows, standards organizations and trade associations. But even these contacts require caution.

Prohibitions

In all contacts with competitors, avoid discussing pricing policy, terms and conditions, costs, inventories, marketing and product plans, market surveys and studies, production plans and capabilities—and of course, any other proprietary or confidential information.

Collaboration or discussion of these subjects with competitors can be illegal. If a competitor raises any of them, even lightly or with apparent innocence, you should object, stop the conversation immediately, and tell the competitor that under no circumstances can you discuss these matters. If necessary, you should leave the meeting.

In summary, dissociate yourself and IBM from participation in any possibly illegal activity with competitors; confine your communication to what is clearly legal and proper. Finally, immediately report any incident associated with a prohibited subject to IBM legal counsel.

Information About Others

In the normal course of business, it's not unusual to acquire information about many other organizations, including competitors. Doing so is a normal business activity and is not unethical in itself. In fact, IBM quite properly gathers this kind of information for such purposes as extending credit and evaluating suppliers. The company also collects information on competitors from a variety of legitimate sources to evaluate the relative merits of its own products, services, and marketing methods. This activity is proper and necessary in a competitive system.

Acquiring Information

However, there are limits to the ways that information should be acquired and used, especially information about competitors. No company should employ improper means to acquire a competitor's trade secrets or other confidential information.

Such flagrant practices as industrial espionage, burglary, wiretapping and stealing are obviously wrong. But so is hiring a competitor's employees solely to get confidential information. Improper solicitation of confidential data from a competitor's employees or from IBM customers is wrong. IBM will not tolerate any form of questionable intelligence-gathering.

Using Information

Information about other companies should be treated with sensitivity and discretion. Such information is often about individuals. And other companies are rightly concerned about their reputations and the privacy of their people. Adverse information with no business use should not be kept or maintained.

When using sensitive information about other companies, you should use it in the proper context and make it available only to other IBM employees with a legitimate need to know. In presenting such information, you should disclose the identity of the organization or individuals only if it is necessary. If disclosure is not necessary, you should present the information in the aggregate or by some other means . . .

On Your Own Time

What personal activities or circumstances outside work might conflict with your job responsibilities at IBM? What factors should you consider to avoid a possible conflict of interest?

Conflicts of Interest

Your private life is very much your own. Still, a conflict of interest may arise if you engage in any activities or advance any personal interests at the expense of IBM's interests. It's up to you to avoid situations in which your loyalty may become divided. Each individual's situation is different, and in evaluating your own, you will have to consider many factors. The most common types of conflicts are addressed here to help you make informed decisions.

Assisting a Competitor

An obvious conflict of interest is providing assistance to an organization that markets products and services in competition with IBM's current or potential products or service offerings. You may not, without IBM's consent, work for such an organization as an employee, a consultant, or as a member of its board of directors. Such activities are prohibited because they divide your loyalty between IBM and that organization.

Competing Against IBM

Today, many IBM employees are engaged on their own time in routine activities that involve personal computers, software or other products that IBM offers to its customers. Generally, such activities do not result in a conflict of interest. However, employees should be careful not to become engaged in activities that do conflict with IBM's business interests.

Obviously, you may not commercially market products or services in competition with IBM's current or potential product offerings. Such marketing activities are "commercial" if you receive direct or indirect renumeration of any kind. Although marketing competing products and services commercially creates unacceptable conflicts of interest, performing such activities on a noncommercial basis is usually permissible. However, it would not be permissible if IBM decides that such activity has or may have more than a minimal impact on its current or future business.

Because IBM is rapidly expanding into new lines of business and new areas of interest, the company must constantly redraw lines of acceptable activity. Therefore, it is unlikely that you will find definitive answers to many of your questions in published guidelines. It is your responsibility to consult your management or IBM legal counsel before pursuing any activity that might create a conflict of interest with IBM.

Supplying IBM

Generally, you may not be a supplier to IBM, represent a supplier to IBM, work for a supplier to IBM, or be a member of its board of directors while you are an employee of IBM. In addition, you may not accept money or benefits of any kind for any advice or services you may provide to a supplier in connection with its business with IBM. Also, you may not work on any products or services offered by a supplier to IBM.

Use of IBM's Time and Assets

You may not perform outside work or solicit such business on IBM premises or while working on IBM time, including time you are given with pay to handle personal matters. Also, you are not permitted to use IBM equipment, telephones, materials, resources or proprietary information for any outside work.

Public Service

IBM encourages employees to be active in the civic life of their communities. However, such service may, at times, place you in a situation that poses a conflict of interest with IBM. As a board or committee member, you may, for example, be confronted with a decision involving IBM. It might be a decision to purchase IBM equipment or services. Or it might be a decision by a board of tax assessors or a zoning board that affects IBM property. In such circumstances, your interest in IBM and your obligation to the civic organization might pull you in opposite directions. Should you abstain in such a situation?

The Question of Abstaining

There are several considerations. The law may require you to abstain, depending on your position in IBM and whether you stand to gain personally from the decision. On the other hand, there may be circumstances in which the law does not permit you to abstain. Before making your decision, you should get advice from the civic organization's lawyer and from IBM legal counsel.

If the law does not require you to abstain, your participation in such a decision or vote may still cause substantial embarrassment to you, to the board or committee, or to IBM. In considering the possible consequences of your decision, it may be helpful to ask yourself the following questions: How might the story be reported by the press, and how might your fellow townspeople react to such a story? Should you abstain to preserve the public trust in your objectivity and integrity? And, will IBM be needlessly embarrassed by your vote either for or against its interest?

Whether or not you finally abstain, you should make it clear that you are an IBM employee and thereby head off any charges of trying to conceal your association with IBM. And, if you decide to abstain, state clearly that you are doing so because there would be a conflict of interest—or the appearance of one—if you did not.

Your Call—Your Responsibility

Generally, you are the person in the best position to decide whether or not you should abstain. And how you handle the decision is up to you. It follows, of course, that you bear the responsibility for your decision.

Participation in Political Life

IBM will not make contributions or payments to political parties or candidates. In many countries, political contributions by corporations are illegal. IBM will not make such gifts even in countries where they are legal. Also, the company will not provide any other form of support that may be considered a contribution.

In this regard, your work time is the equivalent of such a contribution. Therefore, you will not be paid by IBM for any time spent running for public office, serving as an elected official or campaigning for a political candidate, unless required by law. You can, however, take reasonable time off without pay for such activities, if your IBM duties permit the time off and it is approved by your manager. You also may use vacation time for political activity, or you may be able to make up political-activity time outside your regular work schedule.

Speaking Out

When you speak out on public issues, make sure that you do so as an individual. Don't give the appearance that you are speaking or acting on IBM's behalf.

CHAPTER FOUR

Are Good Ethics Good Business?

Commentary

The opinion that being ethical is good business is regarded by many informed and sensible people as naive, and the opposing view that business is amoral is widely viewed as cynical. The selections found in this chapter suggest that both of these common views possess an element of truth, but that neither by itself is a complete portrayal.

Benjamin Franklin, author of the first selection, is perhaps the best candidate for Father of American Business. True, he was not the first businessman in America, but he was for over a century the model of the self-made man, an entrepreneur from the beginning, reaching out later into politics, science, and culture. He taught industry, thrift, diligence, high-mindedness, public-spiritedness, and broad learning. Generations of Americans—not misled by his appearance of simplicity—regarded him as among the best men ever to grow on American soil. He was *the* example of the kind of human being that freedom and free enterprise make possible.

Have the complexities of business that have arisen since Franklin's time rendered his views obsolete? Amitai Etzioni suggests that in a simple and direct sense, honesty remains the best policy. But the story of Cummins Engine Company is a reminder that honesty is not the only virtue, and that a complex business environment complicates the response of morally alert business leadership.

To explore the issues raised by the Cummins case one has to take seriously the company's argument that it established a *long-term* approach to investment, and that it viewed its ongoing social responsibilities and its responsibilities to its employees in that light. On the other hand, those tempted to forgive all in the name of virtue and long-term planning need to consider that the corporate leadership ran the risk of losing the company or going broke—neither of which would do anyone any good. As Franklin might observe, an empty sack cannot stand up straight. But then, does not competition in the global market place always involve risk?

Lincoln Steffens appears to think that dishonesty may be necessary in business. In his deceptively innocent way, he suggests that it is better to be dishonest and admit it to oneself than to compound it by adding a second vice, hypocrisy. He seems intent on leaving his "student" successful but discontented. Underneath it all, what is his message? That business is not a suitable vocation for a man of integrity? That a man of business cannot be expected to walk away from the prospect of success just because he must work in a corrupt environment? That a decent man cannot rest satisfied with prosperity as the sole measure of his success?

Churchill's remarks are appropriate here only by analogy. He looks at ethics from the standpoint of the statesman who, like the business executive, is *obligated* to achieve a measure of success. Thus, the requisites of success need not be at odds with what many people believe to be sound ethics. But by contrasting the ethics of statesmanship with those of Christianity (or his reading of it), Churchill poses an issue that deserves as much attention from the business leader as from the statesman: what is the connection between our most basic spiritual and moral conceptions, be they Christian or otherwise, and the principles by which we are *obliged* to manage business enterprise?

BENJAMIN FRANKLIN

The Way to Wealth

I stopped my horse lately where a great number of people were collected at an auction of merchants' goods. The hour of the sale not being come, they were conversing on the badness of the times; and one of the company called to a plain, clean old man with white locks, "Pray, Father Abraham, what think you of the times? Will not these heavy taxes quite ruin the country? How shall we ever be able to pay them? What would you advise us to do?" Father Abraham stood up and replied, "If you would have my advice, I will give it to you in short; for A word to the wise is enough, as Poor Richard says." They joined in desiring him to speak his mind, and gathering around him, he proceeded as follows:

"Friends," said he, "the taxes are indeed very heavy, and if those laid on by the government were the only ones we had to pay, we might more easily discharge them; but we have many others, and much more grievous to some of us. We are taxed twice as much by our idleness, three times as much by our pride, and four times as much by our folly; and from these taxes the commissioners cannot ease or deliver us by allowing an abatement. However, let us hearken to good advice, and something may be done for us; God helps them that help themselves, as Poor Richard says.

I. "It would be thought a hard government that should tax its people one tenth part of their time, to be employed in its service; but idleness taxes many of us much more; sloth, by bringing on diseases, absolutely shortens life. Sloth, like rust, consumes faster than labor wears, while The used key is always bright, as Poor

Excerpted from "The Way to Wealth, As Clearly Shown in the Preface of An Old Pennsylvania Almanac Entitled 'Poor Richard Improved'," by Benjamin Franklin, in *Revolutionary Literature—Colonial Prose and Poetry (Third Series)*, William P. Trent & Benjamin W. Wells, Eds. New York: Thomas Y. Crowell Co., no date.

Richard says. But dost thou love life? Then do not squander time, for that is the stuff life is made of, as Poor Richard says. How much more than is necessary do we spend in sleep, forgetting that the sleeping fox catches no poultry, and that there will be sleeping enough in the grave, as Poor Richard says. If time be of all things the most precious, wasting time must be, as Poor Richard says, the greatest prodigality; since, as he elsewhere tells us, Lost time is never found again, and what we call time enough always proves little enough. Let us, then, be up and be doing, and doing to the purpose; so by diligence shall we do more with less perplexity. Sloth makes all things difficult, but industry, all easy; and, He that riseth late must trot all day and shall scarce overtake his business at night; while Laziness travels so slowly that Poverty soon overtakes him. Drive thy business, let not that drive thee; and, Early to bed, and early to rise, makes a man healthy, wealthy, and wise, as Poor Richard says.

"So what signifies wishing and hoping for better times? We make these times better if we bestir ourselves. Industry need not wish, and he that lives upon hopes will die fasting. There are no gains without pains . . . Diligence is the mother of good luck, and God gives all things to Industry. Then plow deep while sluggards sleep, and you shall have corn to sell and to keep. Work while it is called to-day, for you know not how much you may be hindered to-morrow. One to-day is worth two to-morrows, as poor Richard says; and, further, Never leave that till to-morrow which you can do to-day. If you were a good servant, would you not be ashamed that a good master should catch you idle? Are you, then, your own master? Be ashamed to catch yourself idle, when there is so much to be done for yourself, your family, your country, your kin. Handle your tools without mittens; remember that The cat in gloves catches no mice, as Poor Richard says. It is true there is much to be done, and perhaps you are weak-handed; but stick to it steadily, and you will see great effects; for, Constant dropping wears away stones; and, By diligence and patience the mouse ate in two the cable; and, Little strokes fell great oaks.

"Methinks I hear some of you say, Must a man afford himself no leisure? I will tell thee, my friend, what Poor Richard says: Employ thy time well, if thou meanest to gain leisure; and since thou art not sure of a minute, throw not away an hour. Leisure is time for doing something useful; this leisure the diligent man will obtain, but the lazy man never; for, A life of leisure and a life of laziness are two things. Many, without labor, would live by their wits only, but they break for want of stock; whereas industry gives comfort and plenty and respect. Fly pleasures and they will follow you. The diligent spinner has a large shift; and now I have a sheep and a cow, every one bids me good morrow.

II. "But with our industry we must likewise be steady and careful, and oversee our own affairs with our own eyes, and not trust too much to others; for, as Poor Richard says:

> I never saw an oft-removed tree,
> Nor yet an oft-removed family,
> That throve so well as those that settled be.

And again, Three removes are as bad as a fire; and again, Keep thy shop, and thy shop will keep thee; and again, If you would have your business done, go; if not, send; and again:

> He that by the plow would thrive,
> Himself must either hold or drive.

And again, The eye of the master will do more work than both his hands; and again, Want of care does us more damage than want of knowledge; and again, Not to oversee workmen is to leave them your purse open. Trusting too much to others' care is the ruin of many; for, In the affairs of this world men are saved, not by faith, but by the want of it. But a man's own care is profitable; for, If you would have a faithful servant and one that you like, serve yourself. A little neglect may breed great mischief; for want of a nail the shoe was lost, for want of a shoe the horse was lost, and for want of a horse the rider was lost, being overtaken and slain by the enemy; all for want of a little care about a horseshoe nail.

III. "So much for industry, my friends, and attention to one's own business; but to these we must add frugality, if we would make our industry more certainly successful. A man may, if he knows not how to save as he gets, keep his nose all his life to the grindstone, and die not worth a groat at last. A fat kitchen makes a lean will; and

> Many estates are spent in the getting,
> Since women forsook spinning and knitting,
> And men for punch forsook hewing and splitting.

If you would be wealthy, think of saving as well as of getting. . . .

. . . What maintains one vice would bring up two children. You may think, perhaps, that a little tea or a little punch now and then, diet a little more costly, clothes a little finer, and a little entertainment now and then, can be no great matter; but remember, Many a little makes a mickle. Beware of little expenses; A small leak will sink a great ship, as Poor Richard says. . . .

. . . By these and other extravagances the genteel are reduced to poverty, and forced to borrow of those whom they formerly despised, but who, through industry and frugality, have maintained their standing; in which case it appears plainly that, A plowman on his legs is higher than a gentleman on his knees, as Poor Richard says. . . .

. . . And again, Pride is as loud a beggar as Want, and a great deal more saucy. When you have bought one fine thing, you must buy ten more, that your appearance may be all of a piece; but Poor Dick says, It is easier to suppress the first desire than to satisfy all that follow it. And it is as truly folly for the poor to ape the rich, as for the frog to swell in order to equal the ox.

> Vessels large may venture more,
> But little boats should keep near shore.

It is, however, a folly soon punished; for, as Poor Richard says, Pride that dines on vanity, sups on contempt. Pride breakfasted with Plenty, dined with Poverty, and supped with Infamy. And, after all, of what use is this pride of appearance, for which so much is risked, so much is suffered? It cannot promote health nor ease pain; it makes no increase of merit in the person; it creates envy; it hastens misfortune.

"But what madness must it be to run in debt for these superfluities? We are offered by the terms of this sale six months' credit; and that, perhaps, has induced some of us to attend it, because we cannot spare the ready money, and hope now to be fine without it. But ah! think what you do when you run in debt; you give to another power over your liberty. If you cannot pay at the time, you will be ashamed to see your creditor; you will be in fear when you speak to him; you will make poor, pitiful, sneaking excuses, and by degrees come to lose your veracity, and sink into base, downright lying; for, The second vice is lying, the first is running in debt, as Poor Richard says; and again to the same purpose, Lying rides upon debt's back; whereas a freeborn Englishman ought not to be ashamed nor afraid to see or speak to any man living. But poverty often deprives a man of all spirit and virtue. It is hard for an empty bag to stand upright.

. . . When you have got your bargain, you may, perhaps, think little of payment; but, as Poor Richard says, Creditors have better memories than debtors; creditors are a superstitious sect, great observers of set days and times. The day comes round before you are aware, and the demand is made before you are prepared to satisfy it; or, if you bear your debt in mind, the term, which at first seemed so long, will, as it lessens, appear extremely short. Time will seem to have added wings to his heels as well as his shoulders. Those have a short Lent who owe money to be paid at Easter. At present, perhaps, you may think yourselves in thriving circumstances, and that you can bear a little extravagance without injury; but

> For age and want save while you may;
> No morning sun lasts a whole day.

Gain may be temporary and uncertain, but ever, while you live, expense is constant and certain; and, It is easier to build two chimneys than to keep one in fuel, as Poor Richard says; so, Rather go to bed supperless than rise in debt.

> Get what you can, and what you get, hold,
> 'Tis the stone that will turn all your lead into gold.

And when you have got the philosopher's stone, be sure you will no longer complain of bad times or the difficulty of paying taxes.

IV. "This doctrine, my friends, is reason and wisdom; but, after all, do not depend too much upon your own industry and frugality and prudence, though excellent things; for they may all be blasted, without the blessing of Heaven; and, therefore, ask that blessing humbly, and be not uncharitable to those that at present seem to want it, but comfort and help them. Remember Job suffered, and was afterward prosperous.

The Franklin Stove

In order of time I should have mentioned before that, having in 1742 invented an open stove for the better warming of rooms and at the same time saving fuel, as the fresh air admitted was warmed in entering, I made a present of the model to Mr. Robert Grace, one of my early friends, who, having an iron furnace, found the casting of the plates for these stoves a profitable thing, as they were growing in demand. To promote that demand I wrote and published a pamphlet entitled, "An Account of the new-invented Pennsylvania Fireplaces; wherein their Construction and Manner of Operation is particularly explained; their Advantages above every other Method of warming Rooms demonstrated; and all Objections that have been raised against the Use of them answered and obviated," etc. This pamphlet had a good effect. Governor Thomas was so pleased with the construction of this stove, as described in it, that he offered to give me a patent for the sole vending of them for a term of years; but I declined it from a principle which has ever weighed with me on such occasions; namely, that as we enjoy great advantages from the inventions of others, we should be glad of an opportunity to serve others by any invention of ours; and this we should do freely and generously.

Public-Spirited Projects

Peace being concluded, and the association business therefore at an end, I turned my thoughts again to the affair of establishing an academy. The first step I took was to associate in the design a number of active friends, of whom the Junto furnished a good part. The next was to write and publish a pamphlet entitled "Proposals relating to the Education of Youth in Pennsylvania." This I distributed among the principal inhabitants gratis; and as soon as I could suppose their minds a little prepared by the perusal of it, I set on foot a subscription for opening and supporting an academy. It was to be paid in quotas yearly for five years. By so dividing it I judged the subscription might be larger, and I believe it was so, amounting to no less, if I remember right, than five thousand pounds.

In the introduction to these Proposals I stated their publication, not as an act of mine, but of some "public-spirited gentlemen," avoiding as much as I could, according to my usual rule, the presenting myself to the public as the author of any scheme for their benefit.

The subscribers, to carry the project into immediate execution, chose out of their number twenty-four trustees, and appointed Mr. Francis, then attorney-general, and myself to draw up constitutions for the government of the academy; which being done and signed, a house was hired, masters engaged, and the schools opened, I think, in the same year, 1749.

The trustees of the academy after a while were incorporated by a charter from the government; their funds were increased by contributions in Britain and grants of land from the proprietaries, to which the Assembly has since made considerable addition; and thus was established the present University of Philadelphia. I have been continued one of its trustees from the beginning, now near forty years. . . .

In 1751 Dr. Thomas Bond, a particular friend of mine, conceived the idea of establishing a hospital in Philadelphia (a very beneficent design which has been ascribed to me but was originally his) for the reception and cure of poor sick persons, whether inhabitants of the province or strangers. He was zealous and active in endeavoring to procure subscriptions for it, but the proposal being a novelty in America, and at first not well understood, he met with but small success.

At length he came to me with the compliment that he found there was no such thing as carrying a public-spirited project through without my being concerned in it. "For," says he, "I am often asked by those to whom I propose subscribing, 'Have you consulted Franklin upon this business? And what does he think of it?' And when I tell them that I have not (supposing it rather out of your line), they do not subscribe, but say they will consider of it." I inquired into the nature and probable utility of his scheme, and receiving from him a very satisfactory explanation, I not only subscribed to it myself, but engaged heartily in the design of procuring subscriptions from others. Previously, however, to the solicitation, I endeavored to prepare the minds of the people by writing on the subject in the newspapers, which was my usual custom in such cases, but which he had omitted.

The subscriptions afterward were more free and generous; but, beginning to flag, I saw they would be insufficient without some assistance from the Assembly, and therefore proposed to petition for it, which was done. The country members did not at first relish the project. They objected that it could only be serviceable to the city, and therefore the citizens alone should be at the expense of it; and they doubted whether the citizens themselves generally approved of it. My allegation on the contrary, that it met with such approbation as to leave no doubt of our being able to raise two thousand pounds by voluntary donations, they considered as a most extravagant supposition and utterly impossible.

On this I formed my plan; and, asking leave to bring in a bill for incorporating the contributors according to the prayer of their petition, and granting them a blank sum of money, which leave was obtained chiefly on the consideration that the House could throw the bill out if they did not like it, I drew it so as to make the important clause a conditional one, namely: "And be it enacted, by the authority aforesaid, that when the said contributors shall have met and chosen their managers and treasurer, *and shall have raised by their contributions a capital stock of* —— *value,* (the yearly interest of which is to be applied to the accommodating of the sick poor in the said hospital, free of charge for diet, attendance, advice, and medicines,) *and shall make the same appear to the satisfaction of the speaker of the Assembly for the time being,* that *then* it shall and may be lawful for the said speaker, and he is hereby required, to sign an order on the provincial treasurer for the payment of two thousand pounds, in two yearly payments, to the treasurer of the said hospital, to be applied to the founding, building, and finishing of the same."

This condition carried the bill through; for the members who had opposed the grant, and now conceived they might have the credit of being charitable without the expense, agreed to its passage; and then, in soliciting subscriptions among the people, we urged the conditional promise of the law as an additional motive to give, since every man's donation would be doubled; thus the clause worked both ways. The subscriptions accordingly soon exceeded the requisite sum, and we claimed and received the public gift, which enabled us to carry the design into execution. A convenient and handsome building was soon erected; the institution has, by constant experience, been found useful, and flourishes to this day; and I do not remember any of my political maneuvers the success of which gave me at the time more pleasure, or wherein, after thinking of it, I more easily excused myself for having made some use of cunning.

It was about this time that another projector, the Rev. Gilbert Tennent, came to me with a request that I would assist him in procuring a subscription for erecting a new meetinghouse. It was to be for the use of a congregation he had gathered among the Presbyterians who were originally disciples of Mr. Whitefield. Unwilling to make myself disagreeable to my fellow-citizens by too frequently soliciting their contributions, I absolutely refused. He then desired I would furnish him with a list of the names of persons I knew by experience to be generous and public-spirited. I thought it would be unbecoming in me, after their kind compliance with my solicitations, to mark them out to be worried by other beggars, and therefore refused also to give such a list. He then desired I would at least give him my advice. "That I will readily do," said I; "and in the first place, I advise you to apply to all those whom you know will give something; next, to those whom you are uncertain whether they will give anything or not, and show them the list of those who have given; and, lastly, do not neglect those who you are sure will give nothing, for in some of them you may be mistaken." He laughed and thanked me, and said he would take my advice. He did so, for he asked of everybody, and he obtained a much larger sum than he expected, with which he erected the capacious and very elegant meetinghouse that stands in Arch Street.

Our city, though laid out with a beautiful regularity, the streets large, straight, and crossing each other at right angles, had the disgrace of suffering those streets to remain long unpaved, and in wet weather the wheels of heavy carriages plowed them into a quagmire, so that it was difficult to cross them, and in dry weather the dust was offensive. I had lived near what was called the Jersey Market, and saw with pain the inhabitants wading in mud while purchasing their provisions. A strip of ground down the middle of that market was at length paved with brick, so that, being once in the market, they had firm footing, but were often over shoes in dirt to get there. By talking and writing on the subject I was at length instrumental in getting the street paved with stone between the market and the bricked foot pavement that was on each side next the houses. This for some time gave an easy access to the market, dry-shod; but, the rest of the street not being paved, whenever a carriage came out of the mud upon this pavement it shook off and left its dirt upon it, and it was soon covered with mire, which was not removed, the city as yet having no scavengers.

After some inquiry I found a poor, industrious man, who was willing to undertake keeping the pavement clean by sweeping it twice a week, carrying off the dirt from before all the neighbors' doors for the sum of sixpence per month to be paid by each house. I then wrote and printed a paper setting forth the advantages to the neighborhood that might be obtained by this small expense: the greater ease in keeping our houses clean, so much dirt not being brought in by people's feet; the benefit to the shops by more custom, etc., as buyers could more easily get at them, and by not having, in windy weather, the dust blown in upon their goods, etc. I sent one of these papers to each house, and in a day or two went round to see who would subscribe an agreement to pay these sixpences. It was unanimously signed, and for a time well executed. All the inhabitants of the city were delighted with the cleanliness of the pavement that surrounded the market, it being a convenience to all; and this raised a general desire to have all the streets paved, and made the people more willing to submit to a tax for that purpose.

After some time I drew a bill for paving the city, and brought it into the Assembly. It was just before I went to England in 1757, and did not pass till I was gone, and then with an alteration in the mode of assessment which I thought not for the better, but with an additional provision for lighting as well as paving the streets, which was a great improvement. It was by a private person, the late Mr. John Clifton,—his giving a sample of the utility of lamps by placing one at his door,—that the people were first impressed with the idea of enlighting all the city. The honor of this public benefit has also been ascribed to me, but it belongs truly to that gentleman. I did but follow his example, and have only some merit to claim respecting the form of our lamps, as differing from the globe lamps we were at first supplied with from London. Those we found inconvenient in these respects: they admitted no air below; the smoke, therefore, did not readily go out above, but circulated in the globe, lodged on its inside, and soon obstructed the light they were intended to afford, giving, besides, the daily trouble of wiping them clean; and an accidental stroke on one of them would demolish it and render it totally useless. I therefore suggested the composing them of four flat panes, with a long funnel above to draw up the smoke, and crevices admitting air below to facilitate the ascent of the smoke. By this means they were kept clean, and did not grow dark in a few hours, as the London lamps do, but continued bright till morning, and an accidental stroke would generally break but a single pane, easily repaired.

I have sometimes wondered that the Londoners did not, from the effect holes in the bottom of the globe lamps used at Vauxhall have in keeping them clean, learn to have such holes in their street lamps. But, these holes being made for another purpose, namely, to communicate flame more suddenly to the wick by a little flax hanging down through them, the other use, of letting in air, seems not to have been thought of; and therefore, after the lamps have been lit a few hours, the streets of London are very poorly illuminated.

The mention of these improvements puts me in mind of one I proposed, when in London, to Dr. Fothergill, who was among the best men I have known, and a great promoter of useful projects. I had observed that the streets, when dry, were never swept, and the light dust carried away; but it was suffered to accumulate till wet weather reduced it to mud, and then, after lying some days so deep on the pavement that there was no crossing but in paths kept clean by poor people with brooms, it was with great labor raked together and thrown up into carts open above, the sides of which suffered some of the slush at every jolt on the pavement to shake out and fall, sometimes to the annoyance of foot passengers. The reason given for not sweeping the dusty streets was that the dust would fly into the windows of shops and houses.

An accidental occurrence had instructed me how much sweeping might be done in a little time. I found at my door in Craven Street one morning, a poor woman sweeping my pavement with a birch broom. She appeared very pale and feeble, as just come out of a fit of sickness. I asked who employed her to sweep there. She said, "Nobody; but I am very poor and in distress, and I sweeps before gentlefolkses doors, and hopes they will give me something." I bid her sweep the whole street clean, and I would give her a shilling. This was at nine o'clock; at twelve she came for the shilling. From the slowness I saw at first in her working I could scarce believe that the work was done so soon, and sent my servant to examine it, who reported that the whole street was swept perfectly clean, and all the dust placed in the gutter, which was in the middle; and the next rain washed it quite away, so that the pavement, and even the kennel, were perfectly clean.

I then judged that if that feeble woman could sweep such a street in three hours, a strong, active man might have done it in half the time. And here let me remark the convenience of having but one gutter in such a narrow street, running down its middle, instead of two, one on each side, near the footway; for where all the rain that falls on a street runs from the sides and meets in the middle, it forms there a current strong enough to wash away all the mud it meets with; but when divided into two channels, it is often too weak to cleanse either, and only makes the mud it finds more fluid, so that the wheels of carriages and feet of horses throw and dash it upon the foot pavement, which is thereby rendered foul and slippery, and sometimes splash it upon those who are walking. . . .

Some may think these trifling matters, not worth minding or relating; but when they consider that though dust blown into the eyes of a single person, or into a single shop, on a windy day is but of small importance, yet the great number of the instances in a populous city, and its frequent repetitions, give it weight and consequence, perhaps they will not censure very severely those who bestow some attention to affairs of this seemingly low nature. Human felicity is produced not so much by great pieces of good fortune that seldom happen, as by little advantages that occur every day. Thus, if you teach a poor young man to shave himself and keep his razor in order, you may contribute more to the happiness of his life than in giving him a thousand guineas. The money may be soon spent, the regret only remaining of having foolishly consumed it; but in the other case, he escapes the frequent vexation of waiting for barbers, and of their sometimes dirty fingers, offensive breaths, and dull razors. He shaves when most convenient to him, and enjoys daily the pleasure of its being done with a good instrument. With these sentiments I have hazarded the few preceding pages, hoping they may afford hints which some time or other may be useful to a city I love, having lived many years in it very happily, and perhaps to some of our towns in America.

AMITAI ETZIONI

Good Ethics is Good Business

As scandals mount in the financial and commodities markets, economists theorize that the market determines one's ethicality. If "everybody" cheats, those who don't will be wiped out. Like much economic writing, this conclusion is not based on factual observations of ethical traders who went bankrupt, but on abstract theories about "perfect competition."

University of Chicago sociologist Wayne Baker observed that many traders in the pits organize themselves in tight-knit social groups that jealously guard their pits. Often, they do not "hear" better bids shouted by traders who visit from other pits. And

Reprinted from "The Moral Dilemma—Good Ethics is Good Business—Really" by Amitai Etzioni. *The New York Times,* February 12, 1989. Copyright © 1989 by The New York Times Company. Reprinted by permission.

130

they juggle trades to exhaust the capital of those outsiders. More generally, social scientists have found that social ties and other such non-economic factors largely determine whether conduct is ethical. Leading these non-economic factors are local cultures and the social webs that sustain them.

For example, the culture of some pits is more tolerant of un-ethical conduct than the culture of others. Federal Bureau of Investigation agents initially penetrated the Standard & Poor's 500 pit but found little unethical behavior. The agents then moved into the yen and Swiss franc pits, which reportedly have much more lax cultures.

Other differences in culture and regulatory traditions seem to exist among exchanges. In previous years, many investors, believed that the New York Stock Exchange adhered to stricter standards than the American Stock Exchange and over-the-counter market, which in turn were thought of as "cleaner" than certain regional exchanges. (Denver's exchange, for example, is often in the news as the hotbed of often manipulated penny stocks.) Likewise, the Tokyo and Mexico exchanges are believed to be much more "rigged" than, say, the exchanges in London.

Cultures are introduced into behavior by what sociologists call "differential association"—if you join a corrupt organization, pretty soon you are likely to behave accordingly, unless you are one of the very rare people who quit. A study of price fixing in the electrical equipment industry found that "the defendants almost invariably testified that they came new to a job, found price fixing an established way of life, and simply entered into it as they did into other aspects of their job."

The national moral climate is an important factor that pushes local cultures in one direction or another. Sally S. Simpson, who studied antitrust violations between 1927 and 1981, found such violations were more common during Republican than Democratic administrations.

Another economic theorem is that unethical behavior rises in a profit squeeze. To survive trades, financiers and others are pushed, if not forced, to "cut corners." Or, as it is often put, ethical behavior is a "luxury" of those with hefty profit margins. Actually, the implication that ethics is bad for business is simplistic. As the commodities markets already discovered, unethical behavior tarnishes an industry's reputation and drives out customers. It is an effect that lingers for years.

Also, transaction costs are higher the more unethical the market. The less that those who trade can trust one another, the greater is the need for accountants, inspectors, lawyers and regulatory agencies. The current F.B.I. commodity market investigation was reportedly set off after a major agricultural company, Archer Midland Daniels, complained that the cheating in commodities was hurting its business. We tend to forget that the commodity exchanges not only serve those trying to make a fast buck, but also smooth out agriculture and exports.

Finally, any examination of the list of people charged with insider trading suggests that they hardly suffered from a profit squeeze. Most are multimillionaires—the stretch limo crew. Unethical behavior is in large part driven by lack of conscience, unbridled greed, desire to "outperform" the other guy in a game scored in millions of dollars. Others, on the way up, become so accustomed to "cutting corners" and acquire so much hubris in ducking the law, that they fail to change even after they reach the top. Moreover, in each trade and profession, and on all levels of income, there are many who are basically honest.

The cultural and organizational foundations of unethical behavior inform us where the corrections must be made. National leaders, especially the President, can set higher standards. Self-regulation is inadequate. Individuals who are ethically concerned need to join with like-minded others to participate in the difficult task of changing unduly lax cultures. They will often lose business to other markets if they do not shape up. They will always be less able to face their neighbors, community and children, and, one hopes, their better self.

OLIVER F. WILLIAMS

The Example of Cummins Engine

. . . While there are, no doubt, many business organizations
that would qualify as helpful models in formulating a business
ethics, I have recently had the opportunity to study one such
firm, the Cummins Engine Company. For eight days in March,
1981, I visited the Cummins operation in Columbus, Indiana.
The major portion of this time was spent in interviews with
twenty-three managers . . . Persons interviewed ranged from
MBAs with the firm for a year to senior-level executives near
retirement. While I asked a number of specific questions, much of
the time was devoted to discussing more open-ended questions
aimed at making some determination of the ethical quality of the
firm. Cummins stands out not only because it has a good reputation as a profit-making organization, but also because it con-
sciously and deliberately strives to be a leader in the corporate
social responsibility movement. Cummins is the largest independent producer of diesel engines in the world, with twenty-two
thousand employees and seven thousand common stockholders.
In 1980 net sales were $1.7 billion. Significantly, social activists,
typically identified as antibusiness, have praised Cummins for its
ethical sensitivity . . .

The concern for social value questions at Cummins is system-
atically integrated into the organization under the leadership of
the Department of Corporate Responsibility. The department offers a course in management and ethics, provides assistance to
managers who are experiencing difficulties in ethical dilemmas,
and develops policies on social-ethical issues. In addition to this
staff support, the department serves two other functions: it provides research reports on social and political issues in the coun-

Excerpted from "Business Ethics: A Trojan Horse?" by Oliver F. Williams.
California Management Review, Vol. XXIV, No. 4 (Summer, 1982). Copyright
1982 by The Regents of the University of California. Reprinted by permission of
The Regents.

tries where Cummins is present or projected to be present, and it supports top management of specific public policy projects, such as a study commission on South Africa. The department currently has three full-time employees.

There is an ethos at Cummins, a way of life that has developed over the years as moral men and women worked together at a common task. An important means of passing on the "Cummins way" is a set of formal policies called *Cummins Practices.* There is a *Cummins Practice* on ethical standards, questionable payments, meals, gifts, and discounts, financial representations, international distributor accounts, customs declarations, supplier selection, employee participation in political campaigns, and employee participation in noncorporate political activities. Each of these includes a very readable discussion of a practice, a detailing of responsibility for the practice, and a listing of persons to consult should additional information and counsel be necessary.

The *Cummins Practice on Ethical Standards* gives an excellent summary of the moral tone desired by top management.

> For Cummins, ethics rests on a fundamental belief in people's dignity and decency. Our most basic ethical standard is to show respect for those whose lives we affect and to treat them as we would expect them to treat us if our positions were reversed. This kind of respect implies that we must:
>
> 1. Obey the law.
> 2. Be honest—present the facts fairly and accurately.
> 3. Be fair—give everyone appropriate consideration.
> 4. Be concerned—care about how Cummins' actions affect others and try to make those effects as beneficial as possible.
> 5. Be courageous—treat others with respect even when it means losing business. (It seldom does. Over the long haul, people trust and respect this kind of behavior and wish more of our institutions embodied it.)

A strong flavor of an "ethics of consequences" permeates the Cummins Practices . . .

> The reason for such behavior is that, in the long run, nothing else works. If economies and societies do not operate in this way,

the whole machinery begins to collapse. No corporation can long survive in situations where employees, creditors and communities don't trust each other. Since a corporation lives by society's consent, it must plan on earning and keeping that consent for the duration. Successes we have today—in securing sales, completing negotiations, obtaining credit, enlisting employee loyalties—are in major part made possible by the fact that others have learned to expect that Cummins will deal with them fairly. What we do today will maintain or undermine that legacy.

In an interview I had with J. Irwin Miller, long-time chief executive officer and presently chairman of the executive and finance committee of the board, Miller elaborated on his view that "ethical behavior is the best course, for, in the long run, nothing else works." For Miller, this insight is a biblical one and it is confirmed in the experience of life. The teachings of Jesus on honesty, trust, and generosity are taken to be the best guidelines for a rewarding life, even if following them means losing some business on occasion. The Bible, for Miller, tells him the best way to live and realize his God-given destiny. Miller's vision has long been influenced by the Christian faith, and not only in the corporate office. As the first lay president of the National Council of the Churches of Christ in the United States, he was a leader in the civil rights activities of the 1960s. Under Miller's leadership, Cummins began their traditional practice of distributing 5 percent of pretax profits to charity.

. . . It is worth noting that although Cummins practices detail rules of conduct for a whole range of ethical issues, top management does not assume that the rules in themselves will always be sufficient. The assumption is that there will be value conflicts, and it is a stated role of the Department of Corporate Responsibility to assist managers with these conflicts. The sorts of conflicts encountered are illustrated by the following quotes from a cross section of corporate executives interviewed. When asked, "What sort of ethical problems might one expect in your position?" executives answered as follows:

"Nepotism. Requests that we hire friends over others who may be more competent. Contending with the 'old boy' network."

"Requests for illegal money transfers in international business."

"Real estate agents interested in the firm's business may offer unethical 'incentives' to company representatives."

"Engineering design issues. How safe do you make a product? We must do cost-benefit analysis, but where do you draw the line?"

"A serious problem is that people do not tell the truth to each other about poor job performance. Often poor performers are just carried along until economic reasons dictate a cut, and then the person is let go. We need more candid discussions about performance, and we need to learn to be better at bringing people along in their professions."

"Deceptive or unauthorized expense accounts are turned in occasionally."

"Accepting gifts from company suppliers or potential suppliers."

"Determining a fair price for our products."

"Determining fair warranty expenses."

"Problems with confidential compensation reviews."

"How 'honest' must we be with the press?"

"Kickbacks in claims processing."

"Hiring senior-level executives from outside instead of promoting from within is a big ethical problem for me."

"Problems arise in dealing with confidential information about employees."

"Affirmative action always needs more attention."

"What is a 'fair' profit?"

"How do you decide what plants to take up or down in the production process?"

. . . Experience has shown Cummins that talented and ethically sensitive executives may need additional education in business ethics. Beginning in 1978, the Department of Corporate Responsibility developed a course for senior and middle-level managers. Presupposing that the manager is disposed to do the right thing and that the company is so structured that it will support an individual trying to do the right thing, the course is designed to train managers to be better at discerning just what the right thing is in a complex situation with claims in conflict. Specifically, the course outline lists three learning goals:

- To improve recognition of ethical dimensions in management decisions.
- To acquire concepts and methods of ordering and analysis of ethical issues.
- To strengthen the capacity for resolution of ethical issues in managerial decisions.

While the course provides a number of cases from business, participants are urged to suggest cases from their own experience for group discussion. They are also provided with brief lectures and four excellent handouts. The handouts, entitled *What is Ethics?, Understanding Moral Disagreement, Why Managerial Ethics?,* and *Ethical Principles,* are clearly written and capture the best of contemporary thinking on practical ethics. A key paragraph from *Why Managerial Ethics?* highlights the basic self-understanding of Cummins management.

> The underlying philosophy of Cummins Engine Company, Inc., is that business corporations hold a kind of public trust—society requires business enterprise for human well-being, and individual corporations derive their power ultimately from society's consent that the business is fulfilling its public trust. Managers, then, are not simply responsible to "owners" but also to the wider community whose needs call forth the industry and whose cooperation and support is necessary for successful operation. Cummins expresses this philosophy in one of its corporate goals: to develop and maintain "the highest standards of responsibility to all stakeholders." Every member of the community—local and the wider public—who has a stake in Cummins operations deserves consideration when decisions are made affecting them.

Developing this managerial skill to make prudential judgments and to factor social values into economic decisions is no easy matter. It requires a judgment as to the probable consequences of a proposal or policy, and a sense for the moral values and claims in conflict at issue in a situation. The course offered by the Department of Corporate Responsibility serves an important function by providing a support group enabling managers to come together and discuss moral issues with colleagues.

Structured into each of the units on business ethics is an evaluation to be completed by participating managers. On a 1-to-5 scale (unsatisfactory to excellent) the course has been consistently evaluated at 4 or better for meeting each of the learning goals listed above. In my interviews with managers I asked them a number of questions about the course in business ethics. The opening question in each interview was, "What is your general response to the form and style of the series on ethics and management?" All answered this question positively. The following quotes from managers present the range of concerns expressed.

"The cases were good. The workshop was an opportunity to meet other managers in the company and share experiences."

"In general, the workshops were fine. I found the company's position on South Africa unclear; we need to work on this more."

"The experience was excellent. It provided an environment that encouraged us to think seriously about ethical considerations. One could then go back to the office and speak with confidence about ethics."

"The ethical issues identification segment was excellent. Some participants dominated too much while others did not speak out enough."

"Helpful. I learned how to structure an ethical problem."

"Good. It got people thinking ethics, and encouraged trusting relationships."

"Some of the cases were a bit unreal, but the general discussion helped me appreciate differences in people. The role playing didn't seem to add much."

"My MBA program never touched on ethical issues, and the workshop filled an important need for me."

"Fine, but we need more follow-up. Larger groups, for example, a group of comptrollers, marketing persons, and so on should meet together too."

"Fine. There should be more training on company practices, however."

"It was a worthwhile workshop, although they should add more work environment cases."

The question "Do the concepts introduced at the workshops

really help subsequent decision making?" was answered positively by all those interviewed. When asked, "What is the program's most important contribution to individual managers?" the most common response (60 percent) was that the course was an important symbol signalling that ethical concerns were legitimate at Cummins. Many (70 percent) noted that the course was helpful for increasing sensitivity to ethical issues and for thinking clearly about them. A significant number (80 percent) remarked that the course was an excellent opportunity to meet other managers in diverse areas of the firm and to share ideas on increasing the quality of life at Cummins.

While Cummins clearly subscribes to the teaching of business ethics, it is significant that there are very modest claims made for the course. . . . Top management has grasped the fact that character is not shaped by a course or two but rather is a culmination of a long process. The key to ethical management is not only a wholesome environment in the firm and policies and processes that promote and protect essential values, but also the careful selection of personnel. In 1974 the then chairman of the board, J. Irwin Miller, reiterated a description of the sort of person the company should hire. Miller underscored that:

> We must aim at recruiting persons of stable character, who are able to commit themselves to a common undertaking, and who *want* to do good work. We must aim at *secure* persons, who are not afraid to speak up, and who do not think only of themselves. . . . So what are we looking for in our recruiting? Character and maturity before specific skills—every time; intelligence and the capacity to identify responsibility with our common objectives. Such persons are not easy to find. It is not always the habit today to commit oneself to a group or to be able to identify with an institution in an intelligent, responsible manner.

. . . Focusing on the life in a business organization such as Cummins Engine brings to light a crucial corrective for much of the practical ethics done today. Cummins has found that it is important to stress the sort of company it wants to be and the sort of employee it wants to hire, the character of the company and its employees. The Cummins course on business ethics, and much of their literature, offers a vision, a rationale, for acting in certain ways. Rather than an exclusive focus on rules and principles (from a theory of obligation), there is a trend toward an ethics of character (what traditionally has been called a theory of virtue). The really important question from a theory of virtue perspective is not, "What rules or principles are at stake here?" Rather, it is, "What sort of company are we becoming by pursuing this policy?" or "What sort of person am I becoming by acting this way?" . . .

ROBERT JOHNSON

Cummins Shows the Decade's Scars

COLUMBUS, Ind. —In 1919, Clessie Cummins founded a company with the pledge that he would make good engines first and eventually make a profit.

The latter took 18 years. But the values Mr. Cummins instilled in his fledgling company left it in good stead for the better part of six decades: quality products, happy workers, strong community ties.

Indeed, Cummins Engine Co. is a paradigm of the benevolent side of capitalism. As much a fixture in this heartland town of 32,000 people as the old church bells, covered wooden bridges and ice cream fountains, Cummins has over the years built a homeless shelter here and financed drug counseling in the public schools. It has long paid the fees of distinguished architects for public buildings here, and it once even lobbied for a higher state corporate income tax so it could pay more of what it deemed its fair share.

Such largess still left room for handsome profits. By 1979,

Reprinted from "SURVIVOR'S STORY, With Its Spirit Shaken But Unbent, Cummins Shows Decade's Scars" by Robert Johnson. *The Wall Street Journal,* December 13, 1989. Reprinted by permission of *The Wall Street Journal,* ©1989 Dow Jones & Company, Inc. All Rights Reserved Worldwide.

Cummins had earnings of $57.9 million, its 43rd straight year in the black. The annual report that year trumpeted, "The 1980s offer exciting challenges for Cummins."

The '80s did bring challenges, though hardly the excitement Cummins expected. Forces largely outside the company's control have left Cummins struggling for its very survival. Cummins, long secure in its isolation, was buffeted by nearly every major upheaval that swept through the decade's economy.

These included a vicious recession, stiff competition from foreign rivals and the relentless demand for profits emanating from Wall Street-backed corporate raiders. Such forces wreaked havoc throughout industrial America, and many of Cummins's Rust Belt neighbors didn't survive.

Cummins itself has been forced into layoffs and plant closings which have halted the steady flow of Columbus youth into jobs on its factory floors. Just prior to announcing the company's first-ever round of layoffs in 1983, Cummins executives met with 30 of the town's clergymen and prayed.

Meanwhile, the company's insistence on spending big bucks for research and development and pursuing long-term goals at the expense of short-term profits has run Cummins afoul of an increasingly impatient Wall Street and brought a potentially hostile acquirer to Cummins's door twice in the last year.

Unwanted Investors

First, it managed to turn away the unwanted interest of the British conglomerate Hanson PLC, which acquired a 8.8% stake beginning in the fall of 1988.

Hanson is known for its aggressive acquisitions, including its earlier hostile takeover of SCM Corp. Columbus's first family, the Millers, put up $72 million to buy off the British earlier this year. Then came Industrial Equity (Pacific), a Hong Kong investor, which continues to hold a threatening 14.9% of the maker of heavy-duty, diesel engines. Says Kemper Financial Services Inc. chief economist David Hale, "The company could disappear soon."

This is the story of how Cummins, its people and its town survived, yet were inevitably changed. It raises some particularly troubling questions as managers, bureaucrats and policy makers debate America's declining industrial competitiveness. Cummins is by most accounts well-managed. It has protected its market share against foreign competition. And it adheres to the idealized notion of capitalism that private industry should do social good so that government won't have to. Yet it is threatened as never before.

Discussing his company, Cummins's 55-year-old Chairman Henry B. Schacht, sounds more like Jimmy Stewart in "It's a Wonderful Life" than a 1980s-style chief executive. His 1983 annual report to shareholders listed the company's goal as "being fair and honest and doing what is right even when it is not to our immediate benefit."

Balanced Values

Mr. Schacht, who passed up numerous offers from Wall Street to spend 30 years making truck and industrial engines here, now says, "Some say the company's main goal should be to maximize shareholder value. . . . I say no." He speaks instead of achieving "a balanced set of values that ought to permeate the U.S. financial sector."

Those values, in Cummins's view, include giving more to charity than all but 95 of the Fortune 500 companies in 1988, a year when the company itself didn't make a dime; helping to build a school, a clinic and a gymnasium in a slum area near its new factory in Sao Paulo, Brazil, and sending engines and generators, free of charge, to hurricane victims in South Carolina earlier this year. Says Mr. Schacht with obvious pride, "Nobody stopped to say, Hey, we aren't making any money."

Nobody at Cummins, maybe. "Cummins is one big, social slush fund," says Greg Jarrel, former chief economist for the Securities and Exchange Commission, who has written extensively on corporate strategy. "An incredibly naive attitude exists at the company, and I think a lot of people involved with it are going to get their hearts broken."

They may include people like Mihir Patel, a high-school senior whose family moved here from India. "You realize growing up here that a big company isn't just out to make money," he says of Cummins.

Or just about the whole town of Columbus. "This town puts a high value on being needed," says J. Irwin Miller, the 80-year-old patriarch of the investment banking family that began lending money to Clessie Cummins 70 years ago. Losing Cummins, he says, "would be a kind of death."

Columbus is an old farm town, 45 miles south of Indianapolis, surrounded by cornfields, and the road leading into town is lined with weeping willows.

Cummins has paid $9.9 million over the years to get recognized architects to design 24 public buildings here, right down to the new jail by Don Hisaka, a nationally-known architect in Cambridge, Mass., who visited Columbus 12 times and worked nine years on the jail's design. Townsfolk like to call Columbus the "Athens of the Prairie."

The pride in their town has long been equalled only by the pride local residents have in their company.

For many years now, at least one out of every 10 Columbians has worked at Cummins. Wage and benefit packages have historically been so generous, recalls plant manager Mike Cantrell, that when he joined out of college 16 years ago, he was told to name his own salary. When he named a figure he thought more than fair, his Cummins recruiter said it was too low.

The company's emphasis on quality has taken on cult dimensions here. Charles Kessler used to gather his factory-floor trainees around to shame any of one of them who failed to properly tighten a bolt, and the late manager V.E. MacMullen ranted at so much as a momentarily out-of-place oil pan on the assembly line. (People here still talk about long-retired, even dead, employees.)

The main plant is still scrubbed as much as some restaurant kitchens. The clutter of newspapers isn't allowed during breaks on the line, where reading is limited to the bible and technical manuals.

The rejection rate for engines that have to be reworked at the end of Cummins's assembly line is about 1%, fully one-third the industry average. Cummins's engines are pricey equipment under the hoods of the big-truck kings: Kenworth, Navistar and Peterbilt.

"We don't expect to need any major work on a Cummins engine until 600,000 miles," or 100,000 miles more than most other brands, says Andrew Corrado, owner of a 140-truck steel-hauling fleet in Niles, Ohio. Since he switched to trucks with Cummins engines in 1983, he says his fleet's fuel mileage increased to 6.2 per gallon from 4.3.

"The best engines a lot of sweat can build—that's what we believe in," says Donnie Wright, a machine-tool operator for 22 years. He points out Cummins-equipped trucks to his wife whenever they are on the highway. "Ours have a special hum, a rumble all their own. When I see one hauling logs, freight or fuel, it makes me proud to help a trucker feed his family," he says.

It used to be that such pride and commitment could pretty much guarantee success. "From the '50s through the '70s, craftsmanship and higher volume meant you keep doing better," says Robert B. Reich, political economist at Harvard University. "This decade shattered a comfortable world where manufacturers improved profits by doing what they always did—just more of it."

Grappling with Change

Cummins has spent the '80s both bowing to and stubbornly resisting change. It has refused to chop its charitable spending. It won't cut its budget for research and development of improved engines, which annually exceeds $100 million. And it absolutely won't consider leaving Columbus for a lower cost, nonunion site somewhere in the South. Some of the company's young M.B.A.s "say we can reduce this thing to dollars and cents, but we won't," says Cummins president James Henderson, himself a Harvard M.B.A. and a 25-year Cummins veteran.

Cummins's biggest problem has been the threat of foreign competition, which first began stalking the U.S. diesel engine market in 1984. Companies such as Nissan Motor Co., sporting newer factories and cheaper labor, entered the U.S. market with engines selling for as much as 20% less than those of Cummins.

Foregoing short-term profits, Cummins decided that its future depended on holding onto market share—at a heavy price. It began slashing prices even more than the Japanese. It began selling some engines at 40% markdowns. The effect on profit was devastating. Cummins sustained a $107 million loss in 1986.

At the same time, the company has undertaken a decade-long move to modernize its production processes, which has upset just about everyone at the company in one way or another. High technology has come to the factory floor, some factories have been closed, and thousands of jobs have been lost.

"When the supervisor told us robots were coming into our section, I asked how hard we'd have to work to keep them out," says Robert Schilawski, a 25-year veteran engine tester. "The answer was, 'No one can work that hard.'"

Robots have eliminated 40 of the 100 jobs in the testing sections at Mr. Schilawski's plant in the last five years. Each robot tests 20 new engines a day, compared to two by each human.

"We take pride in listening to an engine and knowing if there is something wrong. But more and more, machines do the listening. You have to wonder if the company's dying when there's no young guys coming up for you to pass skills along to," he says.

Until the last few years, it was common for highly rated plant workers to be promoted into management jobs. Larry Kirk, a 26-year veteran, recently shunned such an offer—along with its prestige and 10% raise. "Fifteen years ago my goal was to move up. But it means leaving the union—giving up all protection if there is another cutback. Now I just can't take that chance; I have to stay where I am," he says.

The biggest impact on workers—and on Columbus—has been the layoff of roughly 4,000 people in Columbus during the decade. On his way to work in the morning, Mr. Schacht occasionally passes by a local unemployment office, saddened by the knowledge that many of those he sees inside were put there by him. He says no one waiting in the unemployment line has ever been abusive, although nearly everyone in town recognizes him. "It would be easier if they ranted and raved. But they make it hard by saying, 'I wish things could be different. I wish I could help.'"

Trouble for Columbus

Officials in Columbus attribute what they portray as ominous changes in the social fabric of this town directly to the problems at Cummins. County Sheriff Rick Hill, whose late father worked 30 years on a Cummins assembly line, says his department has investigated 340 cases of domestic disputes in the first 10 months of this year, a 30% increase from the same period four years ago. "A lot of them involve families with someone laid off from Cummins making $15 an hour," he says. "Now he's making $5 an hour flipping burgers. There's disillusionment and tension that goes with that."

The sheriff recently offered 14 new clerical jobs paying $7.75 an hour at the new jail. "We got 200 applications. Ten years ago, people didn't line up in Columbus for that little money," Mr. Hill says.

Mr. Hill also notes that "today, our prisoners are a different breed. We've had our first home invasions in the last couple of years. Violent assaults. It's kind of shocking," he says softly.

Rising crime in Columbus coincides with "jaded values and lower expectations," says Stan Franke, a sheriff's detective who investigates juvenile offenses. High-school graduates could previously aspire to be hired into one of three Cummins plants at top wages. But the company hasn't hired a single new plant worker since 1979. "I'm beginning to hear kids say there isn't a future in Columbus anymore," says Mr. Franke. The county had 200 reported teen-age runaways last year, compared to about a dozen in 1979.

Despite all this gloom, Cummins officials continue to preach to employees, community officials and Wall Street that they do have a survival plan—they just need more time to pull it off. The company now has 54% of the U.S. heavy-duty diesel-engine market. Its research department has successfully developed several smaller engines for use in trucks and speedboats. It says costs are down 22% since 1983, when a reduction program began.

The layoffs and unpopular modernization haven't cost Cummins all of its distinctive workplace culture. The electronic mail slot of Mr. Henderson, the company president, bulges daily with criticisms and suggestions, signed by workers, which he encourages them to send. One worker's note complains that he is receiving overtime pay, while his friends suffer through layoffs. Mr. Henderson responds that he can't bring back workers merely to fill a few orders that take longer than expected.

The company still has the staunch support of the powerful Miller family, which rescued it from the Hanson threat. "In much of the country, the '80s were the decade of the grasshopper in Aesop's fable: spending, consuming and instant gratification," says 33-year-old William I. Miller, son of J. Irwin Miller, president of his family's investment concern and an influential member of the Cummins board. "But we are a town of somewhat nerdy, hard-working ants, taking pride in our labors," he says.

Dashed Hope

The much hoped-for turnaround seemed to have arrived earlier this year, when Cummins recorded two quarters of strong profits. But then came the distractions of the hostile takeover threat, along with a sudden downturn in new truck sales. The company lost $39.7 million in the third quarter. Wall Street was once again dismayed. Says analyst Steve Colbert of Prudential-Bache Securities Inc., Cummins has been "in a long-term mode for 10 years. . . . Schacht sounds great, but at some point there's got to be a payout for all this spending."

Industrial Equity, which is headed by New Zealand-based investor Sir Ronald Brierley, isn't saying what it plans to do with its Cummins stake. But it has made three U.S. acquisitions in the past 18 months, failed in a hostile takeover attempt of tobacco machinery maker Molins PLC, and has stated its corporate goal as "the acquisition of sound, fixed assets and operating businesses."

Meanwhile, Mr. Schacht has been looking for another friendly investor to join with the Miller clan and give Cummins some long-term protection.

"Cummins has a fantastic future because it isn't just factories, machines and cash," says the elder Mr. Miller, a former Cummins chairman and still a close adviser to Mr. Schacht. "It's outstanding people who take intense pride in their work and their community."

"The gloomiest predictions have all been wrong so far," he continues. "My mother used to say the last good year was 1910."

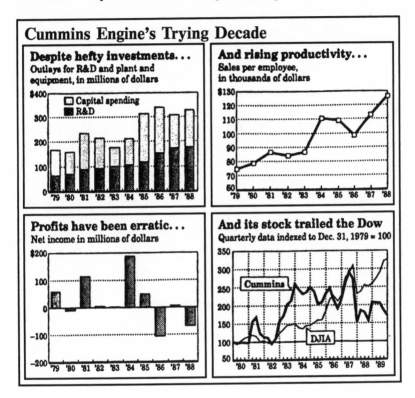

Cummins Engine's Trying Decade

Despite hefty investments...
Outlays for R&D and plant and equipment, in millions of dollars

And rising productivity...
Sales per employee, in thousands of dollars

Profits have been erratic...
Net income in millions of dollars

And its stock trailed the Dow
Quarterly data indexed to Dec. 31, 1979 = 100

Editor's Note:

In July, 1990, as we go to press, Cummins has announced that it has obtained $250 million in fresh capital from Ford, Tenneco and Kubota Ltd. of Japan in exchange for a 27% stake in the company and a seat on the board each for Ford and Tenneco. All three investors are customers of Cummins and management anticipates growing sales to them as well as a partial solution to the company's immediate cash-flow problems, according to a July 16 article in *The New York Times.*

LINCOLN STEFFENS

An Intelligent Unhappy Crook

. . . [T]hat was what was the matter with Boston and me, not
what we did, but what we thought.

You could see it, plain, in Boston, founded by a lot of earnest
Puritans from England who had the 'truth' and wished to be free
to practice it, who came to the new country to set up liberty and
the Right. How can one believe in both liberty and the Right?
The Puritans took liberty for themselves, but they could not
grant it to others who were wrong. They believed in the Christian
ideals, but they founded a system of economics—the only one
they knew—which rewarded, nay, which required, thrift, cunning, and possessions—the ownership of properties which would
enable them to live without the necessity to do work, which they
said they believed in and gradually learned to avoid. As they
succeeded, some of them, and acquired wealth, they mistook
their plutocracy for aristocracy and soothed their Christian ideals with a scholarly admixture of the ideals of the Greek aristocracy. But they always kept their religion and their culture out of
politics and business. They formed, as we all do, watertight com-
partments of the mind, learned from the start to think one way
and do another. As the Puritans went on from agriculture to
industry they kept their principles as convictions in one lobe of
their brains, which they did not let know what the other lobe was
doing. They could corrupt their democratic, agricultural government and social organization to their business uses and still be
honest men and democrats who believed and said what the Governor of Connecticut said: "It is right for us (the aristocrats) who
know what is right to (buy votes and otherwise) influence the
ignorant who do not know what is right." They could believe in
the nobility and discipline of labor and yet justify the accumula-

Excerpted from *The Autobiography of Lincoln Steffens*. New York: Harcourt,
Brace Co., 1931.

tion of riches to save their children from the discipline of labor. They could stand for free speech, a free press, and all that, and tyrannically suppress agitators and buy up or boycott papers that spread discontent. Boston has carried the practice of hypocrisy to the *nth* degree of refinement, grace, and failure. New England is dying of hypocrisy. That was what I wrote into my Boston book, and the remedy I offered was—more hypocrisy.

What I mean by this I can illustrate by reporting a conversation with President Eliot of Harvard. It was at the end of his term, just before he gave way to President Lawrence Lowell. Meeting him one day in the Yard, I joined him and proposed that he let me give a short course to seniors on "the forms in which the first steps to bribery and corruption come to young men in all walks of life." He was interested enough to let me give examples of what I would teach.

"A young lawyer is sent to court to ask for a postponement of a case. He fails to get it, and another, older young attorney goes and gets it. The failure asks the success how he did it, and the success says he tipped the clerk of the court. The failure learns thus a lesson which he applies thereafter so well that some day later you find him in the lobby at Hartford or Albany 'tipping' legislators and never knowing that he is a briber."

President Eliot liked this, an actual story; he stood and drew out more and more. He was moved almost to a consideration of my proposition till he happened to ask me what my course would lead up to.

"You would teach those things to stop the doing of them?" he asked.

"Oh, no," I blurted. "I don't mean to keep the boys from succeeding in their professions. All I want to do is to make it impossible for them to be crooks and not know it. Intelligence is what I am aiming at, not honesty. We have, we Americans, quite enough honesty now. What we need is integrity, intellectual honesty."

That ended me with Mr. Eliot. He gave me a piercing look, a polite bow, and walked on to his office. I would have liked to tell him how about that time President Mellon of the New York, New Haven and Hartford Railroad, a western man, who had acquired what I wished all young men to have, asked me in his office one day how he could get himself and his railroad out of politics. I asked him why he asked that, and the long answer was that he had 'done politics' in the railroad business out west, realized what that meant to him and to society, and had made up his mind, when Morgan called him east, to cut it out. And he was finding that he could not cut it out; when he did not do what had always been done in Massachusetts, Rhode Island, Connecticut, and New York, his railroad was held up and his directors made it hot for him. He had tried, but he was finding that he 'had to' do it.

"Well, that's the answer, Mr. Mellon," I said. "That's what I hear all over this country. You can't run a railroad without corrupting and running the government."

He was amazed that I, a reformer, should say that. "You tell me that? You!" he repeated.

"Yes," I said. "I tell you that; it's evidently a fact, a truth, a hateful truth, which most men who acknowledge it don't feel the hatefulness of, as you do. They excuse it; they ignore it; they are not intelligent."

"But what, then, shall I do?" he almost cried.

My suggestion was that since he knew and hated what he had to do, he should stay on the job and do it up brown. "If we can have all such positions filled with intelligent men who, knowingly corrupt government, it would be a great step ahead of where we are now—betrayed by a lot of honest men who think they are the moral pillars of society."

Mr. Mellon did not seem satisfied with my advice, and a year or two later he resigned. I fictionized this incident in the story of "The Reluctant Briber," and I hope President Eliot read it. He wasn't satisfied with my advice to him either. And there was one other New Englander who was dumbfounded by the idea of, for the present, putting intelligence above morality.

On a train going from Boston to New Haven for a Harvard-Yale football game, Edward A. Filene told me he had just left in the smoking-room one of the steel men who had been indicted in the slight exposure I referred to above: the exposure of collusive bidding for city contracts. I went in and sat beside this young business man and drew from him his story. He was bitter about it, and inclined to be cynical, which is a symptom of defeat, of a failure to think through some emotional experience.

He had been one of those good citizens, he said, who had stood up boldly for the grand jury probe into political corruption, and then when it came he was, to his amazement, one of the first witnesses called. And, by Jove, he was called as an evil-doer, a felon, and—and, yes, he was guilty. Had he not gone into a pool of steel men to agree on bids so that each in turn would get contracts, at a 'fair price'? He had. It was not exactly a pool, but there had been a lot of throat-cutting in the trade; the competitive bidding had cut prices down till no man could make any profit. Really. So the steel men met informally, and—it wasn't a pool; that is to say, they did not call or think of it as a pool, and certainly there was no criminal intent; but, yes, they did agree to agree on prices and on who was to get each contract. "And," he said bitterly, "that was absolutely necessary. It was a crime, but it is necessary. I was not punished, much. I was let off easy, but I was—I was a crook."

"And you still have to be a crook?" I asked, and he was shocked; so I added, "You still have to have some understanding with the other bidders? A pool? Collusive bids?"

He did; slowly he admitted it, and, an honest man, his only pose was—the cynic. That's what I hate, cynicism, and that's what I tried to break with my answer.

"Well," I said, "you are lucky. Your town, this country, is full up with honest men such as you were, who are crooks without ever knowing it. They are good, but they are not intelligent. You are intelligent. If you know that you are a crook and that you have to be a crook, you are, where all Bostoners would like to be and think they are, in the aristocracy of men who know that some of our laws run counter to the forces of nature, to the economic pressure of business."

"What, for example?" He was interested.

"Well, you know, for example, that there is something wrong with an antitrust law that forbids the apparently inevitable formation of pools, which are the first step toward the organization of monopolies."

"But monopolies are wrong, aren't they?"

"There is something wrong about monopolies, I think, either

in their origin or in their private control, but men like you, who see that they are necessary and evil somehow, are on the way to find out just what it is that is wrong and cure it. Good business men—like you, before you were caught and convicted—will never solve a problem that calls for knowledge, study, and insight."

Still in doubt, he looked at me to see if I was serious, and I was. I restated my theorem.

"You are one of the few Boston men who are what they all think they are, good and true. You are in the way of becoming an intelligent and therefore an unhappy crook." . . .

WINSTON S. CHURCHILL

Honor Points the Path of Duty

The Sermon on the Mount is the last word in Christian ethics. Everyone respects the Quakers. Still, it is not on these terms that Ministers assume their responsibilities of guiding states. Their duty is first so to deal with other nations as to avoid strife and war and to eschew aggression in all its forms, whether for nationalistic or ideological objects. But the safety of the State, the lives and freedom of their own fellow countrymen, to whom they owe their position, make it right and imperative in the last resort, or when a final and definite conviction has been reached, that the use of force should not be excluded. If the circumstances are such as to warrant it, force may be used. And if this be so, it should be used under the conditions which are most favourable. There is no merit in putting off a war for a year if, when it comes, it is a far worse war or one much harder to win. These are the tormenting dilemmas upon which mankind has throughout its history been

Excerpted from *The Gathering Storm,* Vol. I, by Winston Churchill. Copyright 1948 by Houghton Mifflin Company. Copyright renewed © 1976 by Lady Spencer Churchill, the Honorable Lady Sarah Audley, and the Honorable Lady Soames. Reprinted by permission of Houghton Mifflin Company.

so frequently impaled. Final judgment upon them can only be recorded by history in relation to the facts of the case as known to the parties at the time, and also as subsequently proved.

There is, however, one helpful guide, namely, for a nation to keep its word and to act in accordance with its treaty obligations to allies. This guide is called *honour.* It is baffling to reflect that what men call honour does not correspond always to Christian ethics. Honour is often influenced by that element of pride which plays so large a part in its inspiration. An exaggerated code of honour leading to the performance of utterly vain and unreasonable deeds could not be defended, however fine it might look. Here, however, the moment came when Honour pointed the path of Duty, and when also the right judgment of the facts at that time would have reinforced its dictates.

CHAPTER FIVE

Is Regulation the Route to Ethical Business Conduct?

Commentary

There has never been a shortage of American critics of business and of the behavior of businessmen. John Winthrop, in *The History of New England from 1630 to 1649* recounts with satisfaction the censure and punishment inflicted on one merchant Mr. Robert Keaine for, among other grievous errors, holding to the principle "That a man might sell as dear as he can, and buy as cheap as he can." Thomas Jefferson sees virtues in farming and the rural life that he cannot find in the corrupt commercial cities: "The mobs of great cities add just so much to the support of pure government, as sores do to the strength of the body." When manufacturing firmly takes hold in the 19th century, the chorus of dissenting voices rises to a high pitch, and as the 1890's merge into the first decades of the 20th century the abuses of the big corporations—combinations to fix prices and to squeeze out rising competitors, sweatshops, low wages and miserable working conditions—culminate in the well-known trust busting campaigns of the first Roosevelt, the rise of the labor unions, and the increasing regulation of business by the federal government.

Our readings begin in the first third of this century with the contrasting views of Herbert Hoover and Franklin D. Roosevelt. Hoover, as Secretary of Commerce in 1924, already alarmed at the rapid rise of government efforts to regulate industry and

commerce, counsels business leaders that denouncing the interference of government in their affairs is not a sufficient response,
and he proposes enlightened self-regulation by means of trade
associations and chambers of commerce.

Roosevelt, speaking in the depths of the Depression, and before a business audience in San Francisco, just a few weeks prior
to his election in 1932, sets forth a wide-ranging review of the
history of government-business relations in the United States. He
argues that "private economic power is . . . a public trust as
well." And government, he says, owes it to the public to curb
private excesses when they occur, to provide a balance of forces,
and to use its powers wisely to prevent another depression.

Perhaps no one has ever taken a stronger stand in principle
against regulation than Alan Greenspan in a 1963 article entitled
"The Assault on Integrity." Permission to reproduce that article
here has been refused, so we provide instead a summary of the
main lines of his argument, as follows: it is quite wrong to think
that government regulatory agencies such as the Food and Drug
Administration and the SEC are necessary to protect consumers
against the unscrupulousness and greed of the businessman. In
fact every business has an interest in cultivating a reputation for
honesty and fair dealing. Neither a drug manufacturer nor a
stockbrokerage can afford to risk any loss of trust on the part of
those who purchase their products and services. In an unregulated economy the companies with the best reputations will pros-
per because of this competitive edge. The interest of the supplier
in maintaining such a reputation is the best safeguard of the
consumer. Government regulation, on the other hand, by setting
arbitrary minimum standards, devalues reputation; the minimum
standards "gradually tend to become the maximums as well."
Government regulation is preventative by its very nature; it does
nothing to support the creative effort which produces superior
products and services. By attempting to protect the consumer the
regulator in fact produces the opposite effect: "gradually destroying the only reliable protection the consumer has: competition for
reputation." The collectivists who favor regulation substitute law
enforcement for incentive and reward. They don't understand,
Greenspan concludes, that "Capitalism is based on self-interest
and self-esteem; it holds integrity and trustworthiness as cardinal

virtues and makes them pay off in the marketplace, thus demanding that men survive by means of virtues, not of vices."

Another perspective is provided 26 years later in a reporter's interview with Greenspan (now a prime regulator himself as Chairman of the Federal Reserve Board). The reader will need to judge whether one expert quoted in the interview is right in suggesting that it will be difficult for Greenspan to advocate deregulation of the banking industry in view of his advocacy of deregulation of savings and loan institutions in 1985.

Our final selection for this chapter is a brief essay by Irving Kristol decrying the "bureaucratization of ethics" via the regulatory bodies, but contending at the same time that regulators are filling a vacuum irresponsibly created by businessmen themselves. "The business community should itself," he argues, "get interested, in a serious way, an intellectually thoughtful way, in the issue of business ethics."

HERBERT HOOVER

National Character Cannot Be Built by Law

The advancement of science and our increasing population require constantly new standards of conduct and breed an increasing multitude of new rules and regulations. The basic principles laid down in the Ten Commandments and the Sermon on the Mount are as applicable today as when they were declared, but they require a host of subsidiary clauses. The ten ways to evil in the time of Moses have increased to ten thousand now.

A whole host of rules and regulations are necessary to maintain human rights with this amazing transformation into an industrial era. Ten people in a whole country, with a plow apiece, did not elbow each other very much. But when we put 7,000,000 people in a county with the tools of electric, steam, thirty-floor buildings, telephones, miscellaneous noises, street-cars, railways, motors, stock exchanges, and what not, then we do jostle each other in a multitude of directions. Thereupon our lawmakers supply the demand by the ceaseless piling up of statutes.

. . . Moreover, with increasing education our senses become more offended and our moral discriminations increase; for all of which we discover new things to remedy. In one of our states over 1000 laws and ordinances have been added in the last eight months. It is also true that a large part of them will sleep peacefully in the statute book.

The question we need to consider is whether these rules and regulations are to be developed solely by government or whether they cannot be in some large part developed out of voluntary forces in the nation. In other words, can the abuses which give rise to government in business be eliminated by the systematic and voluntary action of commerce and industry itself? . . .

From "Unfair Competition and Business Ethics," an address by Secretary of Commerce Herbert Hoover, delivered in Cleveland, Ohio, in 1924.

National character cannot be built by law. It is the sum of the moral fibre of its individuals. When abuses which rise from our growing system are cured by live individual conscience, by initiative in the creation of voluntary standards, then is the growth of moral perceptions fertilized in every individual character.

No one disputes the necessity for constantly new standards of conduct in relation to all these tools and inventions. Even our latest great invention—radio—has brought a host of new questions. No one disputes that much of these subsidiary additions to the Ten Commandments must be made by legislation. Our public utilities are wasteful and costly unless we give them a privilege more or less monopolistic. At once when we have business affected with monopoly we must have regulation by law. Much of even this phase might have been unnecessary had there been a higher degree of responsibility to the public, higher standards of business practice among those who dominated these agencies in years gone by. . . .

When legislation penetrates the business world it is because there is abuse somewhere. A great deal of this legislation is due rather to the inability of business hitherto to so organize as to correct abuses than to any lack of desire to have it done. Sometimes the abuses are more apparent than real, but anything is a handle for demagoguery. In the main, however, the public acts only when it has lost confidence in the ability or willingness of business to correct its own abuses.

Legislative action is always clumsy—it is incapable of adjustment to shifting needs. It often enough produces new economic currents more abusive than those intended to be cured. Government too often becomes the persecutor instead of the regulator.

The thing we all need to searchingly consider is the practical question of the method by which the business world can develop and enforce its own standards and thus stem the tide of governmental regulation. The cure does not lie in mere opposition. It lies in the correction of abuse. It lies in an adaptability to changing human outlook.

The problem of business ethics as a prevention of abuse is of two categories: Those where the standard must be one of individual moral perceptions, and those where we must have a determination of standards of conduct for a whole group in order that there may be a basis for ethics.

The standards of honesty, of a sense of mutual obligation, and of service, were determined two thousand years ago. They may require at times to be recalled. And the responsibility for them increases infinitely in high places either in business or government, for there rests the high responsibility for leadership in fineness of moral perception. Their failure is a blow at the repute of business and at confidence in government itself.

The second field and the one which I am primarily discussing is the great area of indirect economic wrong and unethical practices that spring up under the pressures of competition and habit. There is also the great field of economic waste through destructive competition, through strikes, booms, and slumps, unemployment, through failure of our different industries to synchronize, and a hundred other causes which directly lower our productivity and employment. Waste may be abstractly unethical, but in any event it can only be remedied by economic action.

If we are to find solution to these collective issues outside of government regulation we must meet two practical problems:

First, there must be organization in such form as can establish the standards of conduct in this vast complex of shifting invention, production, and use. There is no existing basis to check the failure of service or the sacrifice of public interest. Some one must determine such standards. They must be determined and held flexibly in tune with the intense technology of trade.

Second, there must be some sort of enforcement. There is the perpetual difficulty of a small minority who will not play the game. They too often bring disrepute upon the vast majority; they drive many others to adopt unfair competitive methods which all deplore; their abuses give rise to public indignation and clamor which breed legislative action.

I believe we now for the first time have the method at hand for voluntarily organized determination of standards and their adoption. I would go further; I believe we are in the presence of a new era in the organization of industry and commerce in which, if properly directed, lie forces pregnant with infinite possibilities of moral progress. I believe that we are, almost unnoticed, in the midst of a great revolution—or perhaps a better word, a transformation in the whole super-organization of our economic life. We are passing from a period of extremely individualistic action into a period of associational activities.

Practically our entire American working world is now organized into some form of economic association. We have trade associations and trade institutes embracing particular industries and occupations. We have chambers of commerce embracing representatives of different industries and commerce. We have the labor unions representing the different crafts. We have associations embracing all the different professions—law, engineering, medicine, banking, real estate, and what not. We have farmers' associations, and we have the enormous growth of farmers' co-operatives for actual dealing in commodities. Of indirect kin to this is the great increase in ownership of industries by their employees, and customers, and again we have a tremendous expansion of mutualized insurance and banking.

Associational activities are, I believe, driving upon a new road where the objectives can be made wholly and vitally of public interest. . . .

Three years of study and intimate contact with associations of economic groups whether in production, distribution, labor, or finance, convince me that there lies within them a great moving impulse toward betterment.

If these organizations accept as their primary purpose the lifting of standards, if they will co-operate together for voluntary enforcement of high standards, we shall have proceeded far along the road of the elimination of government from business. . . .

The test of our whole economic and social system is its capacity to cure its own abuses. New abuses and new relationships to the public interest will occur as long as we continue to progress. If we are to be wholly dependent upon government to cure these abuses we shall by this very method have created an enlarged and deadening abuse through the extension of bureaucracy and the clumsy and incapable handling of delicate economic forces. . . .

American business needs a lifting purpose greater than the struggle of materialism. Nor can it lie in some evanescent, emotional, dramatic crusade. It lies in the higher pitch of economic life, in a finer regard for the rights of others, a stronger devotion to obligations of citizenship that will assure an improved leadership in every community and the nation; it lies in the organization of the forces of our economic life so that they may produce happier individual lives, more secure in employment and comfort, wider in the possibilities of enjoyment of nature, larger in its opportunities of intellectual life.

FRANKLIN D. ROOSEVELT

Government Must Protect the Public Interest

. . . Sometimes, my friends, particularly in years such as these, the hand of discouragement falls upon us. It seems that things are in a rut, fixed, settled, that the world has grown old and tired and very much out of joint. This is the mood of depression, of dire and weary depression.

But then we look around us in America, and everything tells us that we are wrong. America is new. It is in the process of change and development. It has the great potentialities of youth, and particularly is this true of the great West, and of this coast, and of California. . . .

But more than that, I appreciate that the membership of this club consists of men who are thinking in terms beyond the immediate present, beyond their own immediate tasks, beyond their own individual interests. I want to invite you, therefore, to consider with me in the large, some of the relationships of Government and economic life that go deeply into our daily lives, our happiness, our future and our security.

The issue of Government has always been whether individual men and women will have to serve some system of Government or economics, or whether a system of Government and economics exists to serve individual men and women. This question has

Excerpted from an address delivered by President Franklin Delano Roosevelt at the Commonwealth Club, San Francisco, September 23, 1932.

persistently dominated the discussion of Government for many generations. On questions relating to these things men have differed, and for time immemorial it is probable that honest men will continue to differ.

The final word belongs to no man; yet we can still believe in change and progress. Democracy, as a dear old friend of mine in Indiana, Meredith Nicholson, has called it, is a quest, a never-ending seeking for better things, and in the seeking for these things and the striving for them, there are many roads to follow. But, if we map the course of these roads, we find that there are only two general directions.

When we look about us, we are likely to forget how hard people have worked to win the privilege of Government. The growth of the national Governments of Europe was a struggle for the development of a centralized force in the Nation, strong enough to impose peace upon ruling barons. In many instances the victory of the central Government, the creation of a strong central Government, was a haven of refuge to the individual. The people preferred the master far away to the exploitation and cruelty of the smaller master near at hand.

But the creators of national Government were perforce ruthless men. They were often cruel in their methods, but they did strive steadily toward something that Society needed and very much wanted, a strong central State able to keep the peace, to stamp out civil war, to put the unruly nobleman in his place, and to permit the bulk of individuals to live safely. The man of ruthless force had his place in developing a pioneer country, just as he did in fixing the power of the central Government in the development of Nations. Society paid him well for his services and its development. When the development among the Nations of Europe, however, had been completed, ambition and ruthlessness, having served their term, tended to overstep their mark.

There came a growing feeling that Government was conducted for the benefit of a few who thrived unduly at the expense of all. The people sought a balancing—a limiting force. There came gradually, through town councils, trade guilds, national parliaments, by constitution and by popular participation and control, limitations on arbitrary power.

Another factor that tended to limit the power of those who

ruled, was the rise of the ethical conception that a ruler bore a responsibility for the welfare of his subjects.

The American colonies were born in this struggle. The American Revolution was a turning point in it. After the Revolution the struggle continued and shaped itself in the public life of the country. There were those who because they had seen the confusion which attended the years of war for American independence surrendered to the belief that popular Government was essentially dangerous and essentially unworkable. They were honest people, my friends, and we cannot deny that their experience had warranted some measure of fear. The most brilliant, honest and able exponent of this point of view was Hamilton. He was too impatient of slow-moving methods. Fundamentally he believed that the safety of the republic lay in the autocratic strength of its Government, that the destiny of individuals was to serve that Government, and that fundamentally a great and strong group of central institutions, guided by a small group of able and public spirited citizens, could best direct all Government.

But Mr. Jefferson, in the summer of 1776, after drafting the Declaration of Independence turned his mind to the same problem and took a different view. He did not deceive himself with outward forms. Government to him was a means to an end, not an end in itself; it might be either a refuge and a help or a threat and a danger, depending on the circumstances. We find him carefully analyzing the society for which he was to organize a Government. "We have no paupers. The great mass of our population is of laborers, our rich who cannot live without labor, either manual or professional, being few and of moderate wealth. Most of the laboring class possess property, cultivate their own lands, have families and from the demand for their labor, are enabled to exact from the rich and the competent such prices as enable them to feed abundantly, clothe above mere decency, to labor moderately and raise their families."

These people, he considered, had two sets of rights, those of "personal competency" and those involved in acquiring and possessing property. By "personal competency" he meant the right of free thinking, freedom of forming and expressing opinions, and freedom of personal living, each man according to his own lights. To insure the first set of rights, a Government must so order its functions as not to interfere with the individual. But even Jefferson realized that the exercise of the property rights might so interfere with the rights of the individual that the Government, without whose assistance the property rights could not exist, must intervene, not to destroy individualism, but to protect it.

You are familiar with the great political duel which followed; and how Hamilton, and his friends, building toward a dominant centralized power were at length defeated in the great election of 1800, by Mr. Jefferson's party. Out of that duel came the two parties, Republican and Democratic, as we know them today.

So began, in American political life, the new day, the day of the individual against the system, the day in which individualism was made the great watchword of American life. The happiest of economic conditions made that day long and splendid. On the Western frontier, land was substantially free. No one, who did not shirk the task of earning a living, was entirely without opportunity to do so. Depressions could, and did, come and go; but they could not alter the fundamental fact that most of the people lived partly by selling their labor and partly by extracting their livelihood from the soil, so that starvation and dislocation were practically impossible. At the very worst there was always the possibility of climbing into a covered wagon and moving west where the untilled prairies afforded a haven for men to whom the East did not provide a place. So great were our natural resources that we could offer this relief not only to our own people, but to the distressed of all the world; we could invite immigration from Europe, and welcome it with open arms. Traditionally, when a depression came a new section of land was opened in the West; and even our temporary misfortune served our manifest destiny.

It was in the middle of the nineteenth century that a new force was released and a new dream created. The force was what is called the industrial revolution, the advance of steam and machinery and the rise of the forerunners of the modern industrial plant. The dream was the dream of an economic machine, able to raise the standard of living for everyone; to bring luxury within the reach of the humblest; to annihilate distance by steam power and later by electricity, and to release everyone from the drudgery of the heaviest manual toil. It was to be expected that this would necessarily affect Government. Heretofore, Government had merely been called upon to produce conditions within which people could live happily, labor peacefully, and rest secure. Now it was called upon to aid in the consummation of this new dream. There was, however, a shadow over the dream. To be made real, it required use of the talents of men of tremendous will and tremendous ambition, since by no other force could the problems of financing and engineering and new developments be brought to a consummation.

So manifest were the advantages of the machine age, however, that the United States fearlessly, cheerfully, and, I think, rightly, accepted the bitter with the sweet. It was thought that no price was too high to pay for the advantages which we could draw from a finished industrial system. The history of the last half century is accordingly in large measure a history of a group of financial Titans, whose methods were not scrutinized with too much care, and who were honored in proportion as they produced the results, irrespective of the means they used. The financiers who pushed the railroads to the Pacific were always ruthless, often wasteful, and frequently corrupt; but they did build railroads, and we have them today. It has been estimated that the American investor paid for the American railway system more than three times over in the process; but despite this fact the net advantage was to the United States. As long as we had free land; as long as population was growing by leaps and bounds; as long as our industrial plants were insufficient to supply our own needs, society chose to give the ambitious man free play and unlimited reward provided only that he produced the economic plant so much desired.

During this period of expansion, there was equal opportunity for all and the business of Government was not to interfere but to assist in the development of industry. This was done at the request of business men themselves. The tariff was originally imposed for the purpose of "fostering our infant industry," a phrase I think the older among you will remember as a political issue not so long ago. The railroads were subsidized, sometimes by grants of money, oftener by grants of land; some of the most valuable oil lands in the United States were granted to assist the financing of the railroad which pushed through the Southwest. A nascent merchant marine was assisted by grants of money, or by mail subsidies, so that our steam shipping might ply the seven seas. Some of my friends tell me that they do not want the Government in business. With this I agree; but I wonder whether they realize the implications of the past. For while it has been American doctrine that the Government must not go into business in competition with private enterprises, still it has been traditional, particularly in Republican administrations, for business to ask the Government to put at private disposal all kinds of Government assistance. The same man who tells you that he does not want to see the Government interfere in business—and he means it, and has plenty of good reasons for saying so—is the first to go to Washington and ask the Government for a prohibitory tariff on his product. When things get just bad enough, as they did two years ago, he will go with equal speed to the United States Government and ask for a loan; and the Reconstruction Finance Corporation is the outcome of it. Each group has sought protection from the Government for its own special interests, without realizing that the function of Government must be to favor no small group at the expense of its duty to protect the rights of personal freedom and of private property of all its citizens.

In retrospect we can now see that the turn of the tide came with the turn of the century. We were reaching our last frontier; there was no more free land and our industrial combinations had become great uncontrolled and irresponsible units of power within the State. Clear-sighted men saw with fear the danger that opportunity would no longer be equal; that the growing corporation, like the feudal baron of old, might threaten the economic freedom of individuals to earn a living. In that hour, our antitrust laws were born. The cry was raised against the great corporations. Theodore Roosevelt, the first great Republican Progressive, fought a Presidential campaign on the issue of "trust busting" and talked freely about malefactors of great wealth. If the Government had a policy it was rather to turn the clock back, to destroy the large combinations and to return to the time when every man owned his individual small business.

This was impossible; Theodore Roosevelt, abandoning the idea of "trust busting," was forced to work out a difference between "good" trusts and "bad" trusts. The Supreme Court set forth the famous "rule of reason" by which it seems to have meant that a concentration of industrial power was permissible if the method by which it got its power, and the use it made of that power were reasonable.

Woodrow Wilson, elected in 1912, saw the situation more clearly. Where Jefferson had feared the encroachment of political power on the lives of individuals, Wilson knew that the new power was financial. He saw, in the highly centralized economic system, the despot of the twentieth century, on whom great masses of individuals relied for their safety and their livelihood, and whose irresponsibility and greed (if they were not controlled) would reduce them to starvation and penury. The concentration of financial power had not proceeded so far in 1912 as it has today; but it had grown far enough for Mr. Wilson to realize fully its implications. It is interesting, now, to read his speeches. What is called "radical" today (and I have reason to know whereof I speak) is mild compared to the campaign of Mr. Wilson. "No man can deny," he said, "that the lines of endeavor have more and more narrowed and stiffened; no man who knows anything about the development of industry in this country can have failed to observe that the larger kinds of credit are more and more difficult to obtain unless you obtain them upon terms of uniting your efforts with those who already control the industry of the country, and nobody can fail to observe that every man who tries to set himself up in competition with any process of manufacture which has taken place under the control of large combinations of capital will presently find himself either squeezed out or obliged to sell and allow himself to be absorbed." Had there been no World War—had Mr. Wilson been able to devote eight years to domestic instead of to international affairs —we might have had a wholly different situation at the present time. However, the then distant roar of European cannon, growing ever louder, forced him to abandon the study of this issue. The problem he saw so clearly is left with us as a legacy; and no one of us on either side of the political controversy can deny that it is a matter of grave concern to the Government.

A glance at the situation today only too clearly indicates that equality of opportunity as we have known it no longer exists. Our industrial plant is built; the problem just now is whether under existing conditions it is not overbuilt. Our last frontier has long since been reached, and there is practically no more free land. More than half of our people do not live on the farms or on lands and cannot derive a living by cultivating their own property. There is no safety valve in the form of a Western prairie to which those thrown out of work by the Eastern economic machines can go for a new start. We are not able to invite the immigration from Europe to share our endless plenty. We are now providing a drab living for our own people.

Our system of constantly rising tariffs has at last reacted against us to the point of closing our Canadian frontier on the north, our European markets on the east, many of our Latin-American markets to the south, and a goodly proportion of our Pacific markets on the west, through the retaliatory tariffs of those countries. It has forced many of our great industrial institutions which exported their surplus production to such countries, to establish plants in such countries, within the tariff walls. This has resulted in the reduction of the operation of their American plants, and opportunity for employment.

Just as freedom to farm has ceased, so also the opportunity in business has narrowed. It still is true that men can start small enterprises, trusting to native shrewdness and ability to keep abreast of competitors; but area after area has been preempted altogether by the great corporations, and even in the fields which still have no great concerns, the small man starts under a handicap. The unfeeling statistics of the past three decades show that the independent business man is running a losing race. Perhaps he is forced to the wall; perhaps he cannot command credit; perhaps he is "squeezed out," in Mr. Wilson's words, by highly organized corporate competitors, as your corner grocery man can tell you. Recently a careful study was made of the concentration of business in the United States. It showed that our economic life was dominated by some six hundred odd corporations who controlled two-thirds of American industry. Ten million small business men divided the other third. More striking still, it appeared that if the process of concentration goes on at the same rate, at the end of another century we shall have all American industry controlled by a dozen corporations, and run by perhaps a hundred men. But plainly, we are steering a steady course toward economic ogligarchy, if we are not there already.

Clearly, all this calls for a reappraisal of values. A mere builder of more industrial plants, a creator of more railroad systems, an organizer of more corporations, is as likely to be a danger as a help. The day of the great promoter or the financial Titan, to whom we granted anything if only he would build, or develop, is over. Our task now is not discovery or exploitation of natural resources, or necessarily producing more goods. It is the soberer, less dramatic business of administering resources and plants already in hand, of seeking to reestablish foreign markets for our surplus production, of meeting the problem of underconsumption, of adjusting production to consumption, of distributing wealth and products more equitably, of adapting existing economic organizations to the service of the people. The day of enlightened administration has come.

Just as in older times the central Government was first a haven of refuge, and then a threat, so now in a closer economic system the central and ambitious financial unit is no longer a servant of national desire, but a danger. I would draw the parallel one step farther. We did not think because national Government had become a threat in the 18th century that therefore we should abandon the principle of national Government. Nor today should we abandon the principle of strong economic units called corporations, merely because their power is susceptible of easy abuse. In other times we dealt with the problem of an unduly ambitious central Government by modifying it gradually into a constitutional democratic Government. So today we are modifying and controlling our economic units.

As I see it, the task of Government in its relation to business is to assist the development of an economic declaration of rights, an economic constitutional order. This is the common task of statesman and business man. It is the minimum requirement of a more permanently safe order of things.

Happily, the times indicate that to create such an order not only is the proper policy of Government, but it is the only line of safety for our economic structures as well. We know, now, that these economic units cannot exist unless prosperity is uniform, that is, unless purchasing power is well distributed throughout every group in the nation. That is why even the most selfish of corporations for its own interest would be glad to see wages restored and unemployment ended and to bring the Western farmer back to his accustomed level of prosperity and to assure a permanent safety to both groups. That is why some enlightened industries themselves endeavor to limit the freedom of action of each man and business group within the industry in the common interest of all; why business men everywhere are asking a form of organization which will bring the scheme of things into balance, even though it may in some measure qualify the freedom of action of individual units within the business.

The exposition need not further be elaborated. It is brief and incomplete, but you will be able to expand it in terms of your own business or occupation without difficulty. I think everyone who has actually entered the economic struggle—which means everyone who was not born to safe wealth—knows in his own experience and his own life that we have now to apply the earlier concepts of American Government to the conditions of today.

The Declaration of Independence discusses the problem of Government in terms of a contract. Government is a relation of give and take, a contract, perforce, if we would follow the thinking out of which it grew. Under such a contract rulers were accorded power, and the people consented to that power on consideration that they be accorded certain rights. The task of statesmanship has always been the redefinition of these rights in terms of a changing and growing social order. New conditions impose new requirements upon Government and those who conduct Government.

I held, for example, in proceedings before me as Governor, the purpose of which was the removal of the Sheriff of New York, that under modern conditions it was not enough for a public official merely to evade the legal terms of official wrongdoing. He owed a positive duty as well. I said in substance that if he had acquired large sums of money, he was when accused required to explain the sources of such wealth. To that extent this wealth was colored with a public interest. I said that in financial matters, public servants should, even beyond private citizens, be held to a stern and uncompromising rectitude.

I feel that we are coming to a view through the drift of our legislation and our public thinking in the past quarter century that private economic power is, to enlarge an old phrase, a public trust as well. I hold that continued enjoyment of that power by any individual or group must depend upon the fulfillment of that trust. The men who have reached the summit of American business life know this best; happily, many of these urge the binding quality of this greater social contract.

The terms of that contract are as old as the Republic, and as new as the new economic order.

Every man has a right to life; and this means that he has also the right to make a comfortable living. He may by sloth or crime decline to exercise that right; but it may not be denied him. We have no actual famine or dearth; our industrial and agricultural mechanism can produce enough and to spare. Our Government formal and informal, political and economic, owes to everyone an avenue to possess himself of a portion of that plenty sufficient for his needs, through his own work.

Every man has a right to his own property; which means a right to be assured, to the fullest extent attainable, in the safety of his savings. By no other means can men carry the burdens of those parts of life which, in the nature of things, afford no chance of labor; childhood, sickness, old age. In all thought of property, this right is paramount; all other property rights must yield to it. If, in accord with this principle, we must restrict the operations of the speculator, the manipulator, even the financier, I believe we must accept the restriction as needful, not to hamper individualism but to protect it.

These two requirements must be satisfied, in the main, by individuals who claim and hold control of the great industrial and financial combinations which dominate so large a part of our industrial life. They have undertaken to be, not business men, but princes of property. I am not prepared to say that the system which produces them is wrong. I am very clear that they must fearlessly and competently assume the responsibility which goes with the power. So many enlightened business men know this that the statement would be little more than a platitude, were it not for an added implication.

This implication is, briefly, that the responsible heads of finance and industry instead of acting each for himself, must work together to achieve the common end. They must, where necessary, sacrifice this or that private advantage; and in reciprocal self-denial must seek a general advantage. It is here that formal Government—political Government, if you choose—comes in. Whenever in the pursuit of this objective the lone wolf, the unethical competitor, the reckless promoter, the Ishmael or Insull whose hand is against every man's, declines to join in achieving an end recognized as being for the public welfare, and threatens to drag the industry back to a state of anarchy, the Government may properly be asked to apply restraint. Likewise, should the group ever use its collective power contrary to the public welfare, the Government must be swift to enter and protect the public interest.

The Government should assume the function of economic regulation only as a last resort, to be tried only when private initiative, inspired by high responsibility, with such assistance and balance as Government can give, has finally failed. As yet there has been no final failure, because there has been no attempt; and I decline to assume that this nation is unable to meet the situation.

The final term of the high contract was for liberty and the pursuit of happiness. We have learned a great deal of both in the past century. We know that individual liberty and individual happiness mean nothing unless both are ordered in the sense that one man's meat is not another man's poison. We know that the old "rights of personal competency," the right to read, to think, to speak, to choose and live a mode of life, must be respected at all hazards. We know that liberty to do anything which deprives others of those elemental rights is outside the protection of any compact; and that Government in this regard is the maintenance of a balance, within which every individual may have a place if he will take it; in which every individual may find safety if he wishes it; in which every individual may attain such power as his ability permits, consistent with his assuming the accompanying responsibility.

All this is a long, slow task. Nothing is more striking than the simple innocence of the men who insist, whenever an objective is present, on the prompt production of a patent scheme guaranteed to produce a result. Human endeavor is not so simple as that. Government includes the art of formulating a policy, and using the political technique to attain so much of that policy as will receive general support; persuading, leading, sacrificing, teaching always, because the greatest duty of a statesman is to educate. But in the matters of which I have spoken, we are learning rapidly, in a severe school. The lessons so learned must not be forgotten, even in the mental lethargy of a speculative upturn. We must build toward the time when a major depression cannot occur again; and if this means sacrificing the easy profits of inflationist booms, then let them go; and good riddance . . .

NATHANIEL C. NASH

Greenspan's Lincoln Savings Regret

In late 1984, Alan Greenspan, then a private citizen, took on a consulting assignment for the Lincoln Savings and Loan Association of Irvine, Calif., and its owner, Charles H. Keating, Jr. Five years later, Mr. Greenspan, as chairman of the Federal Reserve Board, is finding that four-month job a source of embarrassment and regret.

"When I first met the people from Lincoln, they struck me as reasonable, sensible people who knew what they were doing," Mr. Greenspan said in an interview last week. "I don't want to say I am distressed, but the truth is I really am. I am thoroughly surprised by what has happened to Lincoln."

Lincoln was taken over by Federal regulators in April in an action that is expected to cost taxpayers $2 billion. Mr. Keating was removed from control.

No Conflict Seen

To be sure, no one in Washington is saying that Mr. Greenspan has compromised either his integrity or that of his office. And

Reprinted from "Greenspan's Lincoln Savings Regret" by Nathaniel C. Nash. *The New York Times,* November 20, 1989. Copyright © 1989 by The New York Times Company. Reprinted by permission.

they add that consulting work done when he was a private economist should pose no conflict in his current role as one of the nation's top banking regulators.

Members of Congress and banking analysts say the issue for Mr. Greenspan, a highly respected economist, is one of appearance. And his critics ask why he did not spot the germ of future troubles at Lincoln.

The Justice Department is investigating Mr. Keating, the failure of Lincoln and also the five Senators who accepted contributions from Mr. Keating. The Senate Ethics Committee has hired a special counsel to investigate the Senators' actions.

Mr. Greenspan concedes that he misjudged the ultimate intention of Mr. Keating and Lincoln's management. "Of course I'm embarrassed by my failure to foresee what eventually transpired," he said. "I was wrong about Lincoln. I was wrong about what they would ultimately do and the problems they would ultimately create."

Mr. Greenspan's views in the winter of 1984–85 are being used now by Lincoln's past and present supporters in the fall of 1989 in their own defense.

In late 1984, Mr. Greenspan, head of an economic forecasting firm, Townsend-Greenspan & Company, was retained by the New York law firm of Paul Weiss, Rifkind, Wharton & Garrison for four months. Mr. Greenspan says he does not remember how much he was paid but that it was at his usual rate.

He was asked to conduct a study on real estate investment, known in the savings industry as direct investments, by savings and loan associations. Mr. Keating, Lincoln and its parent company, the American Continental Corporation, were heavily involved in real estate development.

He was also to study Lincoln's financial condition, and if he considered the institution stable, to write officials of the Federal Home Loan Bank of San Francisco supporting an application by Mr. Keating for an exemption for Lincoln to a bank board rule forbidding substantial amounts of such investments. Mr. Greenspan sent such a letter in February 1985. Lincoln did not receive the exemption.

A spokesman for Senator John McCain, Republican of Arizona, and one of the Senators whose intervention with Federal regulators on behalf of Lincoln two years later, in early 1987, is the subject of the Senate and Justice Department inquiries, said that "Senator McCain has cited the Greenspan study many times as a powerful force in his approach to Lincoln."

The other four Senators involved in the inquiry are Democrats: Alan Cranston of California, the majority whip; Dennis DeConcini of Arizona; Donald W. Riegle, Jr., of Michigan and John Glenn of Ohio.

Same Conclusions Today
Mr. Greenspan says that if he had the same assignment today, confronted with the same evidence he had in 1984, his conclusions about Lincoln and about development projects in the industry as a whole would be very much the same.

The issue at the time was whether ownership by savings and loan associations in real estate projects and other commercial ventures posed excessive risk. Mr. Greenspan, long a proponent of deregulation, argued then —and does still—that the laws Congress passed in setting up the savings industry would eventually drive it into a crisis, because institutions would be making their money from interest on 30-year fixed mortgages while having to pay depositors interest rates that at times fluctuated wildly.

Mr. Greenspan and others argued that if the industry could diversify its mix of business by adding more short-term lending, like loans on development projects, savings institutions would be cushioned from the potentially disastrous effects of rising interest rates.

Limitation Was Planned
The Federal Home Loan Bank Board believed that such direct investments posed an excessive risk to the industry. In late 1984, when it was planning to adopt a regulation that would have limited those activities to 10 percent of an institution's activities, Mr. Greenspan was hired by the law firm on behalf of Lincoln.

He submitted his study on direct investment to the bank board, but it adopted the regulation limiting such real estate investments anyway. Then Mr. Greenspan wrote the regulators, asking that Lincoln be given an exemption from the new rule.

Mr. Greenspan described Lincoln's management as "seasoned

and expert in selecting and making direct investments," as having a "long and continuous track record of outstanding success in making sound and profitable direct investments," as succeeding "in a relatively short period of time in reviving an association that had become badly burdened by a large portfolio of long-term fixed-rate mortgages" and that it had "restored the association to a vibrant and healthy state, with a strong net worth position."

View on Direct Investments

Asked last week about his view of direct investments, Mr. Greenspan said: "What I argued then, and argue now, is that direct investments are risky. If you give me two institutions, one that has a mix of short-term direct investments and long-term mortgages properly capitalized, or the same financing structure but invested only in long-term mortgages, I would say the first institution may well be safer."

The problem was that as the economy in the Southwest collapsed in 1986, so did the value of the direct investments made by savings and loan institutions, many of which have since failed. This summer, Congress passed a $159 billion 10-year bailout of the industry.

Although Mr. Greenspan's connections with Lincoln and Mr. Keating were raised at his confirmation hearings in 1987, they were of passing concern. Mr. Greenspan says he has met Mr. Keating twice, and has had no contact with Mr. Keating or Lincoln associates since early 1985.

Troubled by Assertions

What appears to bother Mr. Greenspan most are the assertions of the Senators that his letter to the regulators led them to believe intervention on Lincoln's behalf was warranted.

"How could anyone use any evaluation I would have made in early 1985 as justification more than two years later?" he asks. "No one ever called saying, 'Do you still hold these views.' It's almost as bad as saying, 'I just read a report written two years ago that Amalgamated Widgets is a good stock to buy.' It just doesn't make sense."

Could Mr. Greenspan have seen the handwriting on the wall

on Lincoln, particularly signals that Mr. Keating's plans for Lincoln were far too ambitious and risky, as some critics maintain?

Doubling of Size Cited

Bert Ely, a financial consultant in Alexandria, Va., who recently reviewed the Lincoln case, noted that during 1984—the first year that Mr. Keating owned Lincoln—the institution's financial statements raised red flags. Lincoln doubled in size, from an institution with $1.1 billion in assets at the end of 1983 to one with $2.24 billion a year later. Its depositors' money was going to investments in raw land and unrelated businesses, which soared from $6.6 million to $308 million.

"Any time you double in size, particularly of that magnitude, that should be a warning sign," Mr. Ely said. "Rapid growth is a very risky strategy."

Still, members of Congress and banking experts doubt that the damage to the Federal Reserve's chairman will be great.

Mistake 'Now Meaningless'

"The possible mistake in judgment that was made in 1984 and 1985 is now meaningless," said Kenneth A. Guenther, executive vice president of the Independent Bankers Association. "He has done a superb job as chairman of the Fed."

But Clifford L. Brody, a financial consultant in Washington, warned that while the Keating involvement was not likely to hurt Mr. Greenspan in his conduct of monetary policy, it would make it harder for him to champion bold new deregulatory steps for the banking industry in general.

"I think you will find it will hinder him from being in the forefront of the debate," Mr. Brody said. "Because every time banking deregulation is mentioned, he will be concerned that in the back of people's minds will be the ghost of Charles Keating."

IRVING KRISTOL

Business Ethics and Economic Man

. . . [I]n the current furor over business ethics, not everything is what it appears to be. That it is a hot new issue, in the sense in which Wall Street uses the term, is undeniable—there is clearly active promotion of, and a keen speculative interest in, an issue whose intrinsic merits are anything but obvious. Moreover, a great many "insiders" stand to profit handsomely from going public with this issue. Professors—who regard any code of academic ethics as an infringement on academic freedom—have new courses to offer, new research to be funded, new moral authority to be acquired. Journalists—who regard any code of journalistic ethics as a violation of free speech—have a new field for muckraking. Government bureaucrats—who regard the very idea of a bureaucratic code of ethics as preposterous—have a wider scope for their exercise of power.

So one has the right to be very skeptical about the authenticity of this moralistic fervor, and to suspect its intentions and motives. Much of it—most of it, I would go so far as to say—represents nothing more than an improvised assault against the legitimacy of business enterprise itself, one in which sanctimonious self-righteousness and crude self-interest are neatly wedded. And it has, of course, been enormously successful. Note how "lack of due diligence" by a corporate executive is now legally defined by the SEC [Securities and Exchange Commission] and the courts as a species of "fraud," whereas the same lack of due diligence by a newspaper editor provides no ground whatsoever even for private legal action. Apparently, we are all to be terribly sensitive to any "chilling effect" on journalistic activity, but utterly indifferent to chilling effects on business activity. The fact

Excerpted from *Reflections of a Neoconservative: Looking Back, Looking Ahead* by Irving Kristol. Copyright © 1983 by Basic Books, Inc. Reprinted by permission of Basic Books, Inc., Publishers, New York.

that journalistic activity is, as often as not, itself a form of business activity is conveniently ignored. The upshot is that a presumption that all businessmen would be crooks, did not the media and the bureaucracy keep them honest, is now so widespread that it has become practically impossible even to debate the matter.

Still, after all this has been said and noted, it remains true that there really is such a thing as business ethics, and that business activity does sometimes involve a confrontation with moral dilemmas. (Since business is a human activity, it would be indeed astonishing if this were not the case!) And it is also true that, over these past decades, the business community has not been particularly attentive to, or even interested in, questions of business ethics, blithely leaving such questions to be settled in negotiation between their lawyers and the government's lawyers. But lawyers are just about the last class of people one wants to see involved in these matters, since for a lawyer (and rightly so) the ethical is simply identical with the legal. Unfortunately, this is also precisely the point of view most congenial to politicians and bureaucrats, who then proceed to regulate business activity with enthusiasm.

Business ethics, in any civilization, is properly defined by moral and religious traditions, and it is a confession of moral bankruptcy to assert that what the law does not explicitly prohibit is therefore morally permissible. Yet, curiously enough, this is what businessmen often seem to be saying—therewith inevitably inviting government to expand its code of prohibitions. And the reason this has happened is that businessmen have come to think that the conduct of business is a purely "economic" activity, to be judged only by economic criteria, and that moral and religious traditions exist in a world apart, to be visited on Sundays perhaps.

Such a state of affairs is anything but "natural." After all, business is not a new or peculiarly modern phenomenon. Commercial transactions—like sexual transactions and political transactions—have always been among the most common and important experiences of everyday life. And around that experience there has, over the centuries, grown a huge library of moral commentaries and moral casuistry, in all the world's religions. That businessmen should be unmindful of this tradition is understandable, since the current crop of theologians is, for the most part, itself quite ignorant of it, much preferring superficial "trendiness" to sober learning. Still, it is businessmen who suffer more from this deprivation, since they are likely to be the objects rather than the subjects of moral discourse.

The value and importance of these forgotten ethical traditions is their subtlety and complexity. They apply general rules of moral conduct in the context of circumstances that are always novel in some specific and vital respect. They give no easy answers, because moral practice (as distinct from moral theory) poses no easy questions. We can all easily agree that businessmen should not be dishonest or untrustworthy, on the simple grounds that no one can claim a right to be dishonest or untrustworthy. But nothing is ever simple in the moral life, and an actual businessman will often find himself confronted by perplexing dilemmas.

If the bribing of officials is a common and widespread practice in a foreign nation, should an American corporation participate in such a practice? Only a simpleminded moral absolutist would (as our government has) answer instantly in the negative, and such absolutists—disdaining all casuistry—are of little use when it comes to practical moral problems. A sage moralist would have to take into account the conflict of public interests that are involved. After all, if British and German corporations are free to bribe, while American corporations are not, then American jobs are lost and the American economy as a whole is adversely affected. It is always nice to strike the correct moral posture—but if such posturing is totally ineffectual or very costly, then we are talking about a kind of "conscientious objection" that, in the real world, is not always the most productive kind of moral behavior. This is one of those cases where the general rule is clear enough —bribery is bad and to be discouraged—but where it is not all that easy to come up with specific guidelines appropriate to the specific situation. Priests and rabbis engaged in moral counseling encounter exactly such problems more often than not.

They also frequently encounter problems involving a conflict, not of public interests, but between public morality and private. It is easy to assert glibly that each of us has a moral as well as legal obligation to convey knowledge of any and all illicit activities ("blow the whistle") to the proper authorities. But what if the illicit activity is minor or transient and is committed by a lifelong friend? Or an amiable colleague who has become a close friend? Does that make a difference? Of course it makes a difference. The bonds of friendship are *moral* bonds, and personal loyalty to a friend—or even to an institution one is part of—is a moral sentiment. Here, as elsewhere, the really difficult moral issues arise, not from a confrontation of good and evil, but from a collision between two goods. That is what makes the moral life so intensely interesting—and so eternally perplexing. But one would not know of such perplexities from the quick and easy rhetoric about business ethics that is so popular today.

It is not surprising, therefore, that the solution of our popular moralists to issues of business ethics should be just about the worst of all possible solutions. It involves what can fairly be called the "bureaucratization of ethics," with an array of lofty and contemptuous Sanhedrins (the SEC, the FTC [Federal Trade Commission], the FCC [Federal Communications Commission], and all the rest) issuing moral directives that veer between the dogmatically simpleminded and the incomprehensibly ambiguous. No other group in American life is subject to such mindless, pettifogging tyranny, nor can any reasonable person truly believe that this could possibly result in an elevation of morality, public or private, individual or corporate.

To the degree that the business community protests against this situation, it is in terms of an abuse of power. It is indeed an abuse of power—but power will, in the end, always rush in to fill any available moral vacuum. It is that vacuum which is at the root of the problem. The business community should itself get interested, in a serious way, an intellectually thoughtful way, in the issue of business ethics. There are some, if not many, theologians and philosophers who have no particular animus against business and who have worthwhile things to say on the matter. But the business community, for the most part, does not know who they are—or even that they exist.

Once again, modern business is paying the price for conceiving of itself as representing an abstract species of "economic man," rather than as men and women engaged in a fully human activity. It is this self-delusion that has helped so significantly to create the divorce between the business communities and academic-intellectual communities—a divorce that leaves the business community so defenseless when ideas (about morality or anything else) are used unscrupulously as weapons against it.

CHAPTER SIX

Mergers: Who Benefits?

Commentary

Are big corporate mergers generally beneficial or harmful—and to whom? Yale Brozen and the team of Walter Adams and James W. Brock could hardly be further apart in their views on these questions.

Neither Brozen nor Adams and Brock make the moral issue their central theme. Brozen's case rests on economic efficiency, as does the better part of Adams's and Brock's argument. Yet, while Brozen is cool and dispassionate, Adams and Brock clearly feel a sense of moral outrage at the behavior of the deal-makers and their apparent indifference to the social consequences of their actions.

Important questions emerge from this discussion of the wave of mergers experienced by American business in the 1980s. Where does moral responsibility in merger cases begin and end? Some corporate leaders acknowledge a responsibility to all the "stakeholders"—including employees, residents of the community where they operate, customers, suppliers, as well as management and stockholders. Is it sufficient that a merger be economically sound—that is, that the newly merged business flourish as a business enterprise—or must the impact on the "stakeholders" be part of the business calculation? If it is clear that "stakeholders" will suffer, is anyone responsible to address the harm done to them? Is there ever a case, if it cannot be addressed, where the merger should be foregone?

Adams and Brock make a range of public policy recommendations, including changes in tax laws, establishing margin requirements for takeovers and buyouts to limit leveraging, enforcement of existing antitrust laws, and requirement of public impact statements for deals exceeding a specific size. But there is no suggestion that excesses can be corrected except by government regulation. The authors state their view succinctly: "Given the right signals, American business can play the right game"—the "right signals" being the suggested government regulations.

However, must business get its signals from government, or can it develop principles of responsible business activity independent of government? Looking further, does the view that the "signals" must come from the government rest ultimately on the assumption that what is right is what is legal and only what is legal? If what is right is only what is legal, on what basis does the law *itself* declare anything to be wrong? Alternatively, are there not wrongs in business that are simply beyond the effective reach of law, but well within the reach of business leaders themselves?

Finally, one must ask whether the moral dimension of business activity is captured at all by the metaphor of "the game"—a view reflected in Adams and Brock and widely reflected in daily conversation about business—or whether the popular metaphor rather trivializes the role of business in society. Can business leaders who assume their professional activity to be essentially a "game," the "rules" of which are set by legislatures, discover any basis for independent ethical business judgment? If not, what remains of the idea of business *leadership?*

YALE BROZEN

Conglomerate Mergers and Efficiency

In 1979, when Senator Howard Metzenbaum opened the hearings on S. 600, a bill designed to stop conglomerate mergers by corporations with assets or sales exceeding $350 million, he said:

> It's hard to make a convincing case that putting cigarettes, Hawaiian Punch and offshore oil and gas under one corporate umbrella will have any startling effects on the efficiency with which our economy operates. There is of course some argument about capital allocation, managerial skills, and so forth. But the consensus . . . among industrial or organizational economists, is that most large conglomerate mergers, are at best neutral, with respect to efficiency, and actually may have adverse effects in many instances.

Neither Metzenbaum nor any witness at these hearings provided any evidence that conglomerate mergers do not improve efficiency. Dennis Mueller thought he provided such evidence by citing a survey of the research on the profitability of investing in the acquisition of companies. He testified that the survey showed that "no one who has undertaken a major empirical study of mergers has concluded that mergers are profitable, i.e., profitable in the sense of being 'more profitable' than alternative forms of investment." Mueller concluded "that mergers neither increase nor decrease economic efficiency on average."

Financial Evidence That Mergers Improve Efficiency

That acquiring companies, on the average, earned only normal returns on their investments in acquisitions should not be surprising. The average return on *all* investments is equal to the normal

Excerpted from *Mergers in Perspective* by Yale Brozen. Washington, D.C.: American Enterprise Institute for Public Policy Research, 1982. Reprinted with the permission of the American Enterprise Institute for Public Policy Research, Washington, D.C.

return. Any class of investments on which above average returns can be earned does not long remain in that position unless knowledge of such investments is a secret. Once such investments have become known, investors bid their prices to the level where only normal returns are earned. If the market for acquisitions is competitive, then acquirers can be expected to earn only as much, on average, as they would earn in "alternative forms of investment."

Acquirers of firms listed on the New York Stock Exchange in the postwar years paid substantial premiums for their acquisitions. The premiums averaged 25 percent from 1955 through 1976 on the price prevailing before each merger or tender offer announcement. Even these preoffer values were influenced by the expectation that a bid would be forthcoming. They would have been lower but for that expectation. For the firms acquired when there was no expectation that someone would offer to buy them (the merger offer came as a complete surprise), the premiums averaged more than 50 percent. In recent years, premiums have trended upward, reaching 50 percent in 1979.

The fact that premiums were paid suggests that the acquirers expected to use the acquired assets more efficiently than they had previously been used. Premiums would be offered only if the buying firms expected to produce returns of greater value to their stockholders than the value to the acquired firms' stockholders of the expected returns under the old managements. Since the acquirers' stockholders enjoyed returns after the mergers roughly equal to those of all New York Stock Exchange firms (see figure 1), the expectations were accurate. A marked improvement in the value of the returns must have occurred after the acquisition; otherwise the premiums paid would have produced losses in the acquiring companies. They would have suffered below normal returns, with a consequent loss to their stockholders if the premiums had not been subsequently justified and their value sustained by improvements in efficiency.

Paul Asquith points out that findings in his study of postwar mergers show that

> mergers cause a change in real activity, and this change produces a real gain for the combined firm. That is, the firms are worth more when they are combined than when they are alone. . . .

FIGURE [1]

RETURNS TO STOCKHOLDERS OF ACQUIRING FIRMS IN RELATION TO THE AVERAGE NEW YORK STOCK EXCHANGE FIRM

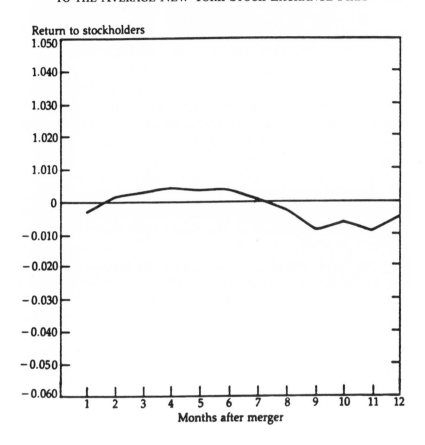

NOTE: Figure shows monthly cumulative average residual return to stockholders of acquiring firms after completion of merger (in percentage of investment in acquiring firm at date of merger).
SOURCE: Paul Asquith, "Mergers and the Market for Acquisitions," mimeographed (January 1979).

Furthermore, the results suggest that the resource which is being acquired in a merger is . . . [an] inefficient[ly] manage[d] . . . target firm.

Other Evidence of Conglomerate Efficiency

That conglomerates are more efficient, or at least use their labor more productively, than single-industry enterprises was demonstrated by Victor Fuchs in his examination of the company statistics portion of the 1954 Census of Manufactures. Fuchs found that value added per employee in conglomerates exceeded that in single-establisment companies by 28 percent. It exceeded that in multi-unit, single-industry companies by 11 percent. Conglomerates paid their employees 9 percent more than single-unit firms and 4 percent more than multi-unit, single-industry firms. On average, conglomerates produced 22 percent more with each worker than single-industry firms and paid their workers 7 percent more in 1954 (see table 1).

An analysis of the 1963 Census of Manufactures enterprise statistics shows even greater productivity and pay rates in conglomerates, in relation to single-unit and multi-unit, single-industry companies, than in 1954. The amount by which value added per employee in conglomerates exceeded value added in single-unit firms rose from 28 percent in 1954 to 38 percent in 1963. Value added per employee in conglomerates rose from 11 percent to 15 percent more than in multi-unit, single-industry firms between 1954 and 1963. Pay rates in conglomerates rose from 9 percent more than in single-unit firms in 1954 to 13 percent more in 1963. Wage rates in conglomerates rose from 7 percent more than in single-industry firms in 1954 to 11 percent more in 1963 (see table 1).

This disequilibrium in 1963 may have been one of the more important reasons for the conglomerate merger wave of the 1960s. Why the increase in the disequilibrium occurred, between 1954 and 1963, we do not know. Whatever the reason, the rise in conglomeration in the 1960s brought the economy back toward a structural equilibrium between 1963 and 1972. Value added per employee fell from 30 percent greater in conglomerates than in single-industry firms in 1963 to 17 percent greater in 1972 (measured by arithmetic means) as a result of the reallocation of resources from single-industry to multi-industry firms (see table 1). This suggests that it was the less efficient single-industry firms

TABLE [1]

VALUE ADDED AND WAGES PER EMPLOYEE IN CONGLOMERATE FIRMS AND SINGLE-INDUSTRY FIRMS, 1954–1972

Ratio of Conglomerate Firm Employee Productivity (or Wage) to Single-Industry Firm Employee Productivity (or Wage)	Number of Enterprise Industries in Each Range of Employee Productivity Ratios			Number of Enterprise Industries in Each Range of Wage Rate Ratios		
	1954	1963	1972	1954	1963	1972
2.00 and over	1	4	1	—	—	—
1.90–1.99	2	3	1	—	—	—
1.80–1.89	—	2	—	—	—	—
1.70–1.79	1	3	3	—	—	—
1.60–1.69	3	2	2	—	—	—
1.50–1.59	1	5	1	1	1	1
1.40–1.49	6	6	6	—	3	2
1.30–1.39	7	13	7	8	3	5
1.20–1.29	14	14	12	22	13	8
1.10–1.19	19	31	23	27	38	28
1.00–1.09	13	16	11	18	36	32
0.90–0.99	7	6	14	2	14	14
0.80–0.89	4	2	8	—	—	1
0.70–0.79	—	—	2	—	—	—
Total number of industries	78	107	91	78	107	91
Median	1.15	1.19	1.13	1.07	1.10	1.09
Mean	1.22	1.30	1.17	1.07	1.11	1.10

NOTE: Dashes indicate 0.
SOURCES: Bureau of the Census, *Enterprise Statistics: 1963*, pt. 1, *General Report on Industrial Organization* (1968, table 5A; *Enterprise Statistics* (1977), table 2.

that conglomerates acquired. It was in these that conglomerates could bring about improvements in output per employee.

In this respect, the conglomerate merger wave of the 1960s may have been similar to the horizontal mergers of the 1930s and 1940s. Most of the firms acquired in those horizontal mergers had suboptimal capacity. Combining their assets by merger formed firms with a larger, more economic scale of operation. These mergers achieved efficiencies without creating excess capacity and driving some firms of less than optimum size into bankruptcy or voluntary liquidation—a more costly way of increasing productivity.

Sources of Conglomerate Efficiency

The sources of the greater productivity of employees of conglomerates have not been determined. Perhaps the joint use of warehouses, delivery trucks, and sales forces and the use of pool car shipments result in economies in some product-extension mergers. Perhaps conglomerates replace incompetent managers in acquired firms. Perhaps they are quicker to take action when performance in a division lags. Perhaps they move more rapidly than single-industry companies to discontinue inefficient or unproductive operations and to put their employees and capital to more productive uses. Perhaps they do not throw good money after bad. Perhaps their ability to raise capital at less cost than smaller or less diversified firms enables them to use more capital-intensive technology. Perhaps their internal capital markets in a day of shortened product-life cycles work more efficiently than impersonal capital markets.

The opportunity to use an internal capital market rather than go to external sources can be crucial when financing is necessary to make use of proprietary information. A firm seeking capital from outside the company to apply new technology developed in its research department may have to disclose some of the information on its new development to obtain funds. But disclosing the information may dissipate some of its value since competitors may, as a consequence, come into the market more quickly:

> The subsidiaries of a conglomerate can disclose proprietary information to corporate headquarters, and thus the corporation can

allocate its capital based on a full information set. . . . This is
. . . why the internal capital market of a large firm may be a
more efficient allocator of capital than the external capital market.
(Jay R. Ritter, "Innovation and Communications: Signaling with
Partial Disclosure")

Richard Nelson, in his paper "The Simple Economics of Basic
Scientific Research," concluded that conglomerate firms obtain a
better return on their investments in research and development
because they "have their fingers in many pies." Their interests in
many fields enable them to produce and market a larger proportion of the unexpected inventions that occur in their research
efforts, and they make more use of basic research. According to
Nelson:

A broad technological base insures that, whatever direction the
path of research may take, the results are likely to be of value to
the sponsoring firm. . . . It is not just the size of the companies
that makes it worthwhile for them to engage in basic research.
Rather it is their broad technological base, the wide range of products they produce or will be willing to produce if their research
efforts open possibilities. . . . Strangely enough, economists have
tended to see little economic justification for giant firms not built
on economies of scale. Yet it is the many-product giants, not the
single-product giants, which have been most technologically dy-
namic.

Conglomerates, by increasing their size through their acquisitions, may also economize in staff functions. A study by Peter
Pashigian of the 284 respondents (most of them conglomerates)
to a questionnaire on legal costs sent to the leading 500 industrial
firms found a strong inverse relationship between legal costs per
million dollars of sales and size (see table 2). If the average cost
of other staff functions per dollar of sales drops anywhere near as
rapidly as legal costs, these economies may be a factor in the
willingness of conglomerates to pay substantial premiums for
their acquisitions. They make it possible to earn a normal return
on these investments despite the large premiums paid.

Perhaps, as Harold Geneen, former president of International
Telephone and Telegraph, explained, a conglomerate "has nu-

TABLE 2

LEGAL COSTS PER MILLION DOLLARS
OF SALES, BY FIRM SIZE

Average Sales of Firms ($ millions)	Average Legal Costs per $1 million of Sales (dollars)
300	2,227
750	1,527
1,000	1,085
2,000 and over	440

SOURCE: B. Peter Pashigian, "The Legal Costs of Firms: Prevention versus Legal Defense" (Paper presented at the Law and Economics Workshop, University of Chicago, May 20, 1980).

merous individual specialists and experienced managers in many fields, and . . . the very untraditional outlook such a company brings to an industry is the key to innovation and new progress." When Mobil acquired Montgomery Ward, it placed its own credit management specialists in Ward's troubled credit operation and lent real estate experts and location specialists from its filling-station-location group to Ward's store-location group. It also applied its retailing expertise and its purchasing know-how to Ward's operation. The superior management and staff of a firm may enable it to improve operations in other firms lacking such management and such staffs.

The "Consumption" of Capital by Acquirers

Opponents of the merger movement frequently argue that the use of borrowings (for example, by du Pont to acquire Conoco or by Mobil to acquire General Crude Oil) would do more for the nation if used by acquirers to build new plant, to do more innovating, or to find new oil rather than to acquire already discovered oil and already built plants. They believe that the use of capital for acquisitions denies capital to real capital formation.

The simple correlation of assets acquired by manufacturing and mining firms with spending on the creation of new assets is very high. The correlation coefficient is 0.85. The acquisition of old and new assets is not a process in which spending on old assets diverts capital from the creation of new assets. An increase in the demand for old assets encourages the creation of new assets. We recognize this in the case of housing yet do not apply the same reasoning to other assets. That an increase in the demand for old houses will increase the demand for new houses is a part of the conventional wisdom. The same principle applies to other assets.

The fact that a firm finds it cheaper to buy already discovered oil than to engage in discovery itself or add to its current discovery effort simply says that it is less efficient at discovery than others or that the added effort would be less efficient. By buying already discovered oil, it increases the demand for discovered oil. Those who *have* discovered oil and are more efficient in discovery sell their reserves and are provided with the capital to engage in additional discovery. Those who earlier invested in companies that discovered oil are, when their companies are acquired, provided with the capital to invest in more discoveries of oil. The result is additional investment in new discovery whether the capital is invested directly by a Mobil or indirectly by its purchase of already discovered reserves. Even if those who sell their positions in already discovered oil do not themselves reinvest in more discovery, others are encouraged to invest by the demand for discovered oil.

To put this another way, an acquisition does not consume the real resources required for the creation of new assets. The purchase of one company by another simply transfers title. It does not divert the real resources used to create new assets to noncreative uses. If anything, acquisitions of existing assets attract additional real resources into creating more new real assets. Remember the correlation between the purchase of existing assets and the creation of new assets.

When firms choose to buy existing assets, such as already discovered oil, where that is cheaper than discovering their own, the process of creating new assets, such as newly discovered oil, is made more efficient. Those who are most efficient at discovery will engage in it and sell to those who are less efficient. To bar such acquisitions will make the discovery process less efficient and reduce the amount of oil discovered both for this reason and because of the forced reduction in the demand for already discovered oil.

Whether conglomerates increase the efficiency of the American economy is a question that has baffled many observers. How can putting cigarettes and Hawaiian Punch under one corporate umbrella have any startling effects on efficiency? Whether or not the answer is apparent to the naked eye is irrelevant. There may be as many different reasons for an increase in efficiency resulting from conglomerate mergers as there are efficient mergers, not one or a few answers applicable to a wide variety of cases. For this reason, no single answer can be discovered. There have been and will continue to be instances in which it is clear, after the fact, that a merger was a mistake. But it should be even clearer that to prevent mistakes government would have to prevent people from making decisions. If our capital, labor, material, and product markets function competitively, they will accord rewards to those that are efficient and losses to those that are not.

Many acquisitions have been mistakes. Some conglomerates overreached themselves. Some large firms overexpanded. But the market cured this. Would-be conglomerates that failed to manage acquired assets as competently as others, as apparently was the case at Whittaker Corporation and Ling-Temco-Vought, were forced to disgorge some of their acquisitions and reorganize their operations to stay alive. American Brands, W. R. Grace, and other conglomerates have sold portions of their acquisitions to finance their activities and to confine their operations to what they can manage well. As William G. Shepherd found: "Many mergers are divestitures rather than a combination of two free-standing companies. Such selling off of branches rose in 1975 to 54 percent of all acquisitions (by number), up from 11 percent in 1967 and 39 percent in 1973."

What is surprising is that evidence of greater relative efficiency in conglomerates shows so strongly in the data (table 1). It would not do so if the economy were in a long-run, static structural equilibrium. With full adjustment to tastes, resources, and technology, wage rates and productivity would be no higher in multi-industry than in single-industry firms. Only to the extent that capital is less expensive to conglomerates would we see higher output per labor-hour in conglomerates when the economy is at or near a secular equilibrium. In this situation, we would also see lower rates of return in the multi-industry firms.

The data showing larger than normal disparities in value added per employee hour in different enterprises, as in 1963, indicate a disequilibrium that could be expected to produce the structural rearrangements of the sort seen in the latter 1960s. A disequilibrium means that resources are not being allocated to their most productive uses. Conglomerates, by moving employees and capital from less to more productive applications (perhaps by simply improving the management of those resources in their current use), contributed to growth and to improvements in the level of living.

On average, acquirers improved asset management, provided stockholders of poorly managed firms with an improvement in the value of their holdings, reallocated capital and labor from less to more productive uses, and improved the economic health of the country. They brought us closer to a long-run, efficient equilibrium in the allocation of resources, despite the continuing movement of the equilibrium position. . . .

Should Horizontal Mergers Be Restrained?
Whether conglomerate mergers should be encouraged and horizontal mergers discouraged may, however, be best left to the market. There may be some circumstances in which most economies of size can be realized by one route and other circumstances in which greater economies can be realized by the alternative route to large size. No blanket policy fits the varied circumstances of different markets, different technologies, different supplies of inputs, or differing levels and types of managerial competence.

In some markets and industries, small size may be more efficient than large size. If those markets are concentrated by mergers, they are soon deconcentrated by competition. Or if small relative size becomes more economic in a market in which large size was formerly more efficient, competition soon deconcentrates the industry. Markets remain concentrated, in the absence of governmental restrictions on entry or expansion by small firms, only if that is the structure that yields the most efficiency.

But we still face the question whether a few firms dominating a market might cause high prices through a lack of sufficient competition. What is the number of firms required to maintain the competition that will yield the lowest prices to consumers? Trying to maintain too many firms in a market can cause high prices. With the maintenance of an overlarge number of businesses in an industry, we lose the economies of scale and the benefits of markedly superior management. The number of superior management teams is small in such industries as are the benefits of innovation in cases where only a few firms in an industry constantly lead the innovation parade (which soon leads to high concentration, if the benefits are passed on).

It can be argued that these benefits will come from internal expansion even when mergers are blocked. But will internal expansion provide those benefits as rapidly? Will capital be wasted and stability be sacrificed by driving the less efficient or the less innovative or the under-optimum-scale firms into bankruptcy on the road to an efficient industrial structure when the merger path is closed by a strict anti-merger policy?

From the evidence available, it does not take many competitors to cause economies of scale or size to be passed on to buyers. The evidence also points to the fact that those industries that are highly concentrated or that become more concentrated tend to reduce costs more rapidly than those that are less concentrated. As a result, their prices rise less rapidly than those of the less concentrated. This is exemplified by the 1900–1925 experience shown in figure (1). Where major consolidations occurred, prices at first fell while those industries with no consolidations had rising prices. In the later inflationary period, prices in the former group of industries rose only half as rapidly as those in the latter.

The postwar experience exhibits a similar pattern. In the industries that were more than 50 percent concentrated, prices rose by only 93 percent of the average rise in all prices. Another study shows that prices declined from 1958 to 1966 in those industries that were more than 75 percent concentrated while prices in less concentrated industries rose. The bromine industry provides a dramatic example of price decline as the industry went from high concentration to very high concentration. From 1958 to 1979, prices in constant dollars fell by 60 percent as four-firm concentration rose from 80 to 95 percent. To judge from these experiences and those of major consolidations that tried raising prices, such as American Sugar and American Can, where prices fell back to competitive levels and their shares fell back to 75 and 60 percent (from 98 and 90 percent) respectively, mergers that put together as much as 50 percent of an industry's capacity will not have a price-raising effect as long as there are at least two major competitors or open entry. In the case of United Shoe Machinery, another consolidation, one minor competitor was sufficient to keep its prices competitive.

Concentration, Conglomeration, and Antitrust

In the Alcoa case (1946) the Court ruled that Alcoa had violated the antitrust laws solely by virtue of its large market share and its simultaneous stimulation of demand and expansion of capacity in anticipation of the enlarged demand to maintain its position. With that precedent and the Celler-Kefauver 1950 amendment to the Clayton Act, mergers that increased concentration or that could be called the beginning of a trend toward concentration, however speculative the possibility of the trend, were condemned by the Court up to the time of the General Dynamics decision (1974). In the General Dynamics litigation, in which the government contended that the merger of the General Dynamics subsidiary United Electric Coal with the Freeman Coal Company was illegal simply on the basis that concentration was increased by the merger, the Court held that statistical data are "not conclusive indicators of anticompetitive effects." The Court went on to say that "only a further examination of the particular market —its structure, history, and probable future—can provide the appropriate setting for judging the probable anticompetitive effect of the merger."

The Court shifted ground from possibilities to reality. This should be recognized in the new guidelines now being formulated. The old guidelines assume that structure determines conduct and performance. But the reality is that conduct and performance are more likely to determine structure and that, in the absence of governmental intervention, structure will be forced by the market in the direction dictated by efficiency. Mergers occur largely because of market pressures, because of the existence of this road to greater efficiency, and because they lead more efficiently than internal expansion to the achievement of greater efficiency. Where mergers do not result in greater efficiency, they are mistakes that are costly to the merger makers.

An examination by Bjorn Eckbo of 259 horizontal and vertical mergers in mining and manufacturing industries, of which 183 were challenged by the government, concluded that the mergers were not motivated by monopolizing intentions. The Antitrust Division and the Federal Trade Commission had simply blocked the efficient road to greater efficiency. Eckbo summarizes his findings in the following words:

> This paper tests the hypothesis that horizontal mergers generate positive abnormal returns to stockholders of the bidder and target firms because they increase the probability of successful collusion among rival producers [or achievement of market power]. Under the collusion [or market power] hypothesis, the rivals of merging firms should benefit from the merger since successful collusion [or use of market power] limits output and raises product prices. This simple proposition is tested on a large sample of horizontal mergers. . . . While we find that the antitrust law enforcement agencies systematically select relatively profitable mergers for prosecution, there is no evidence indicating that the mergers were expected to have . . . anti-competitive effects. Since the data also indicate that the enforcement agencies . . . impose costs on defendant firms, we conclude that past antitrust policy has distorted resource allocation by making some efficient mergers unprofitable.

A shift in the Court's view with respect to conglomerate mergers has also occurred. The Procter and Gamble merger with Clorox was condemned on the ground that Procter and Gamble was perceived as a potential entrant *de novo* (and that it would carry on Clorox's business at a lower cost than Clorox could attain on its own). The Court has since added restrictions on the use of the perceived potential entrant doctrine, and it has eliminated efficiency as a basis for condemning mergers. In *U.S.* v. *Marine Bancorporation,* it said that

> a market extension merger may be unlawful if the target market is substantially concentrated, if the acquiring firm has the character-

istics, capabilities, and economic incentive to render it a perceived potential *de novo* entrant, and if the acquiring firm's premerger presence on the fringe of the target market in fact tempered oligopolistic behavior on the part of existing participants in that market.

The Court's opinion in the Procter and Gamble case had accepted as fact that the liquid bleach industry was oligopolistic, in spite of the presence of 200 competitors, and had speculated that price competition was not vigorous. It had not found it necessary to determine whether Procter and Gamble's potential entry had "in fact tempered oligopolistic behavior." It simply asserted, with no evidence beyond some speculation on its part, that "it is clear that the existence of Procter at the edge of the industry exerted considerable influence on the market." Justice John M. Harlan, in his concurring opinion, disagreed with the majority's view that the "anticompetitive effects with which this product-extension merger is fraught can easily be seen." He went on to say that "assumption is no substitute for reasonable probability." And he indicated that there was no support for the proposition that there was "a reasonable probability that Procter would have entered this market on its own."

In light of the Court's shift in its tests for the legality of conglomerate mergers, the new guidelines should not suggest that such mergers will be challenged solely on the ground that a potential entrant is acquiring a firm with a share greater than 25 percent of some market or greater than 10 percent in a highly concentrated market, as the 1968 guidelines do.

Conclusion

Mergers and acquisitions facilitate "the reallocation of resources and the adapt[ation] of firm sizes and market structures to changes in relative demands, technology, and competitive conditions." (John J. McGowan, "International Comparisons of Merger Activity.") Surges in merger activity are manifestations, and a consequence, of changing circumstances and vigorous competition. If competition were not vigorous, changes in technology, the relative prices of labor and capital, or rates of growth in demand would not cause some firms to expand more rapidly than others and to acquire others. Instead, each would rest comfortably in its market niche, refrain from competing, and accept its share of growth. Firms with apparently widely different efficiencies would quietly coexist. "That the less efficient are able to survive [would be] an indication that competition lacks the vigor which would force them to improve or retire from the field [through merger or liquidation]." (McGowan, ibid.)

Since a high level of merger activity is a sign of robust competition and expanding opportunities, the cries of alarm with which surges in merger activity are greeted are simply perverse from the point of view of improving efficiency, spurring growth, and adapting to changing circumstances. Only to the extent that we wish to remain frozen in a tradition-bound state with all the old familiar places, businesses, and occupations forever with us and progress abolished should we adopt any policy toward mergers other than one of neutrality, neither encouraging nor discouraging them. The possibility of temporary monopoly may be a reason for scrutinizing closely horizontal mergers encompassing more than 50 percent of an industry's capacity in times when there is no excess capacity in the industry, but there is no reason at all for discouraging conglomerate or vertical mergers.

Instead of being alarmed by a high volume of mergers, we should be alarmed by the opposite. "Low merger rates may . . . be cause for concern. For lower merger activity . . . may indicate that competition lacks the vigor which would compel rapid adjustment to changing market conditions." (McGowan, ibid.)

WALTER ADAMS & JAMES W. BROCK

The Big Business Establishment

. . . The top managers of America's corporate complexes sit at the apex of the largest, most influential organizations in the country. To describe the firms they manage as states within a state is

Excerpted from *Dangerous Pursuits: Mergers and Acquisitions in the Age of Wall Street,* by Walter Adams and James W. Brock. Copyright © 1989 by Walter Adams and James W. Brock. Reprinted by permission of Pantheon Books, a division of Random House, Inc.

no exaggeration. Measured by annual dollar receipts, Exxon is bigger than California by a third, and three times larger than the state of Texas. General Motors is bigger than Michigan, Ohio, and Pennsylvania *combined.* At times the nation's largest industrial corporation, at times the second largest, GM can boast of 876,000 employees, approximately 1 million stockholders, sales of $103 billion, $72 billion in assets, and net profits of $3 billion. As described by one Detroit executive, "General Motors is the kind of institution whose like doesn't exist elsewhere in Western civilization. It is America's Japan." The value added of giants like Exxon, General Motors, and IBM exceeds that of most nations of the world.

The top managements of America's 200 largest industrial firms —a group any moderately sized auditorium could comfortably accommodate—collectively preside over 43 percent of the nation's value added in manufacturing, and 61 percent of its total corporate manufacturing assets. Because they direct multistate, multiplant production operations, their decisions have a profound impact on the welfare of communities and states, and on the health of the economy as a whole. The kinds of products they choose to produce, the investments they choose to make, the plants they choose to build and keep running, the research and development they choose to undertake—all these decisions critically affect the nation's economic performance. They have a profound influence on our ability to generate jobs, on the standard of living, on the rate of technological advance, and on our international competitiveness (or lack thereof).

At the same time, the vast size of these corporate complexes gives them considerable political clout. Procter & Gamble, for example is the nation's 17th largest industrial concern: "The company's sheer size—$15.5 billion in annual sales, almost 75,000 employees, plants in more than 50 cities and towns across the U.S. —gives P&G tremendous access [to government]. . . . Its facilities are spread over 25 states, giving it ready entree to about half the members of the Senate. On the House side, almost 20% of the 435 members have a P&G plant in or near their districts. . . . There's a P&G facility in Fort Worth—home base of [former] House Speaker James Wright, D-Tex.—and another in Modesto, which is represented by [former] House Majority

Whip Tony Coelho, D-California. A quarter of the membership
of the tax-writing House Ways and Means Committee represents
a municipality containing a P&G plant" . . .

For the chieftains of big business, faith in the economic virtues
of giant corporate size is fundamental. According to the Business
Roundtable, an organization composed of chief executive officers
of 200 of the very largest American firms, giant firms are "an
integral and important part of the total economic picture. The
country's economy could not function as it does without big enterprises that are large enough to have the assets, the credit and
the talent to be able to think and act long term. Such companies
can direct their planning, research and finance in ways which
. . . will enable them to become corporations for all seasons—
companies capable of responding to and meeting the nation's
needs through good times and bad." Corporate bigness, they insist, "enables the business enterprise to have a policy and to have
a special policy-making body which is sufficiently removed from
the actual day-to-day problems to take the long view, and to take
into account the relationship between the organization and society." Bigness, they believe, "has the means, capabilities, and experience to perform large-scale economic tasks in a socially responsible manner when given the opportunity and flexibility to
do so."

Top managements of these industrial empires are not averse to
corporate mergers, acquisitions, and consolidations—provided
they are the ones who initiate the deals, and so long as the deals
are conducted in "friendly" fashion. In fact, during the 1960s
and 1970s, the nation's 200 largest industrial firms typically accounted for 50 to 60 percent of the very largest corporate mergers consummated (acquisitions valued at $10 million or more), a
pattern that concentrated even greater control over the country's
manufacturing base in the hands of fewer, bigger firms. According to the Business Roundtable, this is as it should be, because
the leaders of big business "are seasoned veterans of one or many
mergers and acquisitions." They "know from hands-on experience that mergers and acquisitions can be a useful and productive
mechanism which is helpful in maximizing efficiency in the marketplace." Friendly mergers are "useful mechanisms by which
corporations can expand and grow and their efficiency and profit-

ability can be improved." Such friendly fusions, they insist, "are conducted with careful thought, concern for the corporate constituents, the free exchange of information to assure informal negotiation, and negotiations that provide the surest means of arriving at a price that is fair to all."

The LTV-Republic consolidation is precisely the friendly kind of merger the Business Roundtable applauds. But incumbent managements have nothing but contempt for raiders who launch hostile takeover assaults on their firms. They denounce the raiders on at least six grounds:

First, as they see them, hostile raids are dangerously speculative games of financial chicanery. "Once before in this century we lost sight of what business and corporations were all about," the Business Roundtable warns. "That was in the 1920s when—as now—the game was playing with corporations rather than running them, and it was dominated, not by entrepreneurs and managers, but by people interested only in fast returns on speculative risks. We all know the consequences of that exercise in corporate game playing. What reason is there to think the end result of this round of the game will be any different?"

Second, this speculative profiteering is facilitated by junk bonds—what incumbent managements call "a destructive new weapon in the corporate raiders' arsenal." Junk bonds, they say, enable corporate raiders to borrow virtually 100 percent of the cost of an acquisition in advance, with little or no security, on the promise that they will break up the target company to repay the loan. According to Fred L. Hartley, president of Unocal, and the target of a hostile takeover raid, junk bonds "are weapons created and used solely for the corporate quick kill. With them, a raider can convert a company's equity into debt, slash research . . . milk assets and take the money and run."

Third, incumbent managements argue that the raiders' fast-buck, quick-kill profiteering destroys good economic performance. The chairman of the Phillips Petroleum Company, a target of two successive hostile raids, compares the raiders to "a farmer who does not rotate his crops, does not periodically let his land lie fallow, does not fertilize his land by planting cover and creating wind breaks. In the early years, he will maximize his return from the land. . . . But inevitably it leads to a dust bowl and economic disaster. . . . Day after day, the takeover entrepreneurs are maximizing their returns at the expense of future generations that will not benefit from the research and development and capital investments that takeover entrepreneurs are forcing businesses to forego." The chairman of Goodyear Tire & Rubber warns that under the Damocles sword of hostile takeovers, "Long-term planning and long-term investment will become relics of the past, and so will any hope of a significant American position in the arena of global competition." As he sees it, "America's economic strength was built on the bedrock of long-term commitments, not on the crumbled clay of one-night stands."

Fourth, regarding the raiders' claim that they train their gunsights on underperforming managements, David M. Roderick, chairman of U.S. Steel Corporation, expresses grave doubts "whether the financial paper pushers have a demonstrated track record that would qualify them to identify inefficient management." He asks, "Have they manifested their managerial skills so that we can with confidence entrust these financiers with more efficiently and effectively running a target enterprise?"

Fifth, incumbent managements warn that hostile raids are burying American firms under mountains of debt, which further erodes economic performance and renders the economy more susceptible to a financial collapse. Even when target firms are able to fend off the raiders, incumbent managements argue, the surviving firm is mortally wounded; it will be financially devastated, highly leveraged with debt, and vulnerable to economic downturns, while important decisions concerning R&D and capital investment will have been delayed and distorted because of the distractions of fighting off unwanted suitors.

Sixth, incumbent managements contend that the important constituencies of large corporations comprise far more than the stockholders alone, and that the interests of these other groups— employees, customers, suppliers, communities—are ignored by takeover "buccaneers." According to Goodyear Tire & Rubber, "All of these constituencies must be served fairly. . . . All, in one way or another, are stakeholders in the company. Their destinies are interwoven in many ways, including the broad issue of American industry's ability to be internationally competitive."

In sum, as incumbent management sees them, the corporate raiders are nothing but financial barbarians—modern-day pirates. The "raiders are wreaking havoc with U.S. industry, reducing competition and throwing thousands of skilled people out of work. . . . Raiders have looted target companies, taken immense personal profits, and left remaining stockholders crushed with new debt. . . . These raids and bust-up takeovers have not inspired one new technological innovation; they have just drained off investment capital. They have not strengthened companies; they have weakened them . . . they have not strengthened the nation's economy; they have weakened it." The raiders are plunderers. They can tear down, but they cannot build up. They are enemies of the nation's economic vitality, and a deadly threat to its future.

But what of big managements' own economic performance? Viewed in the light of their track record over the past two decades, criticisms of the raiders by incumbent managements seem more than a little hypocritical, and rather blatantly self-serving.

For example, haven't incumbent managements built up big, bloated bureaucracies poorly suited for effective economic performance? Haven't they spawned what Richard Darman, former investment banker and now director of the Bush administration's Office of Management and the Budget, has criticized as "corporacy"—that is, "corporate America's tendency to be like the government bureaucracy that corporate executives love to malign: bloated, risk-averse, inefficient and unimaginative." In their candid moments, some chief executives admit as much. Former GM president Elliott M. Estes once confided: "Chevrolet is such a big monster that you twist its tail and nothing happens at the other end for months and months. It is so gigantic that there isn't any way to really run it. You just sort of try to keep track of it." Even current GM chief executive Roger Smith confesses that the main reason for the failures of the American automobile industry "was not exchange rates, differential tax burdens or other external economic factors. . . . It was management—of both people and work processes."

Hasn't the poor performance of these lumbering bureaucracies inflicted substantial damage on the economy? In automobiles and steel, for example, the inefficiencies, high costs, low productivity, and technological stagnation of corporate bigness have led to the loss of markets at home and abroad, massive plant closings, lay-offs of hundreds of thousands of workers, and economic devasta-tion for scores of afflicted communities across the country. More generally, the Fortune 500 firms collectively *lost* an estimated 4 to 5 million jobs between 1970 and 1985—this at a time when the rest of the economy created 30 million new jobs. Is this what the chieftains of big business mean when they wax eloquent about their deep concern for their broader constituencies and "stake-holders"? Is this congruent with their self-proclaimed superiority at engaging in long-term planning? Does their own record sup-port the claim that they are best qualified to direct America's economic affairs?

What about the deplorable record of failed "friendly" mergers, acquisitions, and consolidations effectuated by these same chief-tains of big business? Examining the merger record of 33 large, prestigious U.S. firms over the period 1950 to 1986, Michael Por-ter describes their performance as "dismal." More than half the acquisitions they made subsequently failed and were sold off. For conglomerate acquisitions, the record was even worse—a star-tling 74 percent failure rate. The failure rates of the mergers they consummated include: ITT (52%), General Foods (63%), Gen-eral Electric (65%), Xerox (71%), General Mills (75%), RCA (80%), and CBS (87%).

Haven't these "friendly" mergers and acquisitions wasted stockholders' funds, exacerbated the burden of corporate bureau-cracy, and aggravated poor economic performance? Evaluating Goodyear Tire & Rubber's conglomerate acquisition spree, for example, British raider Sir James Goldsmith points out that top management "strayed into industries about which it knew noth-ing, jeopardizing the very heart of Goodyear's business and the security of all those associated with it." With compelling logic, he claims that the approximately $2 billion Goodyear spent on conglomerate acquisitions "should have been invested to build the most modern, state-of-the-art, frontier-breaking industrial in-frastructure to produce better tires, cheaper, and to ensure that

Goodyear's operations could compete with anything, including imports, no matter what their origin. Instead the market share for imported tires rose from 12 percent in 1982 to 24 percent in 1985 in the replacement tire market."

And what of LTV-Republic? Two years after the deal, in 1986, the LTV-Republic combine collapsed in the single biggest corporate bankruptcy in American business history! In clinical fashion, the *Wall Street Journal* observed that the firm's disastrous post-merger performance calls "into question the premise behind some large mergers—that the combined resources of two ailing companies can create more strength than either could must alone." It demonstrated that when you combine two losers, you create an even bigger loser.

Finally, haven't incumbent managements presided over corporations as if they were their personal fiefdoms, replete with golf courses, sumptuous corporate headquarters, and a personal air force of private jets? Haven't they built monuments to gratify their egos, rather than forging world-class competitive economic organizations? In a front-page cover story examining LTV's woes, for example, the *Wall Street Journal* reports: "LTV Corp. is fighting to survive, but you'd know that from its posh new corporate headquarters here [in Dallas] atop the 50-story LTV Center. A gleaming black marble staircase swirls through three of LTV's five floors, and original Western paintings grace mahogany walls. LTV Chairman Raymond Hay calls it 'one of the most prestigious landmarks west of the Mississippi River.' "
Haven't incumbent managements exploited their "stakeholders" in providing for their own palatial lifestyles—luxuriating in lavish, million-dollar compensation rates virtually divorced from performance, and three times greater than the amounts paid their Japanese counterparts? Have they not, as a result, become insulated, isolated, and out of touch with the realities of the marketplace, and the preferences of the customers it is ostensibly their duty to serve? And are not incumbent managements responsible for allowing all this to occur on their watch? . . .

WALTER ADAMS & JAMES W. BROCK

Big Deals: Playing the Game

In the annals of corporate history, the 1980s will go down as the decade of the deal: Billion-dollar deals fusing corporations together. Billion-dollar deals busting them apart again. Friendly deals, and slashing attacks by hostile raiders. Buyout deals to take companies private, and "reverse" buyouts to take them public again. Horizontal deals between competitors, vertical deals between buyers and suppliers, and conglomerate deals across industries and markets. "Greenmail" deals to put corporations "in play," and "white knight" deals to take them out of play. A saturnalia of debt, equity, tender offers, and leverage—a churning and turning of corporate paper ensnarling Wall Street and the economy.

Statistics tell the story. The game exploded from 1,565 corporate deals in 1980, having a combined value of $33 billion, to 3,487 deals valued at $227 billion in 1988—a more than two-fold increase in number, and a spectacular 580 percent in value. Individual deals valued at $1 billion or more skyrocketed from 3 in 1980, to 42 in 1988. In all, some 26,000 corporate deals were consummated in the 1980–1988 period, totaling more than one trillion dollars in value.

Debt has been the high-octane fuel powering this deal-mania. In the manufacturing sector, for example, corporate debt outstanding nearly doubled (93 percent) over the 1980–88 period, while corporate profits before taxes increased by only 20 percent. As one result, interest payments to service debt loads have continued to claim an ever larger share of corporate earnings, from 16 percent on average in the 1960s, to 30 percent in the 1970s, climbing above 50 percent in the 1980s. In particular, issues of "junk" bonds—"the fake wampum of the '80s"—have exhibited

Prepared statement for the Subcommittee on Economic and Commercial Law, U.S. House of Representatives, January 30, 1990.

an explosive growth, from $900 million in 1980, to $27,000 million in 1988. The fraction of merger- and deal-related junk bonds has also risen phenomenally, from an estimated 11 percent in 1980, to more than 90 percent in 1988.

Playing the Wrong Game
But is deal mania the right economic game for American business to play? . . . The answer is a resounding "No."

1. *The Rape of the Small Investor.* Far from benefitting from it, small investors—and at times large ones too—lose in corporate deal mania. A raft of statistical studies show that the stock value of acquisitive firms typically *falls* an average 1 to 7 percent in the first year, and a cumulative 16 percent over the three years following corporate takeover, rendering shareholders significantly worse off than they would have been had their firms refrained from engaging in acquisitions. Moreover, these losses typically cancel out gains in the stock value of target firms at the time of takeover. In other words, considered as a group, stockholders lose on balance.

Nor are leveraged buyouts a boon for small investors: When publicly held firms are bought out and "taken private" by an elite group of insiders, only to be later sold back to the public, the small investor seldom shares in the bonanza. Instead, the lion's share of the gains accrues primarily to the insiders who contrive these deals. For example, the Gibson Greeting Card Company was taken private by a group which paid stockholders $80 million; just eighteen months later, the firm was sold back to the public for $290 million—more than three times the amount paid to the original stockholders. In other words, small investors part with stocks whose value is subsequently proven to be far in excess of the amount they receive—sometimes by several thousand percent.

Bondholders large and small also have been slaughtered by corporate deal mania, as high takeover premiums, high debt-equity ratios, and astronomical fixed interest charges have combined to erode the value of the bonds they hold. In the wake of Robert Campeau's takeover of Federated Department Stores, for example, Federated's bonds fell more than 17 percent in value, while RJR-Nabisco bonds plummeted $800 million as a result of that firm's leveraged buyout. In all, bondholders—who also are investors—are estimated to have lost tens of billions of dollars in the corporate deal mania of the 1980s.

2. *Destructive Economic Consequences.* Nor does deal mania promote better economic performance, improved production efficiency, or superior technological innovativeness.

Generalized statistical studies show that the average merger is followed by deteriorating profit performance, and losses—not gains—in operating efficiency. Nor is merger mania a boon for technological innovation. In a recent feature story, for example, the *Wall Street Journal* reported that the "vast majority of acquisitions of high-technology companies by large corporations have ended in disaster." An important reason, the *Journal* found, is that the "giants' many layers of bureaucracy often paralyze the freewheeling entrepreneurial style typical in the high-tech world." *Forbes* diagnoses the malady as "Bear Hug" disease: "Big companies buy little companies and usually end up destroying the very thing they coveted the small company for."

The American steel industry poignantly illustrates the futility of the merger game: The industry giants are the product of some eight decades of mergers and acquisitions, beginning with the formation of U.S. Steel Corporation in 1901 as a consolidation of hundreds of formerly independent plants, and continuing down to the LTV-Republic consolidation of 1983. But, alas, America's steel giants are anything but models of economic efficiency. They have lost jobs and market share, not only to foreign producers abroad, but to small, super-efficient and hyper-advanced steel minimills at home. The collapse into bankruptcy of the LTV-Republic combine in 1986 only underscores the failure of mergers to promote better economic performance in steel.

In airlines, successive mega-mergers have resulted in the creation of monopolistic fortress hubs, the escalation of air fares, and the deterioration of service. Shackled by their huge, merger-induced debt, the carriers will be hard put to replace their aging fleets. The prospects are hardly a traveler's Shangri-la!

Most generally, the economic infirmities of mergers, takeovers and acquisitions are graphically illustrated by their atrocious failure rate. As summarized by *Business Week,* a half to two-thirds of all mergers don't work, with one in three later undone. Management expert Peter Drucker puts the record in even starker terms: on average, he concludes, two mergers out of five are "outright disasters," two "neither live nor die," and one "works"—hardly a stirring testimonial for claims that merger mania benefits the nation's economy.

Additional evidence of the untoward economic consequences of deal mania is reflected in the rising default rate on corporate debt, particularly with regard to junk bonds. Despite six years of economic recovery following the recession of 1981/82, defaults on corporate debt have continued to rise, reaching nearly $7 billion by 1987. For 1989, the default rate climbed even higher, to $11.5 billion. For junk bonds, defaults are now estimated to be running at a rate of nearly 40 percent. At the same time, junk bond values have plunged over the past year, with portfolios and mutual funds concentrated in junk bond holdings exhibiting sizable negative returns.

It is noteworthy that, in order to generate additional cash flows to service their interest expenses, highly leveraged firms are raising the prices of their goods and services—price boosts that clearly do not aid the country's battle for competitiveness in world markets. In a provocative recent article, "Who's Really Picking Up the Tab," *Forbes* reports: "To help pay their heavy debts, leveraged companies like RJR Nabisco, Trans World Airlines and Ohio Mattress are raising prices on groceries, airline tickets and mattresses." In the case of RJR Nabisco, "With the Consumer Price Index running at less than 5%, [the president of the firm] will raise prices on various food products by an average of 9.2%. He also plans to raise cigarette prices by about 12%. . . . Altogether, RJR Nabisco price increases this year will contribute as much as $900 million of additional cash flow to help meet the company's yearly cash debt service costs of $2 billion." This suggests that the leveraged buyout craze may now be contributing to the resurgence of inflationary pressures in the economy . . .

3. *The Damning Record of History.* These failures of corporate deal mania are not new. In the turn-of-the-century trust movement, and again in the roaring '20s, the lust for lucrative promoter profits generated a frenzy of corporate deals. Then, as now, producing deals took precedence over producing goods.

Then, as now, blizzards of stocks, bonds and corporate funny-money swirled through the economy. Corporate deal mania rose to the height of speculative frenzy—only to collapse, as reality pricked speculative delusions, and as the arithmetic of reverse leverage relentlessly ground out its dreary results.

This was especially the case in the 1920s, when speculation flourished and corporate debt exploded. As one contemporary of the day put it, the "fruits of financial activity were so inviting that bankers began to operate with more and more regard for these fruits and with less and less regard for the effect of such activity upon the businesses involved. The feet of the gentlemen of Wall Street began to leave the hard ground upon which stood factories and shops; these gentlemen began to float higher and higher in a stratospheric region of sheer financial enterprise—a region of reorganizations and mergers and stock split-ups and trading syndicates and super-super holding companies and investment trusts."

An observation recorded in 1933 by the Twentieth Century Fund, in a report evaluating the role of debt in the 1929 stock market crash and the ensuing financial conflagration, is especially notable. The proliferation of highly leveraged corporate holding company structures during the 1920s, the report point out, "had been lavishly lauded because of the proclaimed economies in management, which were promised through consolidation and co-ordination, through system planning, and through centralized financing." But, the report continued, "The basic weakness in the financial structures was the over-payment for the properties and the excessive fixed charges which resulted from the combinations. The purchases were largely made under competitive bidding between holding company groups. The prices paid were not only high enough to induce the local owners of the properties to sell, but to outbid other competitive groups . . . Even under normal circumstances, the holding company systems would probably have found themselves in difficulty to support the extravagant financial structures which were erected. Only through gross overcharges to the operating companies for various fanciful services, could they expect to sustain their elaborate organizations. But with the financial collapse of 1929, the situation was rapidly changed." The public attitude toward holding companies, the report concluded, "swiftly shifted from simple faith to cynicism."

Contrived upon nothing more than the shifting sands of speculative artifice, one after another of the ramshackle corporate structures and utility "holding companies" eventually toppled, dragging the financial system and the nation's economy down with them. Fabulous profits for deal makers and investment banks—not mundane considerations of real economic performance—drove the process. In the end, the country paid the price.

Nor did the "go-go" conglomerate merger craze of the 1960s open the door to a new golden age. Constructed on the hubris of "synergy" (i.e., $2 + 2 = 5$), the brave new conglomerates subsequently crashed on the reefs of "reverse synergy" (i.e., $2 + 2 = 3$). What bold new strategy are these conglomerates practicing today? *De*-conglomeration! They are selling off hundreds of previously acquired businesses and operations. In recent years, ITT has shed some 100 operations; Gulf & Western (now Paramount) has sold off some sixty businesses; General Mills has divested itself of loss-ridden acquisitions that included restaurants, Play Doh, Monet jewelry and Parker Brothers games; while the big oil companies have struggled to extricate themselves from a series of disastrous forays into conglomerate expansionism. They are concentrating on what they know best, jettisoning the rest, and striving to improve their economic performance in the process.

Nor are the failures of merger mania limited to the United States. Beginning in the 1950s, in an effort to counteract what they feared as the American challenge, West European governments encouraged mergers and consolidations in order to create "national champions" able to slug it out toe-to-toe with their American rivals. Merger-induced corporate size, they believed, would produce world-class economic performance. Instead of the anticipated results, however, these "national champions"—like British Leyland in automobiles, and the British Steel Corporation —became "lame ducks." They typically have suffered deteriorating economic performance, job losses and serious erosions in market shares. They have required more or less constant support, subsidy and bailouts by their home governments. The London *Economist* has written a fitting epitaph to the British Leyland experience: "Merger after merger . . . was supposed to create a creature strong enough to stop the rot, to realise economies of scale and face up to foreign competition. Then another one was needed." The firm's history "is a parable of how such lumping together of good with bad is no match for winnowing out the bad and running the good competitively. Its successive mergers and reorganisations produced a ragbag range of cars that never settled down to win market share from the car companies of America, Japan, France, West Germany and Italy."

4. *The "Opportunity Cost" of Deal Mania.* Corporate deal mania inflicts a further, possibly more destructive cost on the nation's economy. This is because for a nation, as for individuals, there is no such thing as a free lunch. Every action exacts an "opportunity cost"—the cost of not having done something else. Hence, a decade of managerial energy devoted to concocting (or fighting off) corporate deals is, at the same time, a decade during which managerial energy has been diverted from the critically important task of investing in new plants, new products, new state-of-the-art manufacturing techniques, and new jobs. The one trillion dollars spent since 1980 on exchanging paper claims through takeovers, buyouts and acquisitions represents a trillion dollars *not* spent directly on productivity-enhancing equipment or on research and development. The hundreds of millions of dollars absorbed by legal fees and bankers' commissions in corporate deals are, by the same token, hundreds of millions of dollars *not* plowed into the nation's industrial base.

Viewed in opportunity cost terms, it is especially sobering that in 1986, corporate America spent more on mergers and acquisitions ($204 billion) than it did on research and development ($55 billion) and net new plant investment ($81 billion) *combined.*

Playing the wrong game has a particularly deleterious effect on R&D activity. In a recent study, for example, the Battelle Memorial Institute reported that company R&D spending in 1989 would rise by only 4.5 percent. Such spending, Battelle indicates, is being held down by corporate restructurings and buyouts that force managements to concentrate on cash flow to pay interest on the heavy borrowing that invariably accompanies these deals. A National Science Foundation study of 24 companies, while conceding that it is too early to assess the long-run effects, reported that 16 companies which had undergone mergers and acquisi-

CORPORATE EXPENDITURES ON MERGERS, R&D, AND NET NEW INVESTMENT ($ BILLIONS)

Year	Mergers and Acquisitions	Industry-financed R&D	Net New Nonresidential Investment
1980	$ 33.0	$ 30.9	$ 88.9
1981	67.3	35.9	98.6
1982	60.4	40.1	65.5
1983	52.6	43.5	45.8
1984	126.0	49.1	91.1
1985	145.4	52.6	101.5
1986	204.4	55.7	81.0

Sources: *Mergers & Acquisitions,* May–June 1988; *Statistical Abstract of the United States, 1988; Economic Report of the President, 1988.*

tions showed a 4.7 percent drop in R&D spending in 1986 and 1987, while 8 companies that had undertaken LBOs or other restructurings showed an even steeper 12 percent drop.

In a survey released just this month, the National Science Foundation reports that—for the first time in 14 years—spending on corporate research and development in the United States has not even kept pace with inflation, raising concerns that the nation is lagging in its efforts to achieve a competitive edge in high technology. While corporations spent $68.8 billion on R&D in 1989, compared to $66.5 billion in 1988, when adjusted for inflation this represents a decline of nine-tenths of 1 percent—the first drop since 1975. Among the factors explaining this deemphasis on R&D are an increasing focus by corporate managers on short-term profitability and the cost-cutting that accompany corporate restructurings, mergers and leveraged buyouts. "We have moved from research and development as being a corporate asset to where it's what a raider looks for first," says William J. Spencer, the Xerox Corporation's vice president for research and development. "They can make significant cuts and get cash flow. I haven't seen a takeover yet where they increased research and development activities." Says Charles F. Larson, executive director of Washington's Industrial Research Institute: "Research and development is becoming less prominent in American companies exactly at the time when it should be becoming more prominent." Obviously, this does not bode well for our efforts as a nation to enhance industrial productivity and achieve international competitiveness.

The Campeau Case

The meteoric rise and crash of Campeau is a fitting parable for our time. Rebuffed in his 1980 effort to take over one of Canada's largest financial firms, Mr. Campeau redirected his proclivity for corporate dealmaking south of the border. In a short two-year period, and as the result of two celebrated mega-deals, Campeau came to control one of the largest department store retailing empires in the United States.

In 1986, Campeau acquired Allied Stores Corporation, including Allied's Ann Taylor, Brooks Brothers, Jordan Marsh, Maas Brothers, The Bon, and Stern's retailing divisions. The acquisition price was high, $3.7 billion, and was financed by assuming a heavy debt load. In fact, at its inception, Allied/Campeau faced interest payments of $460 million—compared with earnings of only $290 million!

Two years later, in 1988, Campeau launched an even bigger takeover deal, this time for retail giant Federated Stores. At the time of the takeover, Federated ranked as the nation's 5th largest department store operator, with annual sales in excess of $11 billion. Following a fierce bidding war, and with the advice and support of First Boston, Campeau gained control of Federated by paying an estimated $6.6 billion. To his extensive Allied holdings, Campeau now added a star-studded list of some of America's most well known retailers: Bloomingdale's, Filene's, Abraham & Straus, Burdine's, Lazarus, Bullocks Wilshire, I. Magnin, Rich's and Gold Circle, as well as the Ralph's grocery chain. Once again, debt enabled Campeau to undertake and complete the deal: At the very outset, Federated/Campeau faced $600 million in interest charges—compared with $400 million in earnings!

At last, Campeau controlled a retailing colossus. Assembling the empire, however, had necessitated the assumption of an equally colossal debt load, amounting to approximately $13.4 billion. But according to the financial calculus of the 1980s, all was well. Couched in the now familiar hubris of the day, one prominent dealmaker characterized Campeau as "one of the few deals where there are no losers." In fact, Campeau's annual corporate report, issued in June 1989, was replete with extravagant references to the company's "skilled management direction of this new group of entrepreneurs," the firm's "strategic vision" for the future, its "expense streamlining and reallocation," its "merchandising and operational synergies," its commitment to "value creation," and its prowess as "a strategic buyer of quality assets."

Despite these pronunciamentos, financial trouble quickly engulfed the Campeau empire. Operations sold to raise funds in order to service Campeau's enormous debt load fetched far less than anticipated. At the same time, cash flows and operating revenues fell short of projections, and fell further below interest expenses. Meanwhile, interest payments on debt left Campeau cash-strapped and unable to pay its suppliers. In late-1988, Campeau was compelled to issue $750 million in junk bonds, in an effort to staunch the financial hemorrhage. By early-1989, Campeau was unable to pay off a $1.1 billion bridge loan. By midyear, Campeau's losses widened to $191 million, despite increased sales revenues. By September 1989, Campeau's mounting financial problems necessitated another $250 million in loans, while advisors counseled their vendor clients to halt shipments of goods to Allied and Federated—at the peak of the season for Christmas orders. Campeau's losses continued to escalate. The value of its junk bonds plunged 80 percent by December, and precipitated a half-year collapse in the general market for junk. Finally, lenders began to balk when approached for even more loans.

The denouement came quickly. On January 15, 1990—less than two years after acquiring Federated, and with a total debt of $7.5 billion—Campeau's empire was forced to declare bankruptcy, in the single largest mercantile failure and the 4th largest corporate failure in American history. Caught in the collapse are 394 stores with more than 100,000 employees spread across 28 states, along with a train of some 300,000 unpaid creditors, vendors and suppliers. In the financial markets, Campeau's junk bonds are trading for as little as four cents on the dollar.

As the *Wall Street Journal* put it, Campeau learned that leverage is an unforgiving and inflexible master. "Instead of ringing up big bucks," *Business Week* summarized, "Bob Campeau's shopping spree has wiped out billions."

The Campeau bankruptcy marks the latest development in the corporate deal mania of the 1980s. It is the latest addition to a growing list of tottering, debt-laden deals—a list that now includes Revco Drug, Dart Drug Stores, Braniff Airlines, Eastern Airlines, Bonwit Teller, B. Altman, Fruehauf, Leaseway, Southland (7-11 stores), Integrated Resources, Resorts International, SCI Television, and the Jim Walter Corporation, among others. It underscores the price the nation pays for playing the wrong economic game.

Choosing the Right Game

In the final analysis, a nation *chooses* the kind of economic game it plays. A nation chooses, either explicitly or by default, the kinds of skills it will encourage by virtue of the rewards it provides. A nation also chooses the economic consequences it will have to endure, based on the kind of economic game it chooses to play.

If the objective is improved productivity, enhanced efficiency, and accelerated technological progress, then corporate deal mania is simply the wrong game to play.

The challenge, we submit, is to channel business activity away from speculative capitalism, and into creative capitalism. This distinction is crucial: Creative capitalism generates productive wealth; speculative capitalism merely redistributes what has already been produced. Creative capitalism builds new factories; speculative capitalism merely trades their ownership. Creative capitalism gives birth to new goods, services and production techniques; speculative capitalism merely rearranges control over the productive process. Creative capitalism contributes to economic growth; speculative capitalism is a sterile zero-sum game.

Henry Ford personifies creative capitalism at its best. He took the automobile, considered as a luxury for the few, and turned it into an affordable commodity for the many. He did it by building, not by buying—by creating, not by trading what already existed. He understood (in his words) that a manufacturer is "an instrument of society and he can serve society only as he manages his enterprises so as to turn over to the public an increasingly better product at an ever-decreasing price, and at the same time to pay to all those who have a hand in his business an ever-increasing wage, based upon the work they do. In this way and in this way alone can a manufacturer or any one in business justify his existence." Speculation in things already produced, he said, "is not business. It is just more or less respectable graft." He was a hands-on industrial entrepreneur par excellence.

Fortunately, Ford is not an anachronism from a bygone age. America is still blessed with innovative entrepreneurs like Edwin Land, inventor of the instant camera and founder of the Polaroid Corporation; Chester Carlson, inventor of xerography and founder of the Xerox Corporation; Kenneth Iverson, president of Nucor, and Gordon Forward, President of Chaparral, innovators of the minimills that have revolutionized a somnolent, lethargic American steel industry; Steven Jobs, the wizard who from his family's backyard garage revolutionized the computer industry with the Apple personal computer; and the legendary H. Ross Perot, . . . who left IBM in 1962, founded Electronic Data Services (EDS) with savings of $1,000, and built it into a multi-billion dollar business.

As a society, we must decide which game we want the business community to play. We must decide between enterprise and speculation. We must decide between creating wealth and trading it. We must decide between investing in the future or wasting it away in an economically counterproductive game.

Public Policy Recommendations
To this end, we invite the Committee's attention to the following proposals:

First, a number of advocates currently argue for a reduction in the capital gains tax in order to stimulate capital formation and enhance the nation's international competitiveness. While we share these goals, we suggest a more effective way to achieve them would be to modify the capital gains tax in a manner that will directly encourage productive real investment while, at the same time, discouraging counterproductive financial speculation. This can best be accomplished with a "sliding" capital gains tax, whereby profits on assets created and held over long periods are taxed less (or not at all), while quick-buck short-term paper profiteering is taxed at a substantially higher rate. As an illustration, profits on assets held longer than 7 years might pay no tax whatsoever; profits on assets held 2 to 7 years might be taxed at a rate of 15 percent; profits on assets held 1 to 2 years might be taxed at a rate of 30 percent; and the most speculative financial gains— those on assets held less than 12 months—might be taxed at the highest rate, say 50 percent or more. The effects of this sliding capital gains tax would discourage unproductive financial speculation, while encouraging long-run investment in plant, equipment, R&D, and state-of-the-art production techniques—the kinds of investments that contribute to what Adam Smith called the real wealth of nations.

Second, financial regulations governing dealmaking can be tightened, in order to further curb dangerous excesses. Some useful steps have recently been taken in this area, such as reducing the capacity to use prior losses incurred by acquired operations to offset current and future taxes, as well as by narrowing the tax deductibility of interest expenses incurred on zero-coupon, "balloon" payment junk bonds. But more can be done. For example, in the aftermath of the Great Crash of 1929, financial regulations were enacted placing an upper limit on the proportion of stock purchases that individuals are permitted to finance through borrowing based on the market value of the stocks to be acquired. This margin requirement is designed to rein in speculative fever by requiring that individuals back up their stock purchases with other tangible assets worth at least 50 percent of the value of the acquired stock. Applying the same margin requirement to takeovers and buyouts—where the assets of the firms to be acquired are essentially pledged as collateral for the loans—would squeeze a considerable degree of speculative fever from the financial markets, curb excessive debt proliferation, and put corporate financing on a sounder and considerably more sober footing. It would especially impede the Campeau genre of highly leveraged deals.

Third, the nation does have an antimerger law already on the books which, if it were enforced, would further slow down corporate deal mania, by arresting anticompetitive mergers, takeovers and buyouts. Throughout the decade of the 1980s, deal mania has raged with virtual immunity from the antitrust laws: In the face of an unprecedented merger, takeover and consolidation movement, the Justice Department challenged a miniscule number of the more than 10,000 corporate deals during the past decade. Scores of anticompetitive agglomerations—such as Campeau's consolidation of leading competitors in department store retailing, monopolistic mergers among airlines, and consolidation in food production, meatpacking and grocery retailing—could have been halted had the antimerger law been enforced.

Finally, perhaps no matter now conscientiously they might be enforced, the antitrust laws may simply be insufficient to cope with the deal mania sweeping corporate America. A multi-billion dollar leveraged buyout such as Beatrice or RJR Nabisco, for example, may not constitute an antitrust violation in any narrow technical sense; but it may nevertheless exact a heavy opportunity cost by diverting billions of dollars of resources into unproductive uses which compromise the nation's economic performance. To remedy this problem, the proponents of any buyout, takeover or merger exceeding a certain size threshold—say, $1 billion—could be required to file a public impact statement to accompany the proposed deal. This public impact statement would require a showing that the proposed deal will enhance production efficiency; that it will contribute to technological innovation; that it will promote the nation's international competitiveness; and that these outcomes cannot be achieved in the absence of the proposed deal. It would force them to demonstrate, with probative evidence rather than public relations hype, that the deal is not only in their selfish interests, but in the national interest as well. Corporations would still be permitted to grow, so long as they do so through internal expansion—by constructing new plants, developing new products, and creating new jobs. Producers would have an incentive to grow by building rather than by buying—by creating new values, rather than by merely acquiring the values already created by others.

Given the right signals, American business can play the right game. It can rise to the challenge of world-class competitiveness.

CHAPTER SEVEN

Does Business Have a Social Responsibility?

Commentary

Corporate executives may flinch with discomfort when issues such as apartheid intrude upon their business plans. Such issues can be inflammatory, often intractable, and complex beyond description. They lie beyond the sphere of ordinary business learning, experience, responsibility, and authority. Business does not exist to make or reshape the society, it will be said, but rather to produce wealth within the existing social structure.

Yet the impact of such issues is often inescapable. By being a major participant in the social structure, especially as an employer, the behavior of the company may well either mitigate the existing injustices or contribute to their continuation and further spread.

How should business react? Anthony H. Bloom, Group Chairman of the Premier Group, confronted that question in South Africa and outlines his response in the 1987 interview with the *Harvard Business Review* with which this chapter opens. His remarks cover a wide range of pertinent issues, one of which is particularly thorny and central to the concern of this chapter:

HBR: But why should business tell government officials what to do day-in and day-out?

Bloom: Because the government is doing such a rotten, lousy job
of it . . . Apartheid is not only morally repugnant, it's
an enormous economic burden.

Bloom minces no words. He also raises implicitly another important question: what is the responsibility of a business when a
social condition is "morally repugnant" but is not an enormous
economic burden, or indeed may be of some direct business benefit to the company?

Peter Drucker and Milton Friedman are both widely respected
and influential writers on business and economics. In the two
essays which follow the Bloom interview, they take virtually opposite positions, Drucker presenting an amplified view of the social responsibilities of business, while Friedman defends a much
more restrictive definition. Both views have long had thoughtful
and intelligent supporters. Their debate also may serve as the
gateway to an even larger question: whether a nation can sustain
prosperity and good social health though its citizens are preoccu-
pied with their personal or private interests. On this question, we
turn to Alexis de Tocqueville, the acute young French observer
who visited America in the 1830s when Andrew Jackson sat in
the White House and the new democracy was spreading rapidly
westward.

One of Tocqueville's best known contributions is his explanation of how Americans of the 19th century solved the problem of
public virtue or responsibility with the "doctrine of self-interest
properly understood." The cornerstone of that idea is that helping others typically turns out to be as much in the interest of the
benefactor as the beneficiary. This is an idea well-suited to periods when the great mass of humanity spends most of its time
trying to satisfy an ever-growing taste for material comforts. It
may offer a basis for settling the moral dilemma with which
Friedman and Drucker struggle, but that requires the extension
of the doctrine from individual behavior to that of corporations.

In the selections we have chosen, Tocqueville goes on to explore the modern quest for comfort with observations that may
be unsettling, for two reasons. First, much of modern business
depends for its growth precisely on that taste for comfort that
Tocqueville thought a "tenacious, exclusive and universal pas-

sion" in the modern world. But is he correct to think that the love of comfort also corrupts us, leaving us "drunk on petty delights" that "in the end shut out the rest of the world and sometimes come between the soul and God"? And secondly, can such a nation retain either its self-respect or the capacity for hard work and creativity on which its long term material prosperity depends? The concerns of Carter and Darman come to mind (Chapter One).

Setting distant goals may, as Tocqueville suggests, offer something of a remedy to what we have come to call the problem of a "consumer society." But then the door opens on another prospect. Tocqueville suggests that with the growth of industrial democracy and its accompanying division of labor, business leaders will develop vast perspectives and long-range habits of thought, while the scope of vision of the ordinary worker will grow narrower and narrower. In that prospect he foresees the rise of what he calls a new aristocracy. To what extent, if any, has Tocqueville's foresight been vindicated in the century and a half since he set forth this view? If such an aristocracy is arising, does it display any attachment to the doctrine of self-interest properly understood? Will a democratic society tolerate such a distinguished class within its midst unless the authority of leadership is exercised with uncommon concern for the general welfare?

BERNARD AVISHAI

Managing Against Apartheid—
An Interview with Anthony H. Bloom

HBR:

What makes doing business in South Africa different from doing business, say, in the United States?

Bloom:

Look, we live in a society—the only one in the world—that is regulated by institutionalized, legislatively entrenched racial discrimination. So domestic pressures on the average South African business are mind-boggling. We have to deal, for example, with a labor movement that is highly politicized because every other avenue of expression for black political grievances has been stifled. The government exacerbates the problem by locking up union leaders for six months or more, then releasing them without ever giving them a trial. These are the very people management has to sit down and deal with. It's a recipe for conflict.

Blacks comprise 80% of our work force, and they're not enamored, to say the least, of the free enterprise system. They see big business as having supported apartheid for years; therefore big business is bad, and anything else is better.

And I haven't addressed perhaps the worst problem, migratory labor, which has become a little better since the Pass Laws were abolished—the laws requiring blacks to seek permission just to travel from one part of the country to another. Industries still recruit low-wage workers from country areas and bring them into the cities where they house them in massive, single-sex gov-

Reprinted from "Managing Against Apartheid" by Anthony H. Bloom (as interviewed by Bernard Avishai). *Harvard Business Review,* November/December 1987. Copyright © 1987 by the President and Fellows of Harvard College; all rights reserved.

ernment hostels. They keep laborers on contract for a year before they're allowed to return to the rural areas for maybe two or three months at a time. Obviously this ruins family life because the husband works 300 or 400 miles away from his wife and family.

More and more, business is being called on to provide an alternative to squalid government housing. My own company built a hostel on the Western Cape. But the social problems it generated were so terrible that we eventually quit. The whole question of conjugal visits—how do you handle that? You've got 300 men living in a hostel.

How do you cope with international pressures on South African companies?

These problems would probably send American businessmen into catatonic shock. Unprecedented pressure is coming from countries as large as the United States and as small as Luxembourg, from Austria to Australia, the Eastern bloc and the Western bloc. And it takes many forms. One of the most serious is financial sanctions, which forced the South African government to impose a moratorium on foreign debt repayment. The impact on my company, of course, is that former access to foreign capital has been entirely cut off, and some existing liabilities have been caught in the moratorium net.

On the export side it's equally difficult. We've been subject to tough trade sanctions. In black Africa, ironically, sanctions are enforced hardly at all—they so badly need what we have and can get it cheaply only from South Africa.

Then there is the matter of imports: we often can't get what we need. More important, there are many obstacles to technology transfers, even in ordinary computers; technological licensing has become very difficult. We've even had to prepare for critical raw materials becoming unavailable. There's always the sword of disruption hanging over our heads.

Can't companies mitigate some of the worst effects of government policy by perhaps building family housing or promoting blacks into management ranks?

Certainly, and it is being done by the more progressive companies. But there are problems—for example, to build housing you need land zoned for *nonwhite* accommodations. That's extremely difficult to get.

Impossible?

Impossible to build the number of houses required. You'd virtually have to build a township. In our corporate group we have 30,000 workers, about 4,000 of whom live in hostels. So you might have to build 15,000 houses. It's out of the question.

As for promoting blacks, we find it very difficult to identify, train, and move capable blacks into management. That sounds like a racist cop-out. It's not. There is a massive educational disparity between whites and blacks: the government spends six times more money on a white student than on a black student. And to the handicaps of black education you must add the commercial inexperience of black families. As a child I sat around a table in the evening where business was discussed—it was part of my environment, part of what I grew up with. That's not true of very many blacks in South Africa.

One more point. Recently, a lot of bright blacks in our companies have turned down promotions. Their communities pressure them, viewing black managers as apart from the struggle, as moving over to the "other side." People have a natural desire to rise up the ranks. They want recognition, money, position. But in South Africa, a managerial job doesn't enable a black to rise out of the morass of legislative ties that hold him down. He can't live where he wants, he can't choose where to send his kids to school. True, he may have more money and a good position. He might have a better house—but it's going to be a better house in a decrepit township. If you promote a man to manager of a plant, instead of going home to an upscale suburb, he's going to get on the same train with his subordinates at night. There's a tendency to sort the fellow out and put the screws on him.

What about the black high school teacher you hired in 1977? Today he's a director of your milling division.

Yes, and it's the most important division in the Premier Group. The man is a roaring success, incredible. He's clawed his way up in the organization simply on merit. But we've had more notable failures, one with a degree from a Harvard program. We've tried everything: last year's bonuses were partly linked to how well executives developed black management. But we're lagging behind our targets.

The Business of Business Is Government

President Botha has scolded a number of prominent businessmen, yourself included, for committing your time and company resources to antiapartheid politics. How do you respond?

There are no profits for business in a disintegrating society, in the midst of civil disorder, violence, and racial antagonism. Unless the recipe is changed, that is where we're heading. It *is* a dangerous road to "one man, one vote," but it's not as dangerous as the road we're on now.

But why should business tell government officials what to do day-in and day-out?

Because the government is doing such a rotten, lousy job of it. It has turned South Africa into an international pariah; polarization of our society has never been more extreme. Apartheid is not only morally repugnant, it's an enormous economic burden. I can't emphasize enough how expensive it is to maintain the whole structure of apartheid—separate entrances, separate signs, burgeoning bureaucratic empires, people in prison, a costly, wasteful "homelands" system—millions and millions of dollars every year.

Although President Botha accuses business of antiapartheid involvement, black leaders see business and apartheid as working hand-in-glove. Who's right?

Both of course. There is no one "business view" in South Africa.

For a start, English-speaking and Afrikaans-speaking business-men tend to be divided. Afrikaner leaders are usually more conservative, more inclined to consult with government than confront issues publicly. But there is division even within the English-speaking business community.

While everybody in business, even Afrikaners, would say they support "reform," a split emerges when you start asking what "reform" means. You'd get a broad consensus that blacks should have trading rights, that no municipal ordinance should restrict black commerce. I think most would agree that the Group Areas Act, which legislates the races into separate residential areas, ought to be repealed.

And yet the business community would divide on the issue of talking to the African National Congress, and on whether Nelson Mandela, the imprisoned leader of the ANC, should be released. But business would probably overwhelmingly agree to retain the State of Emergency.

Incidentally, a significant number of Afrikaans-speaking whites are government employed. The bureaucracy is very well looked after by the government because that's its voting constituency. When P. W. Botha became state president, he promised the white electorate he would reduce the size of the bureaucracy. In fact, he's increased it enormously.

Has the government relied on business to enforce the State of Emergency or racial laws?

Recently, it decided to put a bill before parliament to have business deduct from black workers' salaries unpaid rents resulting from rent boycotts in the townships. I think this is an outrage—I, for one, would not be prepared to do it.

Most houses in black townships are on leasehold, and the visible symbol of the system is the local township authority. Inevitably, blacks have protested against apartheid by withholding rent, the major fund source local authorities have to run the townships —for electricity, garbage collection, and so on. Of course you can't evict 400,000 people. So the government wants to empower local authority to have employers of rent defaulters deduct from wages what rent is owed, and hand the sum to local authorities.

This makes us an absolute anathema to township people: we become the government's enforcer. What hypocrisy! Botha has just delivered a blunt warning to the business community to stick to business and keep out of politics. Yet he plans to throw one of the most explosive political issues straight into our court.

If business wins this round, could it use its influence to dismantle apartheid altogether?

Actually, our confrontation with government over the issue underlines the *limits* of our power as businessmen. People always ask, "Why doesn't the business community do more to overthrow apartheid?" Some ANC people, other black leaders, the Western press—all of them have a fundamentally romantic notion that business has the power to change things in South Africa to a much greater extent than it does. I've been told, "Look, this country cannot run without big business. If you wanted to abolish apartheid tomorrow, you could put enough pressure on the government to do it."

But business, especially English-speaking business, has as much influence on government racial policy as a ping-pong ball bouncing off a stone wall. Black political leaders don't necessarily accept this, and they say, "Well, what business ought to do is stop paying taxes." That's nonsensical because if companies don't pay tax, the government will simply get a judgment and the messenger of the court will arrive and attach the company's assets. I don't think people on the outside, who see things as cut and dried, realize what we're up against. We have influenced legislation, but we do not control it.

Free Enterprise under Black Rule?

Are you worried that "one man, one vote" in South Africa will end free enterprise?

The government argues that black independence in the rest of Africa has resulted only in coup and countercoup, chaos, and starvation. This may be true in many cases, but the comparisons get us nowhere. But the results of "one man, one vote"—actually

"one *person,* one vote"—surely depend on when the vote comes
and under what conditions. Black rule in South Africa is historically inevitable. The question is, under what conditions is change
going to take place?

If it comes about at the end of a war of attrition in which racial
enmity has escalated to civil violence, then I think the chance of
our getting a government of retribution and revenge, a government that might be Marxist-Leninist in its policy, is much greater
than if we sit down today to negotiate a joint future with black
leaders. Unless whites and blacks find each other, free enterprise
will become a victim.

Is that why you met with ANC leaders in Zambia?

There was a meeting, a watershed meeting, between a group of
six white South Africans including myself; Gavin Relly, chairman of the Anglo-American group; and Zach de Beer, a director
of Anglo-American, and leaders of the exiled and banned African
National Congress—the people responsible for most of the "revolutionary onslaught," as the government likes to call it. Included
on the ANC side were Oliver Tambo and its rising star, Thabo
Mbeki. The meeting, which Zambian President Kaunda sat in
on, was supposed to have been off-the-record, but news of it
leaked somehow and made a major impact in the world press.

The meeting was very cordial—and constructive. We did not
call them "terrorists"; they did not call us "odious bourgeois
props of apartheid." We understood that civil war would ruin us
both—business *and* the current black leadership. We shared a
commitment to a nonracial future for South Africa, but differed
on other points of principle. For example, we objected, among
other things, to their economic policy, which presently includes
nationalization of the mines, banks, and what is characterized as
"monopoly capital."

What was their response?

I had the feeling that their economic policy is not cast in concrete. That—at least for the moment—the ANC regards its
struggle as primarily political and military. To be sure, black

leaders justify nationalization. They assert that a few people live at the top of a pyramid, controlling most of the wealth, while blacks live at the base in poverty. If they came to power they would try to flatten the pyramid.

I don't disagree with that goal in principle. But they think the way to redistribution is to get the state's hands on industry. That is the point I disputed; I argued for a distinction between exploitive capitalism, which I oppose as much as they do, and free enterprise. If you look at the winners and losers in the world, the winners are clearly those societies that have embraced the principles of free enterprise, of individual initiative, of giving people something to reach for.

ANC people said, "Look, Tony, would you lose your motivation if you had a different set of shareholders? Instead of X investing in your company, you'd have the government. Why should that affect your initiative?" I had difficulty persuading them tactfully that it would make an enormous difference—it was especially difficult to knock government takeover of key industries with President Kaunda sitting there, who has been nationalizing Zambian companies.

Aren't ANC leaders saying, in effect, that they want to use the state for their social and economic enfranchisement in the same way Afrikaners have?

Exactly. But they would go a bit further because they actually want to take over direct ownership of enterprises, rather than just put their bureaucrats in place as the Afrikaners did. Still, ANC leaders did talk in terms of mixed ownership, not about a plan for total nationalization. They spoke of Scandinavian models rather than Eastern bloc models.

I would venture to say that, in their heart of hearts, the ANC leaders feel that South African blacks are more sophisticated than the rest of black Africa. It's not Tanzania or Central African Republic. South Africa has a developed infrastructure, a complex manufacturing base. We export energy in the form of coal, we export precious minerals. We have a sophisticated telecommunications network, computer systems—we're light-years ahead of the rest of Africa. Black leaders who aspire to political power realize, I think, that these assets must not be destroyed in the struggle to achieve political ends.

Do union leaders show the same sophistication?

The unions have, in fact, adapted to the collective bargaining process much better than management has. They represent well over a million paid-up members. They're aggressive, competent, and work daily to augment their bargaining power. Management comes to collective bargaining only once a year at the annual wage negotiation.

Yet there are enormous contradictions in the attitudes of trade unions. You can fight for days with the head of a union about introducing new technology that may result in the destruction of jobs. He will hit the table and say, "Under no circumstances is one job to be lost! We are fighting to preserve every job!" He'll then walk out of the negotiations and proclaim he's in favor of sanctions and disinvestment, which could destroy hundreds of jobs.

To Disinvest or Not

You have brought us, inevitably, to the subject of disinvestment. How do you respond to Reverend Sullivan's claim that it is futile for U.S. companies to adhere to his code, that they should just pull out?

It's a tragedy. Reverend Sullivan's deadline for the South African government to remove apartheid was unduly naive and idealistic. It's doubly unfortunate because advising American companies to disinvest will help remove a constructive force for change in South Africa.

American companies have been at the cutting edge of change. They've affected the lives and hopes of hundreds of thousands of employees and their families. They've given blacks opportunities for upward mobility, they've desegregated facilities, they've spent huge sums on much-needed training. They've also upgraded skills and initiated philanthropic programs such as schools and day-care centers. American companies have spent nearly $300 million in these areas. Finally, I think they're an unequaled example of civilized corporate behavior. American businesses in other countries are certainly not governed by the stringent ethical standards of the Sullivan code.

What, then, is the consequence of their pulling out?

In the past, South African companies have simply taken over their assets, stepped into their shoes. And South African managers may not follow the same enlightened policies as the American companies did during the ten years that the Sullivan code was operative.

My own company has acquired three businesses from American corporations that have pulled out: the Warner Brothers video business, Dow Chemical's pharmaceutical operation, and Kodak's assets. Kodak ostensibly pulled out of the country "completely." In fact, we acquired most of their residual physical assets—at a more than reasonable price.

But is there no sensible disinvestment policy? Ford Motor Company has recently announced an effort to leave a good part of its stock in an employee trust. Is this something you think reasonable on a broader scale?

Well, perhaps. I started at the opposite end of the question because I don't think disinvestment is in itself reasonable. But having determined to disinvest, companies may proceed in a variety of ways. There is the Kodak way, which is basically to get up and go. Other companies have been the objects of highly leveraged management buyouts. The Ford way is a third. But even Ford had considerable difficulty in getting the black unions to accept a generous employee share ownership scheme. The unions see it as paternalistic, an attempt to seduce their members into accepting the terms of capitalism. Unions want disinvestment, but want to be involved in deciding how the company will be managed. At Ford, for example, management originally took a lot of flak because it didn't consult its employees beforehand. There was similar dissatisfaction among Citibank employees.

I suppose if you're an American CEO, you're damned if you

do and you're damned if you don't. But in my view, disinvestment destroys jobs and damages the economy to everybody's detriment. And it's dubious whether disinvestment will advance the black political cause.

Is there any form of external pressure you think might be effective?

Perhaps pressure alone is the wrong thing. To date it has been all stick—no carrot. The international community should give credit when it is due too. Over the last three years we have seen the abolition of the Mixed Marriages Act, which prohibited interracial marriage, and of the so-called Immorality Act prohibiting blacks and whites from sleeping together.

What happens, however, is that foreign opponents of apartheid move the goal posts every time. Even when the hated Pass Laws were abolished, there was a tendency in the international community to say, "That's cosmetic. That's trivial. What we're talking about is political rights." Of course political rights are fundamental. But rejecting all reform as cosmetic simply reinforces in the minds of the South African political leaders that whatever they do is not going to be enough until they "hand the whole country over to blacks." However, pressure can certainly be helpful. Desegregation in sports began as a result of the international sports boycotts. We need to maintain both domestic and international pressure for reform in order to create an atmosphere in which political enfranchisement of blacks will seem more natural.

Let's move from disinvestment to trade sanctions. Many black leaders in the United States, like Reverend Sullivan, have called for sanctions and for severing diplomatic relations with South Africa. What do you think is the case for sanctions?

I don't think there is a case for sanctions. The theory behind them is that you would inflict such damage on the South African economy that the government would be thrown into a state of shock and disarray and would finally see the futility of its ways. I think that is fanciful. Sanctions will make the South African government, and whites generally, more belligerent and defiant. Just look at the gains made by the right wing in the last elections: they are now the official opposition.

Bishop Tutu and other South African black leaders reject this negative view of sanctions. They say blacks suffer so much already that if they suffer a bit more, they won't notice it. But I think that when a man loses his job and has to tell his family that he cannot pay for food and shelter, he *will* notice it.

Besides, Rhodesia survived for something like twelve years in the face of worldwide economic sanctions and found a way around them. Only now are the stories coming out about how Eastern bloc countries bought Rhodesian tobacco and made barter deals. Polaroid decided to pull out of South Africa maybe 15 years ago, but Polaroid film has been on sale in South Africa ever since. There are any number of jobbers, wholesalers, middle merchants—shadowy characters all over the world—who, for a price, will ensure that the flow of Polaroid film into South Africa is maintained.

How can the international business community, particularly in the United States, help accelerate change?

Stay, expand, gain greater leverage—focus on breaking down discrimination wherever it's encountered.

Frankly, do you see a future to work toward?

Look, recent trends have been very discouraging. There is undoubtedly a brain drain—some of our brightest kids have left the country. Many liberal thinking whites lack a sense of the future. But if you come to South Africa and see the beauty of the land, the wealth, the infrastructure, and the people, you would see why there is too much at stake for us to give up. And surprisingly, there is still a reservoir of goodwill between the races in South Africa. I live with the hope that common sense will prevail. But there is not much time; it's five minutes to midnight. If we lose the opportunity, the consequences will be tragic.

Besides, there's an unfolding drama in South Africa. A businessman here feels on the stage of world history. The chief executive of a major American company in a consumer business like mine rarely has the chance to influence events that give shape to Western values, to democracy. We have this chance.

You're implying that your difficulties are interesting.

They *are* interesting. But one is reminded of the old Chinese curse, "May you live in interesting times." The danger is that things will get too interesting.

PETER DRUCKER

The Responsibilities of Management

. . . Even the most private of private enterprises is an organ of society and serves a social function.

Indeed the very nature of the modern business enterprise imposes responsibilities on the manager which are different in kind and scope from those of yesterday's businessman.

Modern industry requires an organization of basic resources which is radically different from anything we have known before. In the first place, the time span of modern production and of business decisions is so long that it goes way beyond the life span of one man as an active factor in the economic process. Secondly, the resources have to be brought together into an organization—both of material objects and of human beings—which has to have a high degree of permanence to be productive at all. Next, resources, human and material, have to be concentrated in large aggregations—though there is of course a question how large they have to be for best economic performance and how large they should be for best social performance. This in turn implies that the people who are entrusted with the direction

Excerpted from *The Practice of Management* by Peter F. Drucker. New York: Harper & Brothers, 1954. Copyright 1954 by Peter F. Drucker. Copyright © renewed. Reprinted by permission of HarperCollins, Publishers.

of this permanent concentration of resources—the managers—have power over people, that their decisions have great impact upon society, and that they have to make decisions that shape the economy, the society and the lives of individuals within it for a long time to come. In other words, modern industry requires the business enterprise, which is something quite different and quite new.

Historically, society has always refused to allow such permanent concentrations of power, at least in private hands, and certainly for economic purposes. However, without this concentration of power which is the modern enterprise, an industrial society cannot possibly exist. Hence society has been forced to grant to the enterprise what it has always been most reluctant to grant, that is, first a charter of perpetuity, if not of theoretical immortality to the "legal person," and second a degree of authority to the managers which corresponds to the needs of the enterprise.

This, however, imposes upon the business and its managers a responsibility which not only goes far beyond any traditional responsibility of private property but is altogether different. It can no longer be based on the assumption that the self-interest of the owner of property will lead to the public good, or that self-interest and public good can be kept apart and considered to have nothing to do with each other. On the contrary, it requires of the manager that he assume responsibility for the public good, that he subordinate his actions to an ethical standard of conduct, and that he restrain his self-interest and his authority wherever their exercise would infringe upon the commonweal and upon the freedom of the individual.

And then there is the fact that the modern business enterprise for its survival needs to be able to recruit the ablest, best educated and most dedicated of young men into its service. To attract and to hold such men a promise of a career, of a living, or of economic success is not enough. The enterprise must be able to give such men a vision and a sense of mission. It must be able to satisfy their desire for a meaningful contribution to their community and society. It must in other words embrace public responsi-

bility of a high order to live up to the demands the manager of
tomorrow must make on himself.

No discussion of the practice of management could therefore
leave out those functions and responsibilities of management that
arise out of the social character and the public existence of even
the most private of enterprises. In addition the enterprise itself
must demand that management think through its public responsibilities. For public policy and public law set the range for the
actions and activities of the enterprise. They decide what forms
of organization are open to it. They prescribe marketing, pricing,
patent and labor policies. They control the ability of the enterprise to obtain capital and its price. They decide altogether
whether private enterprise is to remain private and autonomous
and to be governed by managements of its own choosing.

The responsibility of management in our society is decisive not
only for the enterprise itself but for management's public standing, its success and status, for the very future of our economic
and social system and the survival of the enterprise as an autonomous institution. The public responsibility of management must
therefore underlie all its behavior. Basically it furnishes the ethics
of management.

. . . [M]anagement, in every one of its policies and decisions,
should ask: What would be the public reaction if everyone in
industry did the same? What would be the public impact if this
behavior were general business behavior? And this is not just a
question for the large corporations. In their totality, small businesses and their managements have fully as much of an impact
on public opinion and policy. And all, large and small, should
remember that if they take the easy way out and leave these
problems to "the other fellow," they only assure that their solution will eventually be imposed by government.

The Social Impact of Business Decisions

. . . [T]he impact of management's decisions on society is not
just "public" responsibility but is inextricably interwoven with
management's responsibility to the enterprise. Still, there is a
responsibility of management to the public interest as such. This

is based on the fact that the enterprise is an organ of society, and that its actions have a decisive impact on the social scene.

The first responsibility to society is to operate at a profit, and only slightly less important is the necessity for growth. The business is the wealth-creating and wealth-producing organ of our society. Management must maintain its wealth-producing resources intact by making adequate profits to offset the risk of economic activity. And it must besides increase the wealth-creating and wealth-producing capacity of these resources and with them the wealth of society . . .

This responsibility is absolute and cannot be abdicated. No management can be relieved of it. Managements are in the habit of saying that they have a responsibility to the shareholder for profits. But the shareholder, at least in a publicly owned company, can always sell his stock. Society, however, is stuck with the enterprise. It has to take the loss if the enterprise does not produce adequate profits, has to take the impoverishment if the enterprise does not succeed in innovation and growth.

For the same reason management has a public responsibility to make sure of tomorrow's management without which the resources would be mismanaged, would lose their wealth-producing capacity and would finally be destroyed.

Management is responsible for conducting the enterprise so as not to undermine our social beliefs and cohesion. This implies a negative responsibility: not to usurp illegitimate authority over citizens by demanding their absolute and total allegiance.

In a free society the citizen is a loyal member of many institutions; and none can claim him entirely or alone. In this pluralism lies its strength and freedom. If the enterprise ever forgets this, society will retaliate by making its own supreme institution, the state, omnipotent.

The tendency today of so many, especially of our larger, enterprises to assume paternal authority over their management people and to demand of them a special allegiance, is socially irresponsible usurpation, indefensible on the grounds alike of public policy and the enterprise's self-interest. The company is not and must never claim to be home, family, religion, life or fate for the individual. It must never interfere in his private life or his citizenship. He is tied to the company through a voluntary and cancellable employment contract, not through some mystical and indissoluble bond.

But responsibility for our social beliefs and cohesion also has a positive component. At least in this country it imposes on management the duty to keep open the opportunity to rise from the bottom according to ability and performance. If this responsibility is not discharged, the production of wealth will, in the long run, weaken rather than strengthen our society by creating social classes, class hatred and class warfare.

There are other areas in which responsibilities can be asserted. I would, for instance, consider it a responsibility of the management of the large company to develop a capital-expenditure policy which tends to counteract the extremes of the business cycle (with Automation such a policy becomes a business necessity). I believe that management has a responsibility to develop policies that will overcome the deep-seated hostility to profits, for the simple reason that this is a threat to our economic and social system. I finally believe that any business, in the present world situation, has the responsibility to make its best contribution to the defensive strength of its country.

But what is most important is that management realize that it must consider the impact of every business policy and business action upon society. It has to consider whether the action is likely to promote the public good, to advance the basic beliefs of our society, to contribute to its stability, strength and harmony . . .

Two hundred and fifty years ago an English pamphleteer, de Mandeville, summed up the spirit of the new commercial age in the famous epigram: "private vices become public benefits"— selfishness unwittingly and automatically turns into the common good. He may have been right; economists since Adam Smith have been arguing the point without reaching agreement.

But whether he was right or wrong is irrelevant; no society can lastingly be built on such belief. For in a good, a moral, a lasting society the public good must always rest on private virtue. No leading group can be accepted on de Mandeville's foundation. Every leading group must, on the contrary, be able to claim that the public good determines its own interest. This assertion is the only legitimate basis for leadership; to make it reality is the first duty of the leaders.

That "capitalism," as the nineteenth century understood the term (and as Europe still too prevalently understands it), was based on de Mandeville's principle may explain its material success. It certainly explains the revulsion against capitalism and capitalists that has swept the Western world during the last hundred years. The economic doctrines of the enemies of capitalism have been untenable and often childish. Their political doctrines have carried the threat of tyranny. But these answers have not been sufficient to quiet the critics of capitalism. Indeed they have usually appeared quite irrelevant to the critics, as well as to the people at large. For the hostility to capitalism and capitalists is moral and ethical. Capitalism is being attacked not because it is inefficient or misgoverned but because it is cynical. And indeed a society based on the assertion that private vices become public benefits cannot endure, no matter how impeccable its logic, no matter how great its benefits. . . .

MILTON FRIEDMAN

The Social Responsibility of Business Is to Increase Its Profits

When I hear businessmen speak eloquently about the "social responsibilities of business in a free-enterprise system," I am reminded of the wonderful line about the Frenchman who discovered at the age of 70 that he had been speaking prose all his life. The businessmen believe that they are defending free enterprise when they declaim that business is not concerned "merely" with profit but also with promoting desirable "social" ends; that business has a "social conscience" and takes seriously its responsibilities for providing employment, eliminating discrimination, avoiding pollution and whatever else may be the catchwords of the

Reprinted from "The Social Responsibility of Business Is to Increase Its Profits" by Milton Friedman. *The New York Times Magazine,* September 13, 1970. Copyright © 1970 by The New York Times Company. Reprinted by permission.

contemporary crop of reformers. In fact they are —or would be if they or anyone else took them seriously—preaching pure and unadulterated socialism. Businessmen who talk this way are unwitting puppets of the intellectual forces that have been undermining the basis of a free society these past decades.

The discussions of the "social responsibilities of business" are notable for their analytical looseness and lack of rigor. What does it mean to say that "business" has responsibilities? Only people can have responsibilities. A corporation is an artificial person and in this sense may have artificial responsibilities, but "business" as a whole cannot be said to have responsibilities, even in this vague sense. The first step toward clarity in examining the doctrine of the social responsibility of business is to ask precisely what it implies for whom.

Presumably, the individuals who are to be responsible are businessmen, which means individual proprietors or corporate executives. Most of the discussion of social responsibility is directed at corporations, so in what follows I shall mostly neglect the individual proprietor and speak of corporate executives.

In a free-enterprise, private-property system, a corporate executive is an employe of the owners of the business. He has direct responsibility to his employers. That responsibility is to conduct the business in accordance with their desires, which generally will be to make as much money as possible while conforming to the basic rules of the society, both those embodied in law and those embodied in ethical custom. Of course, in some cases his employers may have a different objective. A group of persons might establish a corporation for an eleemosynary purpose—for example, a hospital or a school. The manager of such a corporation will not have money profit as his objective but the rendering of certain services.

In either case, the key point is that, in his capacity as a corporate executive, the manager is the agent of the individuals who own the corporation or establish the eleemosynary institution, and his primary responsibility is to them.

Needless to say, this does not mean that it is easy to judge how well he is performing his task. But at least the criterion of performance is straightforward, and the persons among whom a voluntary contractual arrangement exists are clearly defined.

Of course, the corporate executive is also a person in his own right. As a person, he may have many other responsibilities that he recognizes or assumes voluntarily—to his family, his conscience, his feelings of charity, his church, his clubs, his city, his country. He may feel impelled by these responsibilities to devote part of his income to causes he regards as worthy, to refuse to work for particular corporations, even to leave his job, for example, to join his country's armed forces. If we wish, we may refer to some of these responsibilities as "social responsibilities." But in these respects, he is acting as a principal, not an agent; he is spending his own money or time or energy, not the money of his employers or the time or energy he has contracted to devote to their purposes. If these are "social responsibilities," they are the social responsibilities of individuals, not of business.

What does it mean to say that the corporate executive has a "social responsibility" in his capacity as businessman? If this statement is not pure rhetoric, it must mean that he is to act in some way that is not in the interest of his employers. For example, that he is to refrain from increasing the price of the product in order to contribute to the social objective of preventing inflation, even though a price increase would be in the best interests of the corporation. Or that he is to make expenditures on reducing pollution beyond the amount that is in the best interests of the corporation or that is required by law in order to contribute to the social objective of improving the environment. Or that, at the expense of corporate profits, he is to hire "hardcore" unemployed instead of better-qualified available workmen to contribute to the social objective of reducing poverty.

In each of these cases, the corporate executive would be spending someone else's money for a general social interest. Insofar as his actions in accord with his "social responsibility" reduce returns to stockholders, he is spending their money. Insofar as his actions raise the price to customers, he is spending the customers' money. Insofar as his actions lower the wages of some employes, he is spending their money.

The stockholders or the customers or the employes could separately spend their own money on the particular action if they wished to do so. The executive is exercising a distinct "social responsibility," rather than serving as an agent of the stockholders or the customers or the employes, only if he spends the money in a different way than they would have spent it.

But if he does this, he is in effect imposing taxes, on the one hand, and deciding how the tax proceeds shall be spent, on the other.

This process raises political questions on two levels: principle and consequences. On the level of political principle, the imposition of taxes and the expenditure of tax proceeds are governmental functions. We have established elaborate constitutional, parliamentary and judicial provisions to control these functions, to assure that taxes are imposed so far as possible in accordance with the preferences and desires of the public—after all, "taxation without representation" was one of the battle cries of the American Revolution. We have a system of checks and balances to separate the legislative function of imposing taxes and enacting expenditures from the executive function of collecting taxes and administering expenditure programs and from the judicial function of mediating disputes and interpreting the law.

Here the businessman—self-selected or appointed directly or indirectly by stockholders—is to be simultaneously legislator, executive and jurist. He is to decide whom to tax by how much and for what purpose, and he is to spend the proceeds—all this guided only by general exhortations from on high to restrain inflation, improve the environment, fight poverty and so on and on.

The whole justification for permitting the corporate executive to be selected by the stockholders is that the executive is an agent serving the interests of his principal. This justification disappears when the corporate executive imposes taxes and spends the proceeds for "social" purposes. He becomes in effect a public employe, a civil servant, even though he remains in name an employe of a private enterprise. On grounds of political principle, it is intolerable that such civil servants—insofar as their actions in the name of social responsibility are real and not just window-dressing—should be selected as they are now. If they are to be civil servants, then they must be selected through a political process. If they are to impose taxes and make expenditures to foster "social" objectives, then political machinery must be set up to guide the assessment of taxes and to determine through a political process the objectives to be served.

This is the basic reason why the doctrine of "social responsibility" involves the acceptance of the socialist view that political mechanisms, not market mechanisms, are the appropriate way to determine the allocation of scarce resources to alternative uses.

On the grounds of consequences, can the corporate executive in fact discharge his alleged "social responsibilities"? On the one hand, suppose he could get away with spending the stockholders' —or customers' or employes' money. How is he to know how to spend it? He is told that he must contribute to fighting inflation. How is he to know what action of his will contribute to that end? He is presumably an expert in running his company—in producing a product or selling it or financing it. But nothing about his selection makes him an expert on inflation. Will his holding down the price of his product reduce inflationary pressure? Or, by leaving more spending power in the hands of his customers, simply divert it elsewhere? Or, by forcing him to produce less because of the lower price, will it simply contribute to shortages? Even if he could answer these questions, how much cost is he justified in imposing on his stockholders, customers and employes for this social purpose? What is his appropriate share and what is the appropriate share of others?

And, whether he wants to or not, can he get away with spending his stockholders', customers' or employes' money? Will not the stockholders fire him? (Either the present ones or those who take over when his actions in the name of social responsibility have reduced the corporation's profits and the price of its stock.) His customers and his employes can desert him for other producers and employers less scrupulous in exercising their social responsibilities.

This facet of "social responsibility" doctrine is brought into sharp relief when the doctrine is used to justify wage restraint by trade unions. The conflict of interest is naked and clear when union officials are asked to subordinate the interest of their members to some more general social purpose. If the union officials try to enforce wage restraint, the consequence is likely to be wildcat strikes, rank-and-file revolts and the emergence of strong competitors for their jobs. We thus have the ironic phenomenon that union leaders—at least in the U.S.—have objected to Government Interference with the market far more consistently and courageously than have business leaders.

The difficulty of exercising "social responsibility" illustrates, of course, the great virtue of private competitive enterprise—it forces people to be responsible for their own actions and makes it difficult for them to "exploit" other people for either selfish or unselfish purposes. They can do good—but only at their own expense.

Many a reader who has followed the argument this far may be tempted to remonstrate that it is all well and good to speak of government's having the responsibility to impose taxes and determine expenditures for such "social" purposes as controlling pollution or training the hard-core unemployed, but that the problems are too urgent to wait on the slow course of political processes, that the exercise of social responsibility by businessmen is a quicker and surer way to solve pressing current problems.

Aside from the question of fact—I share Adam Smith's skepticism about the benefits that can be expected from "those who affected to trade for the public good"—this argument must be rejected on grounds of principle. What it amounts to is an assertion that those who favor the taxes and expenditures in question have failed to persuade a majority of their fellow citizens to be of like mind and that they are seeking to attain by undemocratic procedures what they cannot attain by democratic procedures. In a free society, it is hard for "good" people to do "good," but that is a small price to pay for making it hard for "evil" people to do "evil," especially since one man's good is another's evil.

I have, for simplicity, concentrated on the special case of the corporate executive, except only for the brief digression on trade unions. But precisely the same argument applies to the newer phenomenon of calling upon stockholders to require corporations to exercise social responsibility (the recent G.M. crusade, for example). In most of these cases, what is in effect involved is some stockholders trying to get other stockholders (or customers or employes) to contribute against their will to "social" causes favored by the activists. Insofar as they succeed, they are again imposing taxes and spending the proceeds.

The situation of the individual proprietor is somewhat different. If he acts to reduce the returns of his enterprise in order to exercise his "social responsibility," he is spending his own money, not someone else's. If he wishes to spend his money on such purposes, that is his right, and I cannot see that there is any objection to his doing so. In the process, he, too, may impose costs on employes and customers. However, because he is far less likely than a large corporation or union to have monopolistic power, any such side effects will tend to be minor.

Of course, in practice the doctrine of social responsibility is frequently a cloak for actions that are justified on other grounds rather than a reason for those actions.

To illustrate, it may well be in the long-run interest of a corporation that is a major employer in a small community to devote resources to providing amenities to that community or to improving its government. That may make it easier to attract desirable employes, it may reduce the wage bill or lessen losses from pilferage and sabotage or have other worthwhile effects. Or it may be that, given the laws about the deductibility of corporate charitable contributions, the stockholders can contribute more to charities they favor by having the corporation make the gift than by doing it themselves, since they can in that way contribute an amount that would otherwise have been paid as corporate taxes.

In each of these—and many similar—cases, there is a strong temptation to rationalize these actions as an exercise of "social responsibility." In the present climate of opinion, with its widespread aversion to "capitalism," "profits," the "soulless corporation" and so on, this is one way for a corporation to generate goodwill as a by-product of expenditures that are entirely justified in its own self-interest.

It would be inconsistent of me to call on corporate executives to refrain from this hypocritical window-dressing because it harms the foundations of a free society. That would be to call on them to exercise a "social responsibility"! If our institutions and the attitudes of the public make it in their self-interest to cloak their actions in this way, I cannot summon much indignation to denounce them. At the same time, I can express admiration for those individual proprietors or owners of closely held corporations or stockholders of more broadly held corporations who disdain such tactics as approaching fraud.

Whether blameworthy or not, the use of the cloak of social responsibility, and the nonsense spoken in its name by influential and prestigious businessmen, does clearly harm the foundations of a free society. I have been impressed time and again by the schizophrenic character of many businessmen. They are capable of being extremely far-sighted and clear-headed in matters that are internal to their businesses. They are incredibly short-sighted and muddle-headed in matters that are outside their businesses but affect the possible survival of business in general. This short-sightedness is strikingly exemplified in the calls from many businessmen for wage and price guidelines or controls or incomes policies. There is nothing that could do more in a brief period to destroy a market system and replace it by a centrally controlled system than effective governmental control of prices and wages.

The short-sightedness is also exemplified in speeches by businessmen on social responsibility. This may gain them kudos in the short run. But it helps to strengthen the already too prevalent view that the pursuit of profits is wicked and immoral and must be curbed and controlled by external forces. Once this view is adopted, the external forces that curb the market will not be the social consciences, however highly developed, of the pontificating executives; it will be the iron fist of Government bureaucrats. Here, as with price and wage controls, businessmen seem to me to reveal a suicidal impulse.

The political principle that underlies the market mechanism is unanimity. In an ideal free market resting on private property, no individual can coerce any other, all cooperation is voluntary, all parties to such cooperation benefit or they need not participate. There are no "social" values, no "social" responsibilities in any sense other than the shared values and responsibilities of individuals. Society is a collection of individuals and of the various groups they voluntarily form.

The political principle that underlies the political mechanism is conformity. The individual must serve a more general social interest—whether that be determined by a church or a dictator or a majority. The individual may have a vote and a say in what is to be done, but if he is overruled, he must conform. It is appropriate for some to require others to contribute to a general social purpose whether they wish to or not.

Unfortunately, unanimity is not always feasible. There are some respects in which conformity appears unavoidable, so I do not see how one can avoid the use of the political mechanism altogether.

But the doctrine of "social responsibility" taken seriously would extend the scope of the political mechanism to every human activity. It does not differ in philosophy from the most explicitly collectivist doctrine. It differs only by professing to believe that collectivist ends can be attained without collectivist means. That is why, in my book "Capitalism and Freedom," I have called it a "fundamentally subversive doctrine" in a free society, and have said that in such a society, "there is one and only one social responsibility of business—to use its resources and engage in activities designed to increase its profits so long as it stays within the rules of the game, which is to say, engages in open and free competition without deception or fraud."

ALEXIS DE TOCQUEVILLE

Self-Interest Properly Understood

How the Americans Combat Individualism by the Doctrine of Self-interest Properly Understood

. . . In the United States there is hardly any talk of the beauty of virtue. But they maintain that virtue is useful and prove it every day. American moralists do not pretend that one must sacrifice

Excerpted from *Democracy in America* by Alexis de Tocqueville, edited by Max Lerner and J. P. Mayer, Translated by George Lawrence. Copyright English himself for his fellows because it is a fine thing to do so. But they boldly assert that such sacrifice is as necessary for the man who makes it as for the beneficiaries.

They have seen that in their time and place the forces driving man in on himself are irresistible, and despairing of holding such forces back, they only consider how to control them.

They therefore do not raise objections to men pursuing their interests, but they do all they can to prove that it is in each man's interest to be good.

I do not want to follow their arguments in detail here, as that would lead too far from my subject. It is enough for my purpose to note that they have convinced their fellow citizens. . . .

The Americans . . . enjoy explaining almost every act of their lives on the principle of self-interest properly understood. It gives them pleasure to point out how an enlightened self-love continually leads them to help one another and disposes them freely to give part of their time and wealth for the good of the state. I think that in this they often do themselves less than justice, for sometimes in the United States, as elsewhere, one sees people carried away by the disinterested, spontaneous impulses natural to man. But the Americans are hardly prepared to admit that they do give way to emotions of this sort. They prefer to give the credit to their philosophy rather than to themselves. . . .

Self-interest properly understood is not at all a sublime doctrine, but it is clear and definite. It does not attempt to reach great aims, but it does, without too much trouble, achieve all it sets out to do. Being within the scope of everybody's understanding, everyone grasps it and has no trouble in bearing it in mind. It is wonderfully agreeable to human weaknesses, and so easily wins great sway. It has no difficulty in keeping its power, for it turns private interest against itself and uses the same goad which excites them to direct passions.

The doctrine of self-interest properly understood does not inspire great sacrifices, but every day it prompts some small ones; by itself it cannot make a man virtuous, but its discipline shapes a lot of orderly, temperate, moderate, careful, and self-controlled

translation © 1965 by Harper & Row, Publishers, Inc. Reprinted by permission of HarperCollins Publishers, Inc.

citizens. If it does not lead the will directly to virtue, it establishes habits which unconsciously turn it that way.

If the doctrine of self-interest properly understood ever came to dominate all thought about morality, no doubt extraordinary virtues would be rarer. But I think that gross depravity would also be less common. Such teaching may stop some men from rising far above the common level of humanity, but many of those who fall below this standard grasp it and are restrained by it. Some individuals it lowers, but mankind it raises.

I am not afraid to say that the doctrine of self-interest properly understood appears to me the best suited of all philosophical theories to the wants of men in our time and that I see it as their strongest remaining guarantee against themselves. . . .

The Taste for Physical Comfort in America

. . . If one tries to think what passion is most natural to men both stimulated and hemmed in by the obscurity of their birth and the mediocrity of their fortune, nothing seems to suit them better than the taste for comfort. The passion for physical comfort is essentially a middle-class affair; it grows and spreads with that class and becomes preponderant with it. Thence it works upward into the higher ranks of society and thence spreads downward to the people.

In America I never met a citizen too poor to cast a glance of hope and envy toward the pleasures of the rich or whose imagination did not snatch in anticipation good things that fate obstinately refused to him.

On the other hand, I never found among the wealthy Americans that lofty disdain for physical comfort which can sometimes be seen among even the most opulent and dissolute aristocracies.

Most of these rich men were once poor; they had felt the spur of need; they had long striven against hostile fate, and now that they had won their victory, the passions that accompanied the struggle survived. They seemed drunk on the petty delights it had taken forty years to gain.

Not but that in the United States, as elsewhere, there are a fairly large number of rich men who, having inherited their property, effortlessly possess a wealth they have not gained. But even these people appear to be no less attached to the delights of the material world. Love of comfort has become the dominant national taste. The main current of human passions running in that direction sweeps everything along with it.

Particular Effects of the Love of
Physical Pleasures in Democratic Times

It might be supposed, from what has just been said, that the love of physical pleasures would continually lead the Americans into moral irregularities, disturb the peace of families, and finally threaten the stability of society itself.

But it does not happen like that. The passion for physical pleasures produces in democracies effects very different from those it occasions in aristocratic societies.

. . . Among . . . [democratic peoples] love of comfort appears as a tenacious, exclusive, and universal passion, but always a restrained one. There is no question of building vast palaces, of conquering or excelling nature, or sucking the world dry to satisfy one man's greed. It is more a question of adding a few acres to one's fields, planting an orchard, enlarging a house, making life ever easier and more comfortable, keeping irritations away, and satisfying one's slightest needs without trouble and almost without expense. These are petty aims, but the soul cleaves to them; it dwells on them every day and in great detail; in the end they shut out the rest of the world and sometimes come between the soul and God.

This, it may be said, can only apply to men of middling fortune; the rich will display tastes akin to those which flourished in aristocratic periods. I contest that suggestion.

Where physical pleasures are concerned, the opulent citizens of a democracy do not display tastes very different from those of the people, either because, themselves originating from the people, they really do share them or because they think they ought to accept their standards. In democratic societies public sensuality has adopted a moderate and tranquil shape to which all are expected to conform. It is as hard for vices as for virtues to slip through the net of common standards.

Wealthy men living in democracies therefore think more of satisfying their slightest needs than seeking extraordinary delights. They indulge a quantity of little wants but do not let themselves give rein to any great disorderly passion. They are more prone to become enervated than debauched. . . .

How Excessive Love of Prosperity
Can Do Harm to It

There is a closer connection than is supposed between the soul's improvement and the betterment of physical conditions. A man can treat the two things as distinct and pay attention to each in turn. But he cannot entirely separate them without in the end losing sight of both.

Animals have the same senses as ourselves and much the same appetites. There are no physical passions which are not possessed in common with them and of which the seed is not found in a dog as much as in ourselves.

Why is it, then, that animals only know how to satisfy their primary and coarsest needs, whereas we can infinitely vary and continually increase our delights?

That which makes us better than the brutes in this is that we employ our souls to find those material benefits to which instinct alone directs them. In man an angel teaches a brute how to satisfy its desires. It is because man is able to raise himself above the things of the body and even to scorn life itself, a matter of which the beasts have not the least notion, that he can multiply these same good things of the body to a degree of which they have no conception.

Whatever elevates, enlarges, and expands the soul makes it more able to succeed even in those undertakings which are not the soul's concern.

On the other hand, whatever enervates and lowers it weakens it for every purpose, the least as well as the greatest, and threatens to make it almost equally impotent in both. Therefore the soul must remain great and strong, if only that it may from time to time put its strength and greatness at the service of the body.

If men ever came to be content with physical things only, it seems likely that they would gradually lose the art of producing them and would end up by enjoying them without discernment and without improvement, like animals.

Why in Ages of Equality and Skepticism It Is Important to Set Distant Goals for Human Endeavor

In ages of faith the final aim of life is placed beyond life.

The men of those ages therefore naturally and almost involuntarily grow accustomed to fix their eyes for years together on some static object toward which their progress is ever directed, and they learn by imperceptible degrees to repress a crowd of petty passing desires in order ultimately best to satisfy the one great permanent longing which obsesses them. When these same men engage in worldly affairs, such habits influence their conduct. They gladly fix some general and definite aim as the object of their actions here below and direct all their efforts toward it. They do not shift from day to day, chasing some new object of desire, but have settled designs which they never tire of pursuing.

That is why religious nations have often accomplished such lasting achievements. For in thinking of the other world, they had found out the great secret of success in this.

Religions instill a general habit of behaving with the future in view. In this respect they work as much in favor of happiness in this world as of felicity in the next. That is one of their most salient political characteristics.

But as the light of faith grows dim, man's range of vision grows more circumscribed, and it would seem as if the object of human endeavors came daily closer.

When once they have grown accustomed not to think about what will happen after their life, they easily fall back into a complete and brutish indifference about the future, an attitude all too well suited to certain propensities of human nature. As soon as they have lost the way of relying chiefly on distant hopes, they are naturally led to want to satisfy their least desires at once; and it would seem that as soon as they despair of living forever, they are inclined to act as if they could not live for more than a day.

In skeptical ages, therefore, there is always a danger that men will give way to ephemeral and casual desires and that, wholly renouncing whatever cannot be acquired without protracted effort, they may never achieve anything great or calm or lasting.

If, with a people so disposed, social conditions become democratic, this danger is increased.

When everyone is constantly striving to change his position, when an immense field of competition is open to all, when wealth is amassed or dissipated in the shortest possible space of time in the turmoil of democracy, men think in terms of sudden and easy fortunes, of great possessions easily won and lost, and chance in every shape and form. Social instability favors the natural instability of desires. Amid all these perpetual fluctuations of fate the present looms large and hides the future, so that men do not want to think beyond tomorrow.

In such a country where unhappily skepticism and democracy exist together, philosophers and the men in power should always strive to set a distant aim as the object of human efforts; that is their most important business.

The moralist must learn to defend his position, adapting himself to his age and country. He must constantly endeavor to show his contemporaries that even in the midst of all the turmoil around them it is easier than they suppose to plan and execute long-term projects. He must make them see that although the aspect of humanity has changed, the means by which men can obtain prosperity in this world are still the same and that, in democracies as elsewhere, it is only by resisting a thousand daily petty urges that the fundamental anxious longing for happiness can be satisfied.

The duty of rulers is equally clear.

It is at all times important that the rulers of nations should act with the future in view. But this is even more necessary in ages of democracy and skepticism than in any others. By giving such a lead, the chief men in democracies not only bring prosperity in public affairs but also teach individuals by their example to conduct their private affairs properly.

They must especially strive to banish chance, as much as possible, from the world of politics.

The sudden and undeserved promotion of a courtier in an aristocratic country causes no more than an ephemeral impression, because the whole complex of institutions and beliefs forces men to progress slowly along paths they cannot leave.

But such events give the worst possible example to a democratic people, for they urge it on down in the direction whither all its emotions are anyhow leading. So it is chiefly in times of skepticism and equality that particular precautions are required to prevent the favor of prince or people, which comes and goes at random, from taking the place due to merit or duties performed. One must hope that all promotion will be seen as the reward of effort, so that no high position should be too easily acquired and men of ambition should be obliged to plan well ahead before they reach their goal.

Governments must study means to give men back that interest in the future which neither religion nor social conditions any longer inspire, and without specifically saying so, give daily practical examples to the citizens proving that wealth, renown, and power are the rewards of work, that great success comes when it has been long desired, and that nothing of lasting value is achieved without trouble.

Once men have become accustomed to foresee from afar what is likely to befall them in this world and to feed upon hopes, they can hardly keep their thoughts always confined within the precise limits of this life and will always be ready to break out through these limits and consider what is beyond.

I have therefore no doubt that, in accustoming the citizens to think of the future in this world, they will gradually be led without noticing it themselves toward religious beliefs.

Thus the same means that, up to a certain point, enable men to manage without religion are perhaps after all the only means we still possess for bringing mankind back, by a long and roundabout path, to a state of faith. . . .

How an Aristocracy May Be Created by Industry

. . . [D]emocracy favors the development of industry by multiplying without limit the number of those engaged in it. We shall now see by what roundabout route industry may in turn lead men back to aristocracy.

It is acknowledged that when a workman spends every day on the same detail, the finished article is produced more easily, quickly, and economically.

It is likewise acknowledged that the larger the scale on which an industrial undertaking is conducted with great capital assets and extensive credit, the cheaper will its products be.

People had formed some inkling of these truths long ago, but it is in our day that they have been demonstrated. They have already been applied to several very important industries, and in due turn even the smallest will take advantage of them.

There is nothing in the world of politics that deserves the lawgivers' attention more than these two new axioms of industrial science.

When a workman is constantly and exclusively engaged in making one object, he ends by performing this work with singular dexterity. But at the same time, he loses the general faculty of applying his mind to the way he is working. Every day he becomes more adroit and less industrious, and one may say that in his case the man is degraded as the workman improves.

What is one to expect from a man who has spent twenty years of his life making heads for pins? And how can he employ that mighty human intelligence which has so often stirred the world, except in finding out the best way of making heads for pins?

When a workman has spent a considerable portion of his life in this fashion, his thought is permanently fixed on the object of his daily toil; his body has contracted certain fixed habits which it can never shake off. In a word, he no longer belongs to himself, but to his chosen calling. In vain are all the efforts of law and morality to break down the barriers surrounding such a man and open up a thousand different roads to fortune for him on every side. An industrial theory stronger than morality or law ties him to a trade, and often to a place, which he cannot leave. He has been assigned a certain position in society which he cannot quit. In the midst of universal movement, he is stuck immobile.

As the principle of the division of labor is ever more completely applied, the workman becomes weaker, more limited, and more dependent. The craft improves, the craftsman slips back. On the other hand, as it becomes ever clearer that the products of industry become better and cheaper as factories become vaster and capital greater, very rich and well-educated men come forward to exploit industries which, up to that time, had been left to ignorant and rough artisans. They are attracted by the scale of the efforts required and the importance of the results to be achieved.

Thus, at the same time that industrial science constantly lowers the standing of the working class, it raises that of the masters.

While the workman confines his intelligence more and more to studying one single detail, the master daily embraces a vast field in his vision, and his mind expands as fast as the other's contracts. Soon the latter will need no more than bodily strength without intelligence, while to succeed the former needs science and almost genius. The former becomes more and more like the administrator of a huge empire, and the latter more like a brute.

So there is no resemblance between master and workman, and daily they become more different. There is no connection except that between the first and last links in a long chain. Each occupies a place made for him, from which he does not move. One is in a state of constant, narrow, and necessary dependence on the other and seems to have been born to obey, as the other was to command.

What is this, if not an aristocracy?

As conditions become more and more equal in the body of the nation, the need for manufactured products becomes greater and more general, and the cheapness which brings these things within reach of men of moderate fortune becomes an ever greater element in success.

Thus there is a constant tendency for very rich and well-educated men to devote their wealth and knowledge to manufactures and to seek, by opening large establishments with a strict division of labor, to meet the fresh demands which are made on all sides.

Hence, just while the mass of the nation is turning toward democracy, that particular class which is engaged in industry becomes more aristocratic. Men appear more and more like in the one context and more and more different in the other, and inequality increases within the little society in proportion as it decreases in society at large.

It would thus appear, tracing things back to their source, that a natural impulse is throwing up an aristocracy out of the bosom of democracy.

But that aristocracy is not at all like those that have preceded it.

First, be it noted that because it only flourishes in industry and in some industrial callings, it is an exception, a monstrosity, within the general social condition.

The little aristocratic societies formed by certain industries in the midst of the vast democracy of our day contain, as did the great aristocratic societies of former days, some very opulent men and a multitude of wretchedly poor ones.

These poor men have few means of escaping from their condition and becoming rich, but the rich are constantly becoming poor or retiring from business when they have realized their profits. Hence the elements forming the poor class are more or less fixed, but that is not true of those forming the rich class. To be exact, although there are rich men, a class of the rich does not exist at all, for these rich men have neither corporate spirit nor objects in common, neither common traditions nor hopes. There are limbs, then, but no body.

Not only is there no solidarity among the rich, but one may say that there is no true link between rich and poor.

They are not forever fixed, one close to the other; at any moment interest, which brought them together, can pull them apart. The workman is dependent on masters in general, but not on a particular master. These two men see each other at the factory but do not know each other otherwise, and though there is one point of contact, in all other respects they stand far apart. The industrialist only asks the workman for his work, and the latter only asks him for his pay. The one contracts no obligation to protect, nor the other to defend, and they are not linked in any permanent fashion either by custom or by duty.

A business aristocracy seldom lives among the manufacturing population which it directs; its object is not to rule the latter but to make use of it.

An aristocracy so constituted cannot have a great hold over its employees, and even if it does for a moment hold them, they will soon escape. It does not know its own mind and cannot act.

The territorial aristocracy of past ages was obliged by law, or thought itself obliged by custom, to come to the help of its servants and relieve their distress. But the industrial aristocracy of our day, when it has impoverished and brutalized the men it uses, abandons them in time of crisis to public charity to feed them.

This is the natural result of what has been said before. Between workman and master there are frequent relations but no true association.

I think that, generally speaking, the manufacturing aristocracy which we see rising before our eyes is one of the hardest that have appeared on earth. But at the same time, it is one of the most restrained and least dangerous.

In any event, the friends of democracy should keep their eyes anxiously fixed in that direction. For if ever again permanent inequality of conditions and aristocracy make their way into the world, it will have been by that door that they entered.

CHAPTER EIGHT

What Difference Does Leadership Make?

Commentary

Corporations get their character from the top. Education and training, codes of conduct and law all influence corporate behavior, but if corporations are to build a business community of which the nation can be proud, that can only be achieved by leaders devoted to high standards of business ethics.

The right of each individual to own property and to employ it as he sees fit is a cherished tenet of American society. But modern business organization makes possible the accumulation and employment of property and other wealth on such a scale as to influence significantly the well-being of others and of the country as a whole. The management of such institutions inevitably raises in our minds questions about the rights of others and the public good. Our idea of a good society makes us at once respectful of the rights of business and suspicious of its power.

Law is an instrument by which the claims of business and of other interests with which business competes are mediated and sorted out. But unless law and its inevitable companion, regulation, are to be allowed to permeate every particle of the sphere in which these claims compete, business must accept responsibility to foresee the limits of its legitimate reach, to exhibit appropriate constraints upon its unregulated conduct, and to set standards for itself above and beyond the minimum requirements of the law.

How are these standards to be established and accepted? The task of business leadership is made more difficult today by the general weakening of those secular and religious convictions that have in the past established standards of conduct that go beyond the simple injunction to obey the law. (The extent of illegal activity that has been exhibited in the savings and loan, junk bond, bribery, and other recent scandals serves as a reminder, however, if any is needed, that obedience to law is the first necessary step toward achieving the very minimum of acceptable ethical conduct.) For many law-abiding business leaders, it appears that little is left in the way of principle that is not expressed in the notion of enlightened self-interest—expressed in the idea that good ethics are good for business, that "honesty is the best policy."

"We grew quickly and we stepped on toes," said Drexel Burnham chief Fred Joseph, by way of explaining the unusual antipathies his firm generated in the 1980s. But it is not difficult to develop a list of questions to which Drexel executives should have given their attention. Are high-yield bonds—"junk bonds" as they came to be known—sound investment instruments *over time?* What responsibility does a business executive have to his customers to make sure he is selling a sound product? What responsibilities do business leaders have to make sure that their employees treat their customers fairly, and to make certain that their employees are provided an example of fair treatment by the way they themselves are regarded by their bosses?

J. C. Penney built a firm that has survived and prospered long beyond the life of its founder. At the core of his thinking about leadership seems to be the idea that the moral posture of the leader is central to the long-term health of the business. It is true that Penney thought "honesty is the best policy" a simple expression of the doctrine of enlightened self-interest. But in the J. C. Penney code of conduct one sees more than selfish calculation. Rather, Penney seems intent on conveying to each employee the idea that the company and the employee together have a responsibility, beyond that demanded by the marketplace, to provide the public "complete satisfaction" for a "fair remuneration" which may indeed be less than "all the profit the traffic will bear."

By contrast, Fred Joseph claims, "we did no more than [others] when they hit periods of unusual competitive advantage." A Penney manager stated the alternative on which Penney's approach seems to have been built:

> The J. C. Penney Company enjoys the reputation of being a character and man builder as well as a builder of profits. It is because there has been and always will be that energetic spirit of efficient honesty, directing and developing its affairs, not because honesty is the best policy, but because honesty is right and always has been and always will be until the end of time.

Penney thought he saw a link between what builds human beings and what builds profits. He conveyed and reinforced that idea throughout his organization so unambiguously that it could be stated with clarity and precision by a company manager:

> There is no question but what the public buys their merchandise from individuals and firms of high standing; from those in whom they have the utmost confidence.

Regarding the link between honesty and humanity, Penney's thinking is equally straightforward:

> An honest man is a whole man, not a fraction of a man. He is not one thing above the line and something else below the line; not one thing at home and something else away from home, but a whole man.

Perhaps there is room in the thinking of sophisticated business leadership for as elegant and simple a proposition as:

> The moral grandeur of independent integrity is the sublimest thing in nature.

So said J. C. Penney. It is difficult these days to summon the imagination to conceive a business leadership in America inspired by such a conviction; it is equally difficult to believe that such a leadership could fail.

BENJAMIN J. STEIN

An Open Letter to Roger Hayes

Mr. Roger Hayes
Office of the U.S. Attorney
For the Southern District
Of New York

Dear Mr. Hayes, Word is out that a plea bargain between Michael Milken and the federal prosecutors, under your capable leadership, has been reached. According to reports, the deal calls for the government to drop any further charges against Milken, and to back off previous demands that he testify against his henchmen in insider trading. . . . In return, Milken pays a large fine—although not large by his standards—and meekly goes off to Lompoc to work on his tennis game and maybe his famous prowess at soccer. With the closure of the deal, Milken essentially is off the hook.

The deal is terrifyingly wrong-headed, anti-investor, and above all, anti-law, for a variety of reasons, all of them important.

First, the purpose of a trial of Milken would be to find out more about his operations. With a plea bargain, that opportunity is lost forever. This would be a tragedy akin to willfully refusing to learn basic facts about the subversion of law, markets, journalism and academe over a 15-year period.

Just a few of the questions to which answers might be found at a prolonged trial are in these areas:

Savings and loans: We now know that Milken was at the epicenter of a good part of the ruination of a number of big S&Ls. Lincoln, Columbia, San Jacinto, CenTrust, Imperial, and other dead or dying S&Ls were basically put together with financing arranged by Milken. They bought each other's junky real estate, jacked up each other's share prices, bought whatever

Reprinted by permission of Barron's, © Dow Jones & Company, Inc. (April 23, 1990). All Rights Reserved.

bonds Milken chose to sell them, and then went bust. This operation left the taxpayers of America holding an empty bag that will take tens of billions to fill. The feds apparently plan to let Milken get off with costing the taxpayers billions without requiring that he even answer charges about his role. If he gets off with no charges at all for this bad conduct, it is an insult to taxpayers.

Looting of stockholders and taxpayers: What the defenders of Michael Milken always seem to forget is that a large number of his defalcations were not against strangers or enemies. They were almost always against stockholders of companies (or limited partners of limited partnerships) that his firm represented. His work largely was aimed at taking away value from people to whom he had a fiduciary duty. Of course, his roles in Resorts International, Triangle Industries (still the most questionable Drexel deal I have ever seen) and TWA are by now well known.

But there is a whole host of other deals of highly questionable nature that have not even been touched. Examples are piling up on my desk, mostly based on calls from former Drexel staffers who are revolted with the way that Milken mistreated stockholders to whom he owed a duty. Deals involving knowing underpayment in buyouts, bribes to brokers to sell worthless stock, deals where net-worth statements in companies were simply made up—all of these will just be dropped down the Orwellian Memory Hole if the plea bargain goes through. Stockholders who lost millions and billions will just be cast adrift, without real hope of ever finding out just how badly maimed they were. This would be an astounding expression of contempt for stockholders and investors generally. . . .

The whole junk bond scheme: Even since yours truly wrote about the question of whether junk was really a Ponzi scheme all along, more data have come out hinting that there is rot at the base of the pyramid. The revelations of the worthlessness of much of the Columbia junk portfolio, the similar sad tidings about First Executive, the knowledge that the Drexel-supplied data about junk defaults turns out to be largely if not entirely spurious, the merry insouciance with which some Drexel players are simply walking away from their indentured obligations—all of these hint that Drexel junk was never anything but a boiler-room scam.

At a trial, certain players could be put under oath, given immunity, and made to talk about just how the whole effort was cooked up, who protected it in government, who were its patrons in journalism and academe. The junk-bond effort was probably the single biggest private financial scandal of the century. It would be disgraceful to simply walk away from it without a major effort to find out who was involved. . . .

A plea bargain for Milken would be a real insult to the whole idea of law. For the SEC to now proclaim to the world that if a swindler is big enough, he gets a slap on the wrist—while a secretary to a bond trader gets proportionately draconian punishment, while ghetto kids who rob 7-Elevens get years in truly horrific prisons—this sends a cruel message, indeed.

But even beyond that, the system rests on *law.* The whole society, including the free market in finance, rests on law. If a very rich man can violate laws on a massive scale, fix prices on a staggering scale in the bond market, fix prices on a smaller scale in the stock market, take money from innocent people, and get away with it, he is striking a devastating blow at what holds this nation together.

Sincerely,
Benjamin J. Stein
Los Angeles

PAUL ASQUITH, DAVID W. MULLINS, JR., & ERIC D. WOLFF

Calculating the Real Return on High-Yield Bonds

The development of the original issue high yield bond market represents one of the most successful innovations in recent financial history. From its inception, a major impetus behind the growth of the new issue high yield bond market has been the argument that risk-adjusted returns are high. Specifically, it is argued that defaults on high yield bonds, while higher than those on investment grade bonds, are low relative to their coupon rate, i.e., that their higher coupon rates more than compensate for the default risk. This apparent market inefficiency has been attributed to outdated conventions used by rating agencies and bond investors, both of whom supposedly fail to see the true risk/return characteristics of high yield bonds. . . .

Default studies of high yield bonds have generally supported a positive view of this market. A series of early studies . . . have documented low default rates for high yield bonds. These studies have reported annual default rates in the 1–3 percent range, with Altman and Nammacher (1987) finding an average default rate of 1.5 percent for 1978–1986. These rates, while higher than the default rate on investment grade bonds, are offset by the 3–5 percent spread in yields between high yield and investment grade bonds. These studies showing consistently low default rates have convinced many of the proposition that the high yield debt market has low risk-adjusted default rates.

There are, however, several problems which bias downward the reported default rates in these high yield studies. One source

Excerpted from "Original Issue High Yield Bonds: Aging Analyses of Defaults, Exchanges, and Calls" by Paul Asquith, David W. Mullins, Jr., & Eric D. Wolff. *Journal of Finance,* Vol. XLIV, No. 4 (September 1989). Reprinted by permission.

of bias is the failure to account properly for exchanges. Some studies drop exchanged bonds from their high yield bond samples. If exchanges reflect increased risk, exchanged bonds should have a higher default rate than initial issues. Even if exchanged bonds are not eliminated from a sample, distressed exchanges may be used to avoid technical default, thereby reducing the reported rate of default. As a result, the reported default rate might understate the actual incidence of financial distress by issuers and losses by bondholders.

Second, traditional studies of high yield bond defaults have not properly considered the aging of the bonds. [These s]tudies . . . measure the default rate by dividing the amount of defaults in a given year by the par value of all outstanding issues. This definition of default rate ignores the important effect of bond age on default risk. If bond default rates are not stationary through time but rise with bond age, and if there is a rapid growth in new issue volume year to year, default rates are severely biased downward by this measure. An alternative way to measure default risk is to consider defaults over time within a cohort of bonds issued at the same time. . . .

The objective of this paper is to present an analysis of the high yield bond market which avoids the two methodological difficulties noted above: failure to consider exchanges and the aging of bonds. It specifically incorporates the concept of aging in an analysis of defaults, exchanges, and calls for an exhaustive data base of all original issue public high yield corporate bonds issued between January 1, 1977, and December 31, 1986. For these 741 bonds, all relevant events are examined through December 31, 1988.

The results are striking. A buy-and-hold investor who purchased a portfolio of all high yield bonds issued in 1977 and 1978 would, by December 31, 1988, experience a default rate of 34 percent. Of the bonds issued in the years 1979–1983, between 19 and 27 percent default by December 31, 1988. Default rates for issue years 1984–1986 range from 3 to 9 percent by December 31, 1988.

The effect of bond age on the default rate is clearly evident in these results. Default rates are lower immediately after issue and rise over time. By the time these defaults occur, the overall market is much larger due to the rapid growth in new issue volume. This growth makes the high default rates of old bonds appear small relative to the size of the overall market, which is dominated by recently issued bonds with low default rates.

This study also examines exchanges because of their potential use in avoiding default through a reorganization of claims. The results confirm that, by December 31, 1988, a significant fraction of bonds issued (up to 31 percent for some years) have been subject to exchanges. However, a significant proportion of exchanges are followed by default and are included in the default results reported above. Thus, these results do not support the argument that exchanges are completely effective in eliminating defaults for high yield bonds. They do, however, point to the importance of not dropping exchanged bonds and their successors from any study of the high yield market.

In addition to defaults and exchanges, this study examines calls of original issue high yield bonds. A significant percentage of the bonds issued were called by December 31, 1988. The percentage called for the earlier issue years 1977–1982, where call protection can be considered to have expired, ranges from 26 to 47 percent.

Summing the aged results for defaults, exchanges, calls, and maturities gives a picture far different from the common perception of a stable market with low defaults. By December 31, 1988, only a relatively small fraction of high yield bonds originally issued in years 1977–1982 remain outstanding. On the down side, approximately one third of bonds issued in these years have defaulted or have been exchanged. An additional one third have been called, requiring investors to reinvest. Only a small fraction of original issue high yield bonds has been paid off through sinking funds or at maturity. By December 31, 1988, the residual issues which have neither defaulted nor been called or matured represent only 28.1 percent of the original issues of 1977–1982.

Results for these early years do not appear anomalous. Early year default results for issue years 1983–1986 are equal to or worse than those for issue years 1977–1982. Of course, these early year results do not necessarily predict similar future default rates. . . .

II. Results

A. Defaults

Table II presents cumulative defaults through December 31, 1988, for high yield bonds issued from 1977 through 1986. Default is defined as declaration of default by the bond trustee, the filing of bankruptcy by the issuing firm, or the assignment of a D rating by S&P for a missed coupon payment. If the bond has been exchanged for other securities, default is also defined as a default of the securities for which the original bond was exchanged.

The results presented in Table II document that default percentages are high for "older" bond issues. An investor who bought and held all high yield bonds issued in 1977 and 1978 would experience, by December 31, 1988, cumulative defaults of 34 percent. Buying and holding all new issues in the years 1979–1983 would, by December 31, 1988, produce cumulative defaults ranging from 19 to 27 percent. Cumulative defaults are much lower for "younger" bonds. The issue years of 1984–1986 produced cumulative defaults of 3–9 percent through December 31, 1988.

The importance of aging on default rates is illustrated clearly in Table III. This table reports year by year default rates and cumulative default percentages for each issue year. Default rates are low for the first several years after issue. In fact, for seven of the ten issue years, there are no defaults in the first year after issue, and, for three of the issue years, there are no defaults in the first two years. These low early year default rates lead to low cumulative default percentages, ranging from 0 to 8 percent three years after issue, with the majority in the 3–6 percent range.

Yearly default rates increase with time, and, thus, older bonds have much higher cumulative default percentages. Seven years after issue, cumulative defaults rise to 18–26 percent for the issue years 1978–1982 although no 1977 issues had defaulted seven years after issue. Eleven and twelve years after issue date, cumulative defaults are 34 percent for the two relevant years, 1977 and 1978. Because a methodology which properly considers aging is

Table II

Cumulative Defaults for Original Issue High Yield Bonds until 12/31/88 by Year of Issue

High yield bonds are all bonds rated below investment grade at issue date by Moody's and Standard & Poor's. Defaults are defined as a declaration of default by the bond's trustee, filing of bankruptcy by the firm, or assignment of a D rating by S&P for a missed coupon payment.

	Total Issued		Total Defaulted*		Cumulative % of Total Defaulted	
Issue Year	Number	Amount ($ Millions)	Number	Amount ($ Millions)	Number	Amount ($ Millions)
1977	26	908	6	308	23.08	33.92
1978	51	1,442	17	494	33.33	34.26
1979	41	1,263	12	312	29.27	24.70
1980	37	1,223	12	337	32.43	27.56
1981	24	1,240	4	260	16.67	20.97
1982	41	2,490	11	646	26.83	25.94
1983	74	6,003	16	1,153	21.62	19.21
1984	102	11,552	15	1,084	14.71	9.38
1985	145	14,463	10	510	6.90	3.53
1986	200	30,949	17	2,519	8.50	8.14
Total	741	71,533	120	7,623		

* If the original bond has been exchanged for other securities and no longer exists, default is also defined as a default of the securities for which the bond was exchanged.

employed, the default percentages presented in Table III are much higher than those reported in many earlier studies.

Table III also indicates no trend toward improvement in aged default rates in more recent issue years. Issue years 1982–1986 have average early year default rates equal to or worse than issue years 1977–1981. In fact, the most recent issue year in the sample, 1986, exhibits the highest first year default rate and is second among all ten issue years in cumulative default percentages two and three years after issue.

Table IV gives unaged yearly default rates calculated by taking the amount of defaults in a given year and dividing by cumulative new issues since 1977. This is similar to the methodology used to calculate default rates . . . [in earlier studies and] by Drexel Burnham Lambert. Table IV demonstrates that replicating this methodology on the sample here yields results similar to those

Table III

Aged Defaults for High Yield Bonds Grouped by Year of Issue

In this table an nth year default is defined as a default within $n \times 365$ days of the issue date. High yield bonds are all bonds rated below investment grade at issue date by Moody's and Standard & Poor's. Defaults are defined as a declaration of default by the bond's trustee, filing of bankruptcy by the firm, or assignment of a D Rating by S&P for a missed coupon payment.

Issue Year	1st	2nd	3rd	4th	5th	6th	7th	8th	9th	10th	11th	12th	Total
Panel A: % of Par Amount Defaulted in nth Year After Issue													
1977	0.00	0.00	0.00	0.00	0.00	0.00	0.00	7.71	3.63	19.27	3.30	0.00*	33.92
1978	0.00	8.32	0.00	1.39	0.00	7.91	4.85	3.12	5.55	1.39	1.73*	—	34.26
1979	0.00	0.00	5.54	1.11	2.38	6.73	1.98	0.00	5.78	1.19*	—	—	24.70
1980	0.00	0.57	2.45	0.00	0.00	13.90	6.30	1.88	2.45*	—	—	—	27.56
1981	0.00	6.05	0.00	8.06	6.85	0.00	0.00	0.00*	—	—	—	—	20.97
1982	1.00	2.41	1.61	11.49	0.00	9.44	0.00*	—	—	—	—	—	25.94
1983	0.00	0.00	6.08	7.83	4.80	0.50*	—	—	—	—	—	—	19.21
1984	2.29	1.99	2.03	3.06	0.00*	—	—	—	—	—	—	—	9.38
1985	0.00	0.80	2.28	0.45*	—	—	—	—	—	—	—	—	3.53
1986	2.73	3.84	1.57*	—	—	—	—	—	—	—	—	—	8.14
Panel B: Cumulated % of Par Amount Defaulted for x Years After Issue													
1977	0.00	0.00	0.00	0.00	0.00	0.00	0.00	7.71	11.34	30.62	33.92	33.92*	33.92
1978	0.00	8.32	8.32	9.71	9.71	17.61	22.47	25.59	31.14	32.52	34.26*	—	34.26
1979	0.00	0.00	5.54	6.65	9.03	15.76	17.74	17.74	23.52	24.70*	—	—	24.70
1980	0.00	0.57	3.03	3.03	3.03	16.93	23.22	25.10	27.56*	—	—	—	27.56
1981	0.00	6.05	6.05	14.11	20.97	20.97	20.97	20.97*	—	—	—	—	20.97
1982	1.00	3.41	5.02	16.51	16.51	25.94	25.94*	—	—	—	—	—	25.94
1983	0.00	0.00	6.08	13.91	18.71	19.21*	—	—	—	—	—	—	19.21
1984	2.29	4.28	6.32	9.38	9.38*	—	—	—	—	—	—	—	9.38
1985	0.00	0.80	3.08	3.53*	—	—	—	—	—	—	—	—	3.53
1986	2.73	6.57	8.14*	—	—	—	—	—	—	—	—	—	8.14

* May be incomplete; i.e., entire sample may not have been outstanding for x years.

reported elsewhere. Annual default rates calculated in this manner average under 2 percent from 1980 to 1986, and the "unaged" cumulative default percentage, calculated as cumulative defaults divided by cumulative new issues, is 10.66 percent by December 31, 1988. This clearly demonstrates that it is the use of the aging methodology, not differences in the database, which causes our higher default percentages.

Table V provides further insight into the reason for these low unaged default rates. This table presents the average issue age of the original issue public high yield bond market. Average issue age is defined as average time since issue date for all bonds in the sample. Because of the rapid growth in new issue volume, the average age of the overall market actually declined for several years and has hovered around two years.

As a result, default rates which do not consider bond age, such as those in Table IV, produce biased results. As the aging analysis in Table III demonstrates, default rates do not increase until several years after issue. By then, the larger default rates on old bonds appear small relative to the size of the overall market, now dominated by bonds issued in the previous year or two. An aging methodology is necessary to produce a clear view of the default experience of a buy-and-hold investor.

The illusion of low unaged default rates calculated as in Table IV can be sustained only as long as the explosive growth in new issues continues. Once growth slows, as it inevitably must, the overall market will no longer be dominated by recently issued bonds with lower default rates. With slower growth in new issue volume, the average age of the overall high yield bond market will grow, revealing higher aged default percentages such as those reported in Table III.

Finally, it should be noted that the aged default rates reported in this paper are not necessarily indicative of future default rates. The sample studied here covers a period of generally falling interest rates, rising stock prices, and good economic conditions (except for a brief 1982 recession). Further adversity in capital markets and/or economic conditions could produce higher default rates. In addition, because of the youth of this market, few of the issuers were required to make principal payments during the sample period. With the added burden of sinking fund and matu-

Table IV

Yearly Default Percentages for Original Issue High Yield Bonds Calculated without Aging

High yield bonds are all bonds rated below investment grade at issue date by Moody's and Standard & Poor's. Defaults are defined as a declaration of default by the bond's trustee, filing of bankruptcy by the firm, or assignment of a D rating by S&P for a missed coupon payment. Default percentages are calculated as the number (or $ amount) of defaults in a given year divided by the universe of all high yield bonds issued through the year.

Year	Number Defaulted	Amount Defaulted ($ Millions)	Total Number Issued Since 1/1/77	Total Amount Issued Since 1/1/77 ($ Millions)	Defaults % Number	Defaults % $ Amount
1977	0	0	26	908	0.00	0.00
1978	0	0	77	2,350	0.00	0.00
1979	1	20	118	3,613	0.85	0.56
1980	1	100	155	4,836	0.65	2.08
1981	2	107	179	6,076	1.12	1.77
1982	7	145	220	8,566	3.18	1.69
1983	4	125	294	14,569	1.36	0.86
1984	8	303	396	26,121	2.02	1.16
1985	13	821	541	40,584	2.40	2.02
1986	37	2,104	741	71,533	4.99	2.94
Total*	120	7,623	741	71,533	16.19	10.66

* From 1/1/77 to 12/31/88.

rity payments, future default rates could be higher even without a worsening of the economy. On the other hand, more underwriter and investor experience with the creditworthiness of high leverage or low rated firms, greater liquidity in the secondary market for high yield bonds, and a more active role for exchange offers may lower future default rates.

B. Exchanges

Exchanges are important in analyzing high yield bonds since they may be used to avoid the event of default by a reorganization of claims. In a distressed situation, a firm may offer bondholders the opportunity to exchange the bond for securities with less current service burden (e.g., by a lower coupon rate, a delayed sinking fund, or a combination exchange of bonds and common stock). Such distressed exchange offers, if not properly

Table V

The Average Issue Age* of All High Yield Bonds Issued After January 1, 1977, Until the Date Given

High yield bonds are all bonds rated below investment grade at issue date by Moody's and Standard & Poor's. Average issue age is defined as the amount of bonds issued multiplied by the time since issue date divided by the total amount issued.

Bonds Issued after 1/1/77 until the Date Below	Average Issue Age Weighted by Par Value of Issues
12/31/77	0.48 years
12/31/78	0.85 years
12/31/79	1.36 years
12/31/80	1.87 years
12/31/81	2.39 years
12/31/82	2.50 years
12/31/83	2.28 years
12/31/84	2.01 years
12/31/85	2.07 years
12/31/86	1.94 years

* Formally, the par amount of each bond is multiplied by the number of days since issue. This weighted amount is summed and then divided by the cumulative par amount issued. for example, if an equal amount of bonds is issued every year for ten years, the average age at the end of ten years is five years. If more bonds are issued at the beginning of the period, the average age is > five years. If more are issued at the end of the period, the average is < five years.

considered, might understate the incidence of firm financial distress as well as the size of losses experienced by bondholders since the terms of the exchange should reflect a significant probability of default on the old debt. Furthermore, if exchanges are not followed afterwards, defaults on the newly issued bonds (and on any residual amount of untendered old bonds) will be ignored.

The results in Table VI confirm that, by December 31, 1988, a significant percentage of the bonds issued in the early sample years have been subject to exchanges. Four of the first five issue years have cumulative exchange percentages in excess of 17 percent. Cumulative exchanges for more recent issue years are between 2 and 14 percent.

Table VI

Cumulative Successful Exchanges for Original Issue High Yield Bonds until 12/31/88 by Year of Issue

This table does not include exchanges subsequent to default or bankruptcy. It also does not include debt-equity swaps. High yield bonds are all bonds rated below investment grade at issue date by Moody's and Standard & Poor's. Defaults are defined as a declaration of default by the bond's trustee, filing of bankruptcy by the firm, or assignment of a D rating by S&P for a missed coupon payment.

Issue Year	Number of Issues Exchanged[a]	Amount of Issues Exchanged ($ Millions)	% of Total Issues Exchanged		% of Total Issues Exchanged with No Subsequent Default[b]	
			Number	Amount	Number	Amount
1977	6	281	23.08	30.95	11.54	15.75
1978	10	290	19.61	20.11	7.84	9.02
1979	4	56	9.76	4.43	2.44	1.11
1980	7	212	18.92	17.33	8.11	6.13
1981	6	365	25.00	29.44	20.83	24.19
1982	4	180	9.76	7.23	4.88	0.80
1983	8	820	10.81	13.66	5.41	7.58
1984	7	555	6.86	4.80	6.86	4.80
1985	7	470	4.83	3.25	4.83	3.25
1986	3	480	1.50	1.55	1.00	1.07
Total	62	3,709	8.37	5.19	5.13	3.48

[a] For an additional eleven issues in the sample (par value $581 million), the issue was exchanged after a default or bankruptcy.

[b] As of 12/31/88. This is the percentage of all issues in the sample that have been exchanged without any subsequent default. A high percentage of exchanged bonds subsequently default. (See Table VII.) A small percentage eventually mature or are called. (See Table VII.).

The results presented in Table VII illustrate, however, that exchange offers have not always been successful in avoiding default. For all issue years, excluding 1984 and 1985, a significant fraction of exchanges, 18–89 percent, are followed by default on the securities received in the exchange offer. These defaults are included in the default results reported in Tables II, III, and IV. Of all exchanges, slightly less than one third are followed by default, more than half are followed by no other event by December 31, 1988, and the remaining 9 percent are called or are paid off at maturity. Table VI shows that exchanges not followed by default are a small fraction of total issue amount for most issue

Table VII

Amounts and Percentages of Successful Exchanges That Have Defaulted, Matured, or Been Called from the Exchange until 12/31/88 by Year of Issue

This table does not include exchanges made subsequent to a default or bankruptcy. Percentages are calculated for the sample of total successful exchanges.

Issue Year	Exchanges/No Other Events				Exchange/Default				Exchange/Call or Maturity			
	Number	Amount ($ Millions)	% Number	% Amount	Number	Amount ($ Millions)	% Number	% Amount	Number	Amount ($ Millions)	% Number	% Amount
1977	0	0	0.00	0.00	3	138	50.00	49.11	3	143	50.00	50.89
1978	4	130	40.00	44.83	6	160	60.00	55.17	0	0	0.00	0.00
1979	1	14	25.00	25.00	3	42	75.00	75.00	0	0	0.00	0.00
1980	2	50	28.57	23.58	4	137	57.14	64.62	1	25	14.29	11.79
1981	3	240	50.00	65.75	1	65	16.67	17.81	2	60	33.33	16.44
1982	1	10	25.00	5.56	2	160	50.00	88.89	1	10	25.00	5.56
1983[a]	4	455	50.00	55.49	4	365	50.00	44.51	0	0	0.00	0.00
1984	6	455	85.71	81.98	0	0	0.00	0.00	1	100	14.29	18.02
1985	7	470	100.00	100.00	0	0	0.00	0.00	0	0	0.00	0.00
1986	2	330	66.67	68.75	1	150	33.33	31.25	0	0	0.00	0.00
Totals[b]	30	2.154	48.39	58.07	24	1.217	38.71	32.81	8	338	12.90	9.11

[a] One of the defaulted bonds in 1983, par value $85 million, was later called when the issuing company was acquired by another firm. To avoid double-counting, the bond is only classified as a default.

[b] Total percentages are of total exchanges and are not the average of the yearly percentages.

years. Thus, these results do not support the argument that exchange offers succeed in eliminating defaults, although they may reduce their number or change their timing.

C. Calls and Maturity

Table VIII reports cumulative call percentages for high yield bonds. Between 26 and 47 percent of the bonds issued in the first six years, 1977–1982, have been called by December 31, 1988. This partially reflects the sharp decline in interest rates beginning in 1982. It may also reflect required calls associated with asset sales or an improvement in some bonds' credit ratings. Thus, for a large percentage of the high yield market, lower interest rates and/or good performance by the issuers are translated into calls, requiring bondholders to reinvest. In contrast, only 3–14 percent of the bonds issued in 1983–1986 have been called by December 31, 1988. Given normal call protection periods and lower coupon rates, this is not surprising.

The high cumulative call percentages for early issue years raise the question of whether call provisions were correctly priced for these issues. In view of the possibility of upgrading lower grade bonds, and the larger inherent equity component, one would expect the call options on such bonds to be more valuable than call options on investment grade debt. Exploring the issue of upgrades, of the 116 calls in our sample, 42.2 percent came after upgrades, 13.8 percent came after downgrades, and 44.0 percent had no change in rating since issue. For A rated bonds issued in 1977–1986, the percentage of calls after upgrade was 29.4 percent, 38.1 percent came after downgrades, and 32.5 percent had no change.

Maturity results are given as part of Table IX. The original issue high yield bond market has been primarily long term, and only 2.19 percent of the total value of all issues in the sample had reached maturity by December 31, 1988. For three of the early years, 1978–1980, no bonds have yet matured.

D. Summary Results on Defaults, Exchanges, Calls, and Maturity

Table IX contains summary aged results for defaults, exchanges, calls, and maturities and presents a more detailed picture of this market than previous studies. By December 31, 1988, about one third (32.5 percent) of the high yield bonds issued in years 1977–1982 have defaulted or have been exchanged. Another third (34.7 percent) of the issues have been called and a small percentage (4.5 percent) have matured. Thus, by December 31, 1988, only 28.1 percent of the original issues of 1977–1982 have not defaulted, exchanged, been called or matured.

Table VIII
Cumulative Calls for all High Yield Bonds until 12/31/88 by Year of Issue

High yield bonds are all bonds rated below investment grade at issue date by Moody's and Standard & Poor's.

Issue Year	Number of Issues Called	Amount of Issues Called ($ Millions)	Cumulative % of Total Issues Called Number	Cumulative % of Total Issues Called Amount
1977	9	296	34.62	32.60
1978	13	373	25.49	25.87
1979	13	414	31.71	32.78
1980	11	368	29.73	30.09
1981	8	345	33.33	27.82
1982	15	1,174	36.59	47.15
1983	12	790	16.22	13.16
1984	14	1,059	13.73	9.17
1985	16	2,024	11.03	13.99
1986	5	937	2.50	3.03
Total	116	7,780	15.65	10.88

Results for more recent issue years show fewer defaults and calls. However, the aging analysis of defaults in [Table] III . . . demonstrates that cumulative defaults for later issue years are similar to those for bonds from early issue years at comparable ages. Call rates are lower, however, due presumably to call protection and a leveling off of interest rates. Thus, while a much

Table IX

Cumulative Disposition of Original Issue High Yield Bonds by Percentage of Par Amount Issued until 12/31/88 by Year of Issue

In this table an *n*th year default is defined as a default within $n \times 365$ days of the issue date. High yield bonds are all bonds rated below investment grade at issue date by Moody's and Standard & Poor's. Defaults are defined as a declaration of default by the bond's trustee, filing of bankruptcy by the firm, or assignment of a D rating by S&P for a missed coupon payment.

Issue Year	Total Issued (% Millions)	Defaults %	Exchanges (Still Outstanding) %	Calls %	Maturities %	Residual Outstanding[a] %
1977	908	33.92	0.00	32.60	9.59	24.12
1978	1,442	34.26	9.02	25.87	0.00	30.86
1979	1,263	24.70	1.11	32.78	0.00	41.41
1980	1,223	27.56	4.09	30.09	0.00	38.27
1981	1,240	20.97	19.35	27.82	2.42	29.44
1982	2,490	25.94	0.40	47.15	10.84	15.66
1983	6,003	19.21	7.58	13.16	5.83	54.22
1984	11,552	9.38	3.94	9.17	4.60	72.91
1985	14,463	3.53	3.25	13.99	0.00	79.23
1986	30,949	8.14	1.07	3.03	0.97	86.68
Total	71,533	10.66	3.01	10.88	2.19	73.27

[a] Does not adjust for sinking funds and partial repurchases. If these were included, the residual percentage would be lower.

larger percentage of recent issues remain outstanding without default, there is no evidence suggesting a fundamental change in the nature of the market.

The summary of aging results also underscores the extent to which the outstanding high yield market is dominated by recently issued "young" bonds. This dominance is due not only to the rapid growth in new issue volume but also to the attrition in outstanding issues due to defaults, calls, and principal payments. This attrition accelerates with issue age, thereby diminishing the outstanding balance of older issues.

E. Other Results

Table X presents data, by S&P rating, on the composition of high yield bond issues and on cumulative defaults. One notable

Table X

Distribution by Issue Year of Original Issue High Yield Bonds by S&P Rating at Time of Issue and Cumulative Defaults from Issue Date until December 31, 1988 by Issue Year and S&P Rating

High yield bonds are all bonds rated below investment grade at issue date by Moody's and Standard & Poor's. Defaults are defined as a declaration of default by the bond's trustee, filing of bankruptcy by the firm, or assignment of a D rating by S&P for a missed coupon payment.

Issue Year	Total Issued ($ Millions)	Share of Market by Rating Class as % of Total Issues			Cumulative Default %			
					Total Market	By Rating Class		
		BB	B	CCC or Below		BB	B	CCC or Below
1977	908	42.62	55.95	1.43	33.92	6.46	55.71	0.00
1978	1,442	28.29	70.87	0.83	34.26	35.54	34.15	0.00
1979	1,263	27.95	65.80	6.25	24.70	33.99	21.42	17.72
1980	1,223	26.00	71.95	2.04	27.56	16.67	32.27	0.00
1981	1,240	24.27	75.73	0.00	20.97	0.00	27.69	NA
1982	2,490	44.38	54.02	1.61	25.94	22.62	26.47	100.00
1983	6,003	27.90	63.85	8.25[a]	19.21	0.00	24.99	39.39[a]
1984	11,552	29.48	59.34	11.18	9.38	2.94	10.80	18.89
1985	14,463	31.72	54.62	13.67	3.53	4.36	3.92	0.00
1986	30,949	13.24	69.05	17.71	8.14	0.00	9.08	10.57
Total[b]	71,533	23.26	63.58	13.16	10.66	5.37	12.44	11.39

[a] One bond issue for $35 million was rated below CCC. This CC bond issue defaulted during its first year out.

[b] This is the total amount and percentages for all years together. It differs from an average yearly percentage with each year weighted equally since later years represent a larger share of all issues.

result is the shift toward CCC rated issues in later issue years. Prior to 1983, the original issue public high yield corporate bond market was comprised almost exclusively of BB and B rates issues. This reduction in initial credit quality since 1983 raises the question of whether defaults may prove higher in future years. Cumulative default percentages by S&P rating demonstrate that B rated issues exhibit higher default percentages than BB rated issues for seven of the ten issue years. While inferences in early issue years about CCC rated issues are limited by the small issue amounts, their cumulative defaults are higher than BB or B rated issues for four of the last five issue years. For the entire sample, the default percentage is 5.37 percent for BB bonds, 12.44 percent for B bonds, and 11.39 percent for CCC bonds. This lower percentage for CCC bonds is probably explained by their lower average age. The average issue age is 2.45 years for BB bonds, 1.90 years for B bonds, and 1.21 years for CCC bonds.

Stratifying the sample by industry shows that neither issues nor defaults are concentrated in a few industries. This is not surprising given the tremendous growth in the high yield bond market and the fact that economic conditions may differ by sectors of the economy. There are at least twenty-seven industries with over $1 billion in par value issued. In addition, there are twelve industries with over $200 million in defaults. These twelve industries are energy, steel, industrial machinery and equipment, miscellaneous manufacturing, toys and sporting goods, ship transportation, utilities, credit companies, mortgage bankers, real estate, motion picture production, and hospitals/healthcare.

Table XI presents underwriter market share and default percentages by issue year for original issue high yield bonds. The dominant underwriter, Drexel Burnham Lambert, increased its new issue market share from under one third during 1977–1980 to 53–63 percent in 1981–1985 before dropping to 45 percent in 1986. Of the total sample of high yield bonds, more than half were underwritten by Drexel. Table XI also presents defaults by underwriter for each issue year. Issues underwritten by Drexel exhibit lower default percentages than do the aggregate issues of all other underwriters. In every year except for 1985, Drexel has a lower cumulative default percentage on its issues than all other underwriters taken together. If the defaults are further categorized by rating class and year of issue, Drexel has lower or equal default rates in each year for all CCC's and for nine of the ten years for both B's and BB's. These differences may be explained by Drexel's experience and expertise in the high yield market and by other underwriters' attempts to penetrate the market by underwriting less creditworthy issues.

Finally, after 1980, high yield debt increasingly began to be used for funding mergers and leveraged buyouts.* LBO high yield debt constitutes 24.2 percent, 24.6 percent, and 21.0 percent of the total par value issued in 1984, 1985, and 1986, respectively,

Table XI

Share of Original Issue High Yield Bonds Issued and Cumulative Default Percentages by Underwriter Measured in Par Value of Issue by Year of Issue with the Entire Issue Allocated to the Lead Underwriter

High yield bonds are all bonds rated below investment grade at issue date by Moody's and Standard & Poor's. Defaults are defined as a declaration of default by the bond's trustee, filing of bankruptcy by the firm, or assignment of a D rating by S&P for a missed coupon payment.

| Year | Total Issued ($ Millions) | Share of Market as % of Total Issues[a] | | Cumulative Defaults % | | |
		DBL[b]	Non-DBL[b]	Total Market	DBL Issues[c]	Non-DBL Issues[c]
1977	908	14.98	85.02	33.92	22.06	36.01
1978	1,442	26.35	73.65	34.26	29.74	35.88
1979	1,263	32.30	67.70	24.70	23.53	25.26
1980	1,223	34.18	65.82	27.56	20.33	31.30
1981	1,240	63.23	36.77	20.97	20.41	21.93
1982	2,490	54.42	45.58	25.94	3.32	52.95
1983	6,003	54.02	45.98	19.21	17.21	21.56
1984	11,552	60.10	39.90	9.38	4.68	16.47
1985	14,463	60.87	39.13	3.53	3.92	2.92
1986	30,949	44.90	55.10	8.14	0.79	14.13
Total	71,533	50.84	49.16	10.66	5.13	16.37

[a] DBL is Drexel Burnham Lambert.

[b] The average issue age (as defined in Table V) is 1.85 years for DBL issues and 2.03 years for non-DBL issues.

[c] The cumulative defaults for DBL and non-DBL are the precentages of DBL and non-DBL issues for a given year that default by December 31, 1988. The weighted average (not the sum) of these two percentages gives the total market cumulative default percentage for each year.

and totals $12.9 billion. This LBO debt is 18.6 percent of the total 1977–1986 sample. Three LBO bonds, totalling $704 million par value, have defaulted by December 31, 1988. All are associated with one transaction, the 1986 LBO of Revco Drug Stores. This makes the default percentage for all LBO debt 5.47 percent, but even fewer implications can be drawn from this subsample given its short history and single defaulting firm. . . .

* The following statistics are only for LBO debt and contain no merger and acquisition debt not related to an LBO.

Editors' Note: According to Professor Asquith, investment-grade bonds default at an approximate rate of 1–2 percent per decade.

HERBERT STEIN

Blame Junk Bond Dealers, Not Junk Bonds

Many people are missing the point about our current experience
with junk bonds. They say: "Well, taking risks is essential for
economic progress. Some risks pay off and some do not. Some
investors win and some lose. That is the way capitalism works.
To complain about the losses is to complain about capitalism."

But the point is not that there have been risks and that some
people have lost money. The point is that many people have
abused their responsibilities and weakened trust in the financial
system. Trust, as George Shultz said in another connection, is the
"coin of the realm." Trust that the people with whom you deal
will not only obey the law but also fulfill the fiduciary responsibilities inherent in their relationships is as essential to the working
of the capitalist system as a sound currency and a reliable legal
system. Those who weaken that trust are sabotaging capitalism.

Revelations about the dealings in junk bonds, such as those of
Drexel Burnham, are making this betrayal of confidence clearer
and clearer. It is not that high-risk, high-interest bonds were
being sold. There is nothing wrong with that per se. What was
wrong was that these bonds were being sold to financial institutions whose investors had no wish to take such risks, had no
knowledge of the risks being taken and, most important, had no
prospect of getting the gains if the risk paid off but were certain
to take the losses if the risk failed. And this was being done at the
deliberate intent of some investment bankers and fund managers
and with the complaisance of regulatory agencies.

Although many of the transactions were of an impenetrable
complexity—which served the purposes of their managers—two
arithmetic examples will illustrate what was going on. Suppose
that XYZ Corp. issues $1,000, 10-year bonds that have a proba-

Reprinted from "Blame Junk Bond Dealers, Not Junk Bonds" by Herbert Stein.
The Wall Street Journal, February 23, 1990. Reprinted by permission of the
author.

ble payoff at maturity of $500. If the interest on the bonds is 13.137%, and if the annual interest payments are certain, the bond has a yield of 10%. If 10% is the prevailing yield on riskless assets, the bond is fairly priced. The bond is sold to a pension fund, whose participants are promised a return of 10%. They get their 10% each year, but at maturity get only $500. The present value of the investment for which they paid $1,000 was $807. Where did the other $193 go? To the managers of the pension fund, to the investment bankers who arranged the deal, and to their lawyers, accountants and economic consultants.

But suppose, as seems to have been the case at least some of the time, the bonds were not fairly priced, and their probable payoff at maturity was not $500 but $250. Then what the savers got was worth only $711. There was $289 to distribute among the "rainmakers," this time including the issuers of the bonds, but mainly to the investment bankers, who had to have a lot of good friends among managers of pension funds, insurance companies and savings and loans in order to sell this paper.

(This paper was not written down to reflect the probable loss until disaster struck, by which time the managers had their gains. Insofar as there was a pretense of revaluing the bonds to reflect the market price, it usually was a very thin and unreliable market, where prices were established by the investment bankers who arranged the original issue.)

Any well-trained economist will tell you that this cannot go on forever. In time savers will learn that they are being robbed by such fund managers and will no longer give them their money to invest. But this may be a long time. As an untrained but practical economist, P.T. Barnum, might have said, "There's an ignorant, trusting saver born every minute."

It probably is correct, however, that people will learn. The question is what they will learn. Here we may turn to the wisdom of another untrained economist, Mark Twain. He said: "A cat that sits on a hot stove once will never sit on a hot stove again. But neither will it sit on a cold stove." The cat cannot distinguish in advance between a hot stove and a cold one. The ordinary saver cannot distinguish in advance between a financial intermediary that will give him a fair shake and one that will not. He will learn not to trust financial intermediaries.

Financial intermediation is a vital organ of the modern capitalist system. Financial intermediaries take investments that are individually risky and illiquid but collectively safe and, by the application of pooling, diversification and expertise, produce assets that are safe and liquid for the passive saver to hold. This enables savings to flow into the kinds of investments that make the economy grow. The process requires that the managers of the intermediaries are free to use their judgment about investments. It also requires that savers trust the managers to use their judgment for the benefit of the savers and not at their expense.

At a minimum, the loss of trust raises the costs of intermediation. Savers require higher returns to compensate them for the risks of dealing with untrustworthy fund managers. Then some businesses that would be profitable and productive cannot be financed. The whole system becomes tilted to risk aversion and growth slows down.

At an extreme, an impasse develops. The private system cannot provide assets of the safety and liquidity that savers demand, and savers turn to what they regard as the only safe and liquid assets—money backed by the government or government securities. Then the system breaks down and high employment cannot be maintained unless the government provides the desired assets by running deficits or restores trust in the private intermediaries by insuring and regulating them—in which case they are no longer so private as they used to be.

This is not a science-fiction story. Something like this happened in the 1930s after trust in the private financial system had been lost. We got federal deposit insurance, federal mortgage insurance, the Securities and Exchange Commission and a battery of new regulations of private finance.

New movements to substitute government for trustworthy private financial institutions can already be seen. Talk of "reregulation" abounds. And there is much interest in the idea of "narrow banks," which would provide all checkable deposits and also other deposits for small savers and which could invest only in government securities. This is a peculiar admission that only the government can provide a safe asset. It raises the question of why the innocent investors in pension funds or in life insurance should bear the risks of the private sector.

Anyone who is concerned about the future of capitalism must see the dangers along this path. Those who want to defend capitalism will not do so by defending the people who have betrayed the trust of savers and by calling such behavior a necessary and beneficial feature of the system. That will only destroy their own credibility and debase the public image of the system. It is time for those businessmen, politicians and intellectuals who consider themselves the champions of capitalism to denounce those who are sabotaging it.

HERBERT STEIN

Milken's Accomplishments Not Such a Big Deal

In a statement at the U.S. Courthouse in Manhattan on April 25, Arthur Liman, Michael Milken's lawyer, said:

"It is an enormous accomplishment for Michael to have been instrumental in finding the capital for hundreds of American corporations, which are generating jobs, providing a livelihood for hundred of thousands of people. . . . It is Michael's hope that in the long run history will see his violation in context and judge him not just on the basis of his lapse but on the basis of the contributions that he made to the economy and to the American people."

This reflects an error that is common among people who have not been exposed to economics. It is like the claim that increasing defense spending creates jobs or that increasing imports destroys jobs. It fails to distinguish between what happens in a part of the economy and what happens to the economy in total, and it fails to recognize that there is an equilibrating mechanism in the economy that tends to keep capital and labor fully employed.

Reprinted from "Milken's Accomplishments: Not Such a Big Deal" by Herbert Stein. *The Wall Street Journal,* May 3, 1990. Reprinted by permission of the author.

No New Capital

Mr. Milken did not save or create the capital that he found for his corporate client. He attracted the capital from the people who saved it—mainly from savers who had put their money in insurance companies, mutual funds and savings and loans. He arranged for the sale of junk bonds to these institutions. If the institutions had not bought the junk bonds they would have invested the money in some other way, presumably in some other corporation but possibly in home mortgages.

Mr. Milken did not increase the net flow of capital into investment. He altered the direction of the flow. There are some corporations that received capital because of his efforts. We know their names and Mr. Milken can point to them. But there are corporations and potential home owners who, as a result of his efforts, were unable to obtain capital. We do not know their names, but they are real and important.

Because he did not increase the total stock of capital, and even if he did, Mr. Milken did not create jobs. Given a reasonably stable monetary environment, and Mr. Milken had nothing to do with that, people who seek jobs find jobs, except for market frictions with which Mr. Milken had nothing to do either. It is wrong to think that the people employed in Mr. Milken's client corporations would not have been employed there or elsewhere if it had not been for him.

The real issue is not the total flow of capital or the total amount of employment. It is whether Mr. Milken's efforts affected the quality of the investment made with the flow of capital and consequently affected productivity and incomes.

Here we must distinguish three kinds of cases:

a) The cases usually described on Mr. Milken's behalf where it is alleged that he corrected a market imperfection and improved the allocation of capital, making it more productive. The argument is that the market had overestimated the risks in junk bonds. As a consequence companies that depended on raising money by issuing junk bonds would have faced an unrealistically high risk premium in their cost of capital and would have been unable to make investments with a higher probable yield than the investments actually made by companies that financed themselves in other ways. By finding a market for these bonds that evaluated these risks more properly, it is said, Mr. Milken helped capital to flow to its more productive uses.

But there are two other kinds of possible cases.

b) Cases in which Mr. Milken nurtured and exploited a market imperfection and by so doing made the allocation of capital worse. These would be cases in which investment decisions were made not by the ultimate savers but by agents and dealers—investment bankers and managers of financial institutions—whose motivation was not the total productivity of the investment but the short-run cash flow that could be extracted as commissions, salaries and trading profits. The money of the passive savers was diverted into investments whose probable yield was less than could have been earned elsewhere and this reduced the productivity of investment.

c) Cases that had no effect on the real productivity of investment but only shifted wealth around. Financial institutions bought junk bonds whose proceeds were used to buy existing equities at prices well above the previous market prices and to pay commissions to the managers of the deals. The corporation does not acquire any additional capital in the process. It is only the shell for the transaction. The previous stockholders have a gain, the managers of the transaction have their fees and the investors in the financial institutions have assets for which they paid much more than markets previously thought they were worth and whose riskiness they did not prefer. In the case of the savings and loans these ultimate investors turned out to be the taxpayers.

I do not know in what proportions these kinds of cases existed, and I do not think that anyone else knows either. But I guess that the second and third kind were most important. I think that partly because, at least toward the end, when the flotation of junk bonds was largest, they came more and more to involve well-established corporations that probably would have had little difficulty raising capital in other ways. Also, I am impressed by the persistence of Mr. Milken's dominance of the junk bond market and by the size of his earnings. I wonder, what was his unique asset that allowed that? His initial insight that junk bonds were undervalued would, I suppose, not have remained unique for very long. But his Daisy Chain of money managers willing to subordinate the interests of clients to whom they had fiduciary responsibilities, and even to take the risk of going to jail, may have been more durable.

But this is only a speculation. If Mr. Milken's contribution to the American economy is to be an important factor in determining his sentence, a more serious effort should be made to evaluate that contribution than has been made to date. But I am not hopeful of finding an answer.

Loss of Confidence

Certainly Mr. Milken can afford to hire an econometrician who can "prove" that his contribution was large and positive. Probably the government can afford to hire an econometrician who will "disprove" it. And even the most objective analyst will probably be unable to render a verdict. By the time enough history has passed to see how Mr. Milken's transactions have come out so many other things will have happened that it will be impossible to isolate the effect of his activities from all the other noise in our data. Moreover, we shall never be able to measure the effect of the loss of confidence in financial markets generally that his activities caused.

Anyway, where is it written that criminals should be evaluated by the size of their contribution to the GNP—especially when the contribution was a byproduct of self-interested action?

The GNP does not include the value added by criminal activities, like prostitution or drug trade, so I don't know whether the Department of Commerce will include Mr. Milken's value added.

BRETT DUVAL FROMSON

Did Drexel Get What It Deserved?

Frederick Joseph, the head of Drexel Burnham Lambert, was precisely where no corporate executive wants to be when bad news hits—out of the office. He had taken a few days off to rest and relax at his farm in New Jersey when Chase Manhattan Bank refused to extend Drexel's credit line. Coming due the following Monday was $30 million of commercial paper for the firm's commodities subsidiary. Says a Drexel managing director: "The bank called up on Friday and said, 'Sorry, fellas, it's too risky for us. We're outta here.' We were caught with our pants down."

There is usually a rough justice in life, but only in novels is it as swift and direct as the fate that overtook Drexel Burnham Lambert Group when it declared Wall Street's largest bankruptcy in mid-February. Greed and mismanagement destroyed the innovative, aggressive firm. Says Irwin Jacobs, a Drexel-financed corporate raider, of the greed that afflicted the firm: "When you grab something that is too heavy, you break your arms. When you carry too much weight on your back—no matter if it is gold—you will break your back." From early 1989, when the firm agreed to plead guilty to six felony counts, it hurtled toward the dissolution that shocked Wall Street a year later.

Why did the end come so fast? Who is to blame? Who will suffer the most?

Joseph's initial surprise turned quickly to consternation that Friday afternoon when he arrived back in his office at the 11th-floor Drexel headquarters on 60 Broad Street in lower Manhattan. The commercial paper was an obligation of the holding company, Drexel Burnham Lambert Group, whose assets consisted of an illiquid junk bond portfolio. The firm's liquid capital was

Reprinted from "Did Drexel Get What It Deserved?" by Brett Duval Fromson. *Fortune,* March 12, 1990. © 1990 Time Inc. Magazine Company. All Rights reserved.

housed in its broker-dealer subsidiary, where there was in excess of $1 billion. The parent had been siphoning cash from the sub to meet its obligations until the transfers came to the attention of regulators at the Securities and Exchange Commission, which put a stop to them. The SEC insisted that the parent borrow against its own assets to raise capital, because the brokerage needed funds to protect its customers.

The firm was in the vulnerable position of having its liabilities and illiquid assets in one entity and its liquid capital potentially unreachable in another. Joseph isn't talking, but one of the top people at the firm says, "They took their eye off the ball when they set up the borrowing at the holding company level. It was just poor management. You have to have alternative sources of liquidity."

Joseph and his senior officers began a round of meetings over the weekend. They wanted a $300 million to $400 million bridge loan from their banks and offered a portion of the holding company's junk bond portfolio as collateral. The junk market had been skidding for months, however, and the SEC was not willing to give the banks an implicit government guarantee for any loans to Drexel. As a result, the banks lost confidence in the firm, which was not likely to be any commercial lender's favorite customer anyway. For years the investment house stole corporate clients from the stodgy banks with the help of junk bond financing.

If the banks delivered the first chop to Drexel's outstretched neck, the Federal Reserve was in charge of the guillotine. Fed Chairman Alan Greenspan and E. Gerald Corrigan, head of the New York Fed, were kept informed over the weekend of Drexel's desire to have the Fed help the firm by backstopping the bridge loan. There was a difference of opinion about whether a loan would save the firm, but it would buy time to liquidate the business in an orderly fashion.

The Fed was apparently no more favorably disposed toward this scheme than were Drexel's bankers. The central bank must have believed the securities markets could withstand Drexel's collapse. Moreover, Fed watchers say Greenspan was sending at least two messages to Wall Street: "We are not bailing out the junk bond business as we have the S&Ls" and "You can't plead guilty to six felonies and expect to be rescued by Uncle Sam."

Drexel executives venture another interpretation shared by many on Wall Street. Says one: "We were tough on the way up. We never made any friends. We stole business from other firms. We made the banks look silly. This was payback time. The Establishment finally got us." Adds G. Christian Andersen, a Drexel managing director in corporate finance: "You've just seen someone try to bury Camelot and pretend it never existed."

Monday was the meltdown. When word spread on the Street that Drexel's banks had withdrawn their credit lines, the firm's institutional customers stopped doing business with it. They feared Drexel would not be able to settle trades. Few were sorry for the firm. Says a New York City money manager: "I can still remember the first time that I was stiffed." In 1982 this fellow had bought some bonds from Drexel at 60 cents on the dollar, and a few weeks later when he wanted to sell them, Milken's traders told him they'd take them at 50 cents even though there had been no change in the creditworthiness of the issuer or the condition of the market. The money manager continues: "I said that I could understand a haircut, maybe 58 cents or even 57 cents—but 50! I was told if I didn't like it I could try selling the bonds through someone else. I won't miss Drexel."

The announcement that the parent company had declared Chapter 11 came on Tuesday, and by Wednesday phones were ripped out of the firm's huge, gray ninth-floor trading room. Says a former Drexel broker who witnessed the scene: "I've never seen anything so depressing in my life. Quotron machines were piled up. People were wandering around, so sad, so bitter. They don't know what happened to them." Adds a managing director in the mergers and acquisitions department: "We knew when we got part of our 1989 bonus in pay-in-kind paper that the firm had a liquidity problem. Heck, that was the stuff we used to sell, not buy. But we had no idea that it would end in bankruptcy."

What caused it to end that way is complex and controversial, and few want to take the rap, or the credit. But there are three people most responsible for Drexel's demise: Michael Milken, Rudolph Giuliani, and Fred Joseph.

Milken took too far an imaginative scheme for giving smaller unrated companies access to the market. The key to Drexel's junk bond machine, and its eventual undoing, was Milken's ability to maintain a market, or the illusion of it, in the junk bonds Drexel underwrote for these issuers. In most cases, he was both the supply and the demand—the only buyer when customers wanted to sell their bonds, and the only seller when customers wanted to buy. As long as everyone had confidence in Milken's ability to control the market, the game went on. By 1986 his machine had made Drexel Wall Street's most profitable firm, with earnings of more than $500 million on revenues of $5.3 billion.

By 1987, however, Milken yielded to the temptation to milk his genius and began underwriting companies that were less creditworthy than earlier ones had been. A source close to Milken admits: "Quantity became more important than quality. If Drexel couldn't market the security, they bought it for their own accounts rather than not do the deal." Unfortunately, when Drexel needed cash, this trash heap of private placements, junk bonds, and bridge loans, carried on the books for $2 billion, could not be sold for anywhere near that price.

Rudolph Giuliani, then U.S. Attorney for the Southern District of New York, began hunting the firm down with the help of Dennis Levine, a Drexel investment banker, and arbitrager Ivan Boesky, a Drexel customer, who both later pleaded guilty to securities-fraud-related offenses. Giuliani, who ran unsuccessfully for mayor of New York City, turned the Big Bertha of criminal prosecution—the Racketeer Influenced and Corrupt Organizations Act (RICO)—on his prey. Previously used to nail organized crime bosses and their henchmen, RICO gave Giuliani the power to close Drexel down *before* the firm's guilt or innocence could be proved in a court of law. The threat of being driven out of business scared Drexel's senior management. Says the Milken source: "Giuliani put the gun on the table and said to us, Either you pick it up and use it on yourself or I will."

Fred Joseph pulled the trigger: He agreed Drexel would plead guilty to six charges of mail and securities fraud, the firm would pay $650 million in fines and penalties, and Mike Milken would be removed from his position. Without Milken, the firm's one important franchise, junk bonds, began to unravel. Many of the biggest customers, like TWA's Carl Icahn and Revlon CEO Ronald Perelman, took their business to other firms that were beginning to poach more effectively on Drexel's theretofore private preserve.

Having painted Drexel into a corner, Joseph failed to find a way out. As the junk bond market weakened in 1989, he approved the underwriting and warehousing of even more dubious bridge loans and junk bonds to protect the so-called franchise. As a result, Drexel wound up with huge positions, for example, in West Point–Pepperell, William Farley's distressed textile company.

In trying to put the best face on a bad situation, Joseph compounded Drexel's problems. What he once described in *Fortune* as his "surprising naiveté" verged on deceit. He said that Drexel would not settle with the government. It did. He said that he would not abandon Milken. He did. He thanked the retail brokers for standing by the firm, and then a few months later he took Drexel out of the retail business. Traders at Drexel's West Coast office began calling him "Fred Isuzu."

Joseph's most disingenuous moment came one week before the bankruptcy, when he told the *Wall Street Journal:* "I see daylight. The worst is behind us." The company released unaudited 1989 financial results that showed Drexel with a plump net worth of $800 million and a mere $40 million loss for 1989. Subsequent events suggest that these numbers were more fiction than fact. The chief investment officer of a large Boston-based mutual fund organization received an unsolicited visit from Joseph before the year-end numbers were released to the public. It was a strange meeting, and Joseph's purpose was to say that Drexel was not going broke. By the end of the visit, however, this man was convinced that not even Joseph believed his own story.

The collapse of the junk bond market in January and February revealed more about Drexel's dire straits than Joseph did. Traders feared that a hard-up Drexel and its equally strapped clients would dump billions of dollars of junk to raise cash. Bids evaporated. Even the best credits could not be sold in volume. What was the market saying? Answers the head junk bond trader for a large insurance company: "Drexel was already dead meat."

So too may be most employees, who will be looking for jobs at other firms in the midst of an industry slump. Some 1,000 of them owned stock in the firm, and those whose retirement depended on cashing in their shares have been wiped out. But don't feel too sorry for senior management; they were paid big salaries and didn't spend it all on $1,000 suits. Says Marc Faber, a managing director of Drexel's Hong Kong office: "I hope they lose a hell of a lot of money, because they are the ones who brought the problems about."

Drexel's institutional customers who bought junk at par and have yet to mark the degraded securities to current market prices will have to own up to enormous losses. Bids for some bonds issued at par have been as low as 10 cents on the dollar. Most vulnerable are insurance companies like troubled First Executive, which loaded up on Drexel private placements and other offerings that were not widely distributed. Also at risk are junk bond mutual funds such as the New America High Income Fund, a closed-end fund with at least 70% of its portfolio invested in securities Drexel underwrote. But most junk bond mutual funds have sufficient cash reserves to meet the anticipated redemptions by justifiably concerned shareholders.

In a comically perverse twist to the story, two of Drexel's largest unsecured creditors could turn out to be Mike Milken and the Securities and Exchange Commission. The firm still owes Milken over $100 million in compensation that was to have been paid in 1988. The SEC stands to lose the final $150 million installment on the penalty that Drexel agreed to pay when it settled with the government in 1989. Will Drexel wind up stiffing them? They wouldn't be the first.

RICHARD BEHAR

We Grew Quickly and We Stepped on Toes—An Interview with Fred Joseph

Q. Many people feel that Drexel Burnham Lambert epitomized raw greed in the 1980s and that there is poetic justice in its demise.
A. That's primarily the result of how we were depicted in the press, and I think it's outrageous. The press has to capsulize things that people can absorb. The fact is, Drexel became the major source of capital for industrial companies in the country. Even our worst enemies think only a handful of people did anything wrong, so it's unfair to the vast majority of people at Drexel to lump them into a two-word tag line. The damage that's been done is absolutely unjustified. We grew quickly and we stepped on toes. But we did no more than other investment banks did when they hit periods of unusual competitive advantage.

Q. In the end, who killed Drexel? Was it the Government, your colleagues, or even you?
A. The destruction of Drexel at some point became inevitable. I'll accept the responsibility, and if I knew we had done things that were wrong, I would accept blame. What happened was a confluence of events, starting with the federal investigation [of Drexel's junk-bond department] and hitting a climax when the firm was forced to plead guilty and pay what we thought were unnecessarily high penalties [$650 million]. Congress then changed the rules by requiring savings and loans to sell their high-yield bonds, and the market for those securities fell. Then Drexel faced yet another rule change, when the regulators suddenly raised our capi-

Reprinted from "We Grew Quickly and We Stepped on Toes" by Richard Behar. *Time,* April 23, 1990. Copyright © 1990 The Time Inc. Magazine Company. All rights reserved. Reprinted by permission.

tal requirements. Literally overnight, they said we could no longer touch the $300 million in excess capital in our brokerage subsidiary.

Q. Shouldn't you have known there was impending doom?
A. We had cut costs 50%, and we believed the firm was going to operate profitably in 1990. The problem is that one day you have $300 million and the next day your banker tells you that you can't use it. That's troublesome. Within a day we were totally shut out of the capital markets.

Q. With a little nudging, couldn't the regulators have got the banks to save Drexel?
A. It's a capitalistic system. The banks and regulators are not charged with saving us, and we never asked for direct Government intervention. We did argue aggressively with the regulators, and there were moments when I was angry. I had hoped that the regulators would give some encouragement to the banks, which I don't think happened. I think Drexel's lack of friends—as perceived by the world—might have made it easier for a midlevel official in one of those agencies to not help us. In their eyes, we were lacking in political constituencies.

Q. Do you have any final words for Rudolph Giuliani, the former U.S. Attorney who launched the Drexel investigation?
A. The federal racketeering law, as applied to financial institutions, is a devastating nuclear bomb. The penalties we paid ended up doing material long-term damage to the firm, costing 11,000 people their jobs and costing the markets what most people will admit was a creative, innovative force for financing companies. All this because of alleged wrongdoing by a handful of people. It just seems unfair.

Q. Drexel was criticized for doling out more than $200 million in cash bonuses just weeks before its collapse.
A. A false picture has been painted. There was no expectation of the collapse at the time the bonuses were paid, and the vast majority of them were obligations from the previous year. . . .

Q. Did you ever fear that junk bonds were a house of cards?
A. I think that's rhetoric from the press and politicians. High-yield bonds are a $300 billion market and there will be cycles, but there's no question of their legitimacy.

Q. But wasn't the market too dependent on one man, former Drexel financier Michael Milken? And did his dismissal from Drexel cause irreparable harm to morale?
A. It's hard to judge midstride, as we are right now, whether the market was too dependent on Milken. It's going to take more time to know. Michael is incredibly knowledgeable, but our high-yield department was a major team effort. We put together the RJR-Nabisco deal after Milken. As for morale, he had some pretty fervent supporters in the company, but I don't think there was any irreparable discontent when he left. . . .

Q. Your colleagues say you always keep your cool. How do you cope?
A. Getting rattled doesn't help you perform. At this point we've taken Drexel's $25 billion of inventory positions down to around $1 billion, and I'm too busy to try to figure out the long-term psychological impact on me. But it's been very sad to watch the dismantling of what we built. We were trying to create the most effective investment bank in the country, and for a moment in time, we achieved that.

JAMES STERNGOLD

Drexel Awaits Permission to Close Shop in Japan

The improbably sudden collapse of the Drexel Burnham Lambert Group shocked Wall Street in February, as did the United States Government's willingness to stand aside as the firm crumbled to financial rubble. But one of those caught most off guard was Masahiko Yamamoto, manager of Drexel's Tokyo branch.

Along with a Drexel executive from New York, Mr. Yamamoto had spent the week before the bankruptcy reassuring his Japanese clients that the firm was sound. Then, after Drexel abruptly caved in, he called the Ministry of Finance to say he had been ordered to liquidate the office immediately. He was told he could not do so.

An Instructive Contrast

"It just was not allowed," Mr. Yamamoto recalled, as the still-shaken branch manager led a visitor through Drexel's now-deserted trading room, occupied only by empty desks, chairs and boxes of ballpoint pens for sale. "They said, 'You have responsibilities to take care of.' "

Robert E. Fallon, who had been managing director of corporate finance here for Drexel, added: "They were calm, but they really couldn't understand how something like this could be allowed to happen. They said, 'We license you—you can't simply close. We have to give you permission.' "

It may be just a footnote to the remarkable Drexel Burnham drama, but the Japanese Government's paternalistic reaction to the firm's demise provides an instructive contrast to how the situation was handled in the United States. It highlighted what

Reprinted from "Drexel Awaits 'Permission' to Close Shop in Japan" by James Sterngold. *The New York Times,* April 23, 1990. Copyright © 1990 by The New York Times Company. Reprinted by permission.

many Japanese see as an incomprehensible American bias toward letting the markets take their course, even if it sometimes causes great pain for some people.

It also underscored the strong Japanese emphasis on maintaining a cooperative relationship between government and business. It is unlikely that Japan would have stood for the kind of bitter and ultimately destructive battle waged with Federal prosecutors by Drexel before it admitted to serious securities law violations and by its "junk bond" mastermind, Michael R. Milken, who was said to have agreed Friday to plead guilty to six fraud charges. The situation would most likely have been handled here with a modest public confession, the resignation of senior executives willing to take the blame to save the firm, and as little disruption of the system as possible.

Daily Reports Demanded

"When we license a securities firm, it has certain responsibilities," explained Nobuchika Mori, deputy director of the Finance Ministry's securities company division and the official who worked closest with Drexel. "And we work with them to see things are done properly."

He added, "Compared to the United States, yes, we probably have a more helpful attitude to firms."

Under the Government's watchful eye—the Finance Ministry demanded daily reports of Drexel's dealings in Japan from the moment its American parent filed for bankruptcy—the liquidation of Drexel's Japanese operations, which once had more than 100 staff members and produced $50 million a year in revenues, was far more orderly than in New York.

"Our Japanese employees, were probably more shocked," Mr. Fallon said, "because they knew this could never happen to a Japanese firm."

Employees had to be given at least a month's notice before being laid off. Some severance payments had to be arranged. Previously agreed-upon pensions had to be guaranteed. Strenuous efforts had to be made to help people find new jobs. Customers' accounts, the Government's top priority, had to be safeguarded and transferred smoothly to other securities houses.

And Mr. Yamamoto, who is 44 years old, and a skeleton staff

are going to have to keep the office here open for another six months or so. That is to insure that all problems are resolved and that anyone with a claim has a chance to present it before the doors of the firm's elegant offices, in a modern Tokyo skyscraper overlooking the Imperial gardens, close for good.

Even when the dust settles, Drexel's collapse will not be forgotten quickly, at least not in Japan.

A Lift for Japanese Firms

Japanese securities houses and banks, which have lost some of their best traders and investment bankers in recent years to American firms, quietly rejoiced at the news. Since American firms generally pay two to five times as much as Japanese competitors, the Japanese could argue to wavering employees only that working for an American house gave them less job security. That argument is much more credible now.

"You hear a comment repeated every day now, 'The Americans are so unreliable,' " said Ann Natori, who had been one of Drexel's top Japanese bond salespeople here. She said she had considered joining a European bank, rather than another American firm.

Mr. Mori of the Finance Ministry said of American securities firms, "The impact on their reputations was not negligible."

Emphasis on 'Junk Bonds'

Drexel opened its branch here in 1985, just about the time that its business in America—underwriting offerings of low-grade, high-yield junk bonds and advising corporate raiders in takeovers and buyouts—was beginning to soar. Mr. Yamamoto, who had spent 16 years at Nomura Securities, the largest securities house in the world, was hired to run the Drexel branch.

It expanded steadily, relying largely on its ability to sell securities to Japanese institutions, particularly junk bonds. When the liquidation was ordered in February, it had 105 staff members here, including a dozen Americans.

About half of Drexel's annual revenues in Tokyo of $50 million came from selling junk bonds and United States Government bonds. The rest came from a combination of Japanese and American stock sales to its clients, Japanese institutions.

Profits of $10 Million a Year

The profits approached $10 million a year, before taxes, Mr. Yamamoto said. In short, the Japanese subsidiary was modest in size but healthy and it had no involvement in the abusive practices that regulators were investigating in the United States.

That generally favorable financial status was one reason Drexel's Japanese employees and the Government could not fathom why the office was shut down without some effort to sell it or keep it together.

"Most of the people thought that what they were hearing was just inconceivable—it was impossible," said Laurence M. Platoni, a vice president of administration in the office. "People were orderly, but the Japanese were saying: 'Such a thing is not possible. This is a good business. How can it just close?' "

Mr. Mori of the Finance Ministry said he was struck most by the fact that American regulators did not seem to have spotted or corrected Drexel's financial problems before they reached a crisis.

"We have early warning systems to catch problems," he said. "When a firm becomes unsound, we take precautions."

Mr. Yamamoto said the Finance Ministry quickly laid down its priorities. First, customer accounts had to be transferred safely to another firm. Second, the office had to maintain a satisfactory financial condition so that other firms would not suffer losses during the liquidation. Finally, new jobs had to be found for as many employees as possible.

"The Ministry of Finance said that they could not accept a lot of people becoming unemployed," Mr. Yamamoto added. "They helped us quite a lot in finding jobs for people."

A Humbling Task

Most of the Japanese employees have found new positions, Mr. Yamamoto said, but a number of the Americans, who face bleak job prospects back on Wall Street, are still unemployed. Drexel had enough money in its accounts to move the Americans and their families home, along with their belongings, Mr. Fallon said.

That move has left Mr. Yamamoto and a handful of his colleagues with the humbling task of sitting in the quiet offices and

handling the few remaining chores. There is no receptionist behind the once-busy front desk, neckties are loosened, and the
days crawl by.

"As a Japanese, I can tell you this could not happen in one day
in Japan," Mr. Yamamoto, standing in sandals before the empty
picture hooks on his sunny office wall, said with some bitterness.
"It's amazing, just amazing. I still think this must have been a
bad dream."

MARY ELLEN OLIVERIO

The J. C. Penney Story

. . . The current focus on ethics in business leads to some interesting questions: "Can a highly successful American company
establish clear, unambiguous rules of conduct and implement
them?" "Is American business too complicated to function according to a single code of ethics?" "Are the leaders of American
business too sophisticated to accept a code of ethics that clearly
establishes standards for all behavior?" "Are Americans living in
too mature a society to accept a single code of ethics?" "Is there
too much cynicism in our business world to improve ethical behavior?" "Is there too much anonymity in the workplace to expect people to care about high quality ethical behavior?"

The Lack of Prescriptions for Ethical Business Behavior
There seems to be little, if any, empirical evidence to answer
questions such as those in the preceding paragraph. Yet, at the
present time, there are concerns that the level of ethical behavior
in business needs improvement.

Possibly, there is value in exploring how ethical behavior was

Excerpted from "The Implementation of a Code of Ethics: The Early Efforts of
One Entrepreneur" by Mary Ellen Oliverio. *Journal of Business Ethics,* Vol. 8
(1989), pp. 367–373. © 1989 Kluwer Academic Publishers. Reprinted by
permission of Kluwer Academic Publishers.

described and encouraged in an earlier era in the United States. There are organizations in the United States that continue to recognize the early concern with ethics. One such company which includes its original code of ethical behavior whenever it reissues a code of conduct is the J. C. Penney Company, Inc. The original code was called The Penney Idea. Fortunately, the JCPenney Archives contain historical information that makes possible a review of how the statement was developed and what was done in the company to implement it.

The Early Observations That Influenced The Penney Idea

In early publications of the J. C. Penney Company, J. C. Penney described some of his observations as a young man that had powerful impact on his attitudes about how business should function. Penney was born on a farm in 1875, the seventh of twelve children. His father was a minister. As a young man he served as a clerk in several retail stores, where he observed the practices of the owners. In one store, he saw the owner pour the same coffee beans into two different tins, and there were two different prices for the tins. On another occasion, he noted that some stockings were marked 25 cents while the same stockings were also marked 2 for 25 cents. When he raised a question about the two prices, the owner of the store informed him that when a customer was unwilling to accept the 25 cent stockings, the customer was to be shown the 2 for 25 cent. Penney wrote that he felt uncomfortable about these practices and believed that they were foolish in the long run . . .

In an interview in 1924 Penney reflected on an early experience where he felt that he must adhere to his beliefs, even though he faced failure in his business venture. He told his story to an interviewer:

> I put all my energy into that business. (A butcher store that he had bought in Longmont, Colorado) I studied it from every point. And yet that shop failed in a single year. And I lost every cent I had. I'll tell you why: The butcher told me at the outset that in order to get business and to hold it you had to make certain inducements to

the cooks in town. The most valuable customer was the cook in the hotel.

The butcher said that the way to obtain his trade was to give him a bottle of whisky every Saturday night. "Now, I had been brought up in a family where liquor was an abhorrence. My father was a strict prohibitionist and so was my mother. I had learned to hate the sight of whisky as a boy, and even now it makes my blood boil to see men drinking. But I did buy a bottle of whisky for that hotel cook the first week. When I had done it my conscience began to trouble me. What would my father say?" kept running through my mind. Then I made the decision which cost me my business but I held to it.

I would buy no more whisky for anyone. The butcher remonstrated with me. He told me that I was bound to lose out, which was true. But I refused, and in a year my shop was cleaned out . . .

In 1899, Penney began working in a store where each item had one price. He observed that it was possible to wait on 1/3 to 1/2 more customers than had been his experience in stores where pricing was done differently. He also believed that the single price was so much fairer—more honest—than the varied prices for a single item. As he wrote:

This way of merchandising had a wonderfully stimulating effect and influence on my life. It was my experience in this honest, one price store that gave me my inspiration for a system of stores. In this environment I fairly felt myself grow in every way. Life in that clean, honest business atmosphere took on an ever greater promise, for I had been taught at home that honesty is the best policy . . .

Opportunities in Retailing in the Early Years of This Century

The early days of this century were highly successful days for a number of retailing establishments. Towns and cities were growing; the need for consumer goods intensified as more people were working for others; the domestic tasks were being somewhat transformed, thus, there was considerable demand for goods produced by others.

At the same time, there was a realization that the practices of the itinerant peddler were unfair and inappropriate for the new retailing establishments. While the itinerant peddler may have believed that the buyer had to beware, the newly established retail stores hoped for return business and found it profitable to develop an image of honesty and integrity.

Penney wrote of his respect for the philosophy of John Wanamaker and Marshall Field. These men, along with others, were changing the character of retailing in the United States . . .

> John Wanamaker instituted a money back guarantee. He believed the retailer had to render a real service to the community . . .

> Marshall Field believed that misrepresentation of merchandise was suicidal to any business. He admonished his employees never to misrepresent any article. They were to make no promise which could not be fulfilled . . .

The Implementation of Beliefs

Penney began to implement his beliefs when he was given the opportunity to become a manager/part owner of a new store in Kemmerer, Wyoming in 1902. The store was 25 by 45 feet; the living quarters for him, his wife, and small son were the upper story of the building. Furniture was cartons from the store. In later years, Penney noted that their physical needs were of secondary importance to them. The primary attention was to the business and its progress. He had borrowed $1500 for his share of the store. He sought to assure the success of the business, so that the debt would be paid off. It was paid off in five years . . .

Earl C. Sams joined Penney in 1907. Sams was 23 years old at the time . . . In reminiscing about the early days, Sams recalled how he and Penney would remain in the store after working hours and talk about business and how they should run theirs. Often the discussion turned to the qualities that were deemed critical for success in business. Much attention was focused on a man's character. These men believed that a man's character was basic . . .

The success of the first store encouraged Penney to venture

forth with other stores. He believed that the success of the business depended on the quality of the men who were selected as owner/managers. He designed a plan that permitted immediate partnership status for any man joining the company. Penney seems never to have forgotten the way in which he was admitted to partnership in the Kemmerer, Wyoming store. He felt that the original owners of the Kemmerer store were very generous toward him. He wanted to treat his associates as he had been treated.

By the time of the 1913 meeting, where the first written code of ethics was presented, there were 34 stores and 325 employees. Sales had reached $3,000,000 a year. Penney believed that a basic code of conduct was needed if there was to be a uniform system of stores. The thinking which he and Sams had done in the early days of the first store had continued. When C. E. Dimmitt joined the company in 1911, he began to participate in thinking about a code of ethics. Dimmitt is credited with shaping up the basic ideas that were to be The Penney Idea. At the 1913 meeting, the final statement was presented to all the men who were managing stores and were also owners. The original statement is shown in Figure 1.

Also, at that first national meeting in 1913, partners were asked to be participants in what was called an "Obligation Ceremony." This required a pledge from each and was designed to encourage the partners to maintain high standards of conduct. Later, the title was changed to the "Affirmation Ceremony." The ceremony was actually more than a pledge of loyalty to a company of partners; it was an affirmation to oneself as well, a personal commitment to a life of honesty, integrity, and moral leadership both within and outside the company . . .

In 1927 while reflecting on the early days, Sams made the following comments:

> . . . Every man who joined our group—in those early days—was personally selected by Mr. Penney. And in the formation of the original [company], the type and kind of associates sought for and obtained were:
>   Men of character and ability
>   Men of unselfish aims

THE PENNEY IDEA

Adopted 1913

1

To serve the public, as nearly as we can, to its complete satisfaction.

2

To expect for the service we render a fair remuneration and not all the profit the traffic will bear.

3

To do all in our power to pack the customer's dollar full of value, quality and satisfaction.

4

To continue to train ourselves and our associates so that the service we give will be more and more intelligently performed.

5

To improve constantly the human factor in our business.

6

To reward men and women in our organization through participation in what the business produces.

7

To test our every policy, method and act in the wise: "Does its square with what is right and just?"

Fig. 1.

Men who, in seeking the opportunity, know full well that dividends would be paid to them only as the result of a demonstration of worthiness.

Men who, in their business and social conduct, would not swerve from a line of procedure and personal action, which was planned to represent that which was right and fair to all, and a living example for others . . .

Reinforcement of Basic Ethical Position

Conventions, letters, bulletins issued from the national company reiterated again and again the basic ethical standards established in 1913. An important communication medium was established in April, 1917 with the monthly publication of the house organ, *The Dynamo*. Every issue in a number of ways included advice and stories related to ethics. Two examples are:

> I believe that honesty wins. The kind of honesty that keeps a man's fingers out of his neighbor's till, of course, but the finer honesty that will not allow a man to give less than his best, the kind of honesty that makes him count not his hours but his duties and opportunities, that finer honesty that constantly urges him to enlarge his information and to increase his efficiency . . .

> Character is the very foundation of our organization. It is what we really are. It is the principle upon which our business exists. It is worth more to us than all else we possess.

> The improving of the character of our organization is the greatest work that we can perform. If we do not build its character it is bound to decrease. . . .

> It is the power of character that creates good will and makes customers. There is no question but what the public buy their merchandise from individuals and firms of high standing; from those in whom they have the utmost confidence . . .

The Personal Position of J. C. Penney

Penney appears to have understood exactly what he believed and to have the ability to translate the beliefs about human behavior into practical, everyday behaviors for those who worked in his organization. His own behavior as well as his communications reinforced what he believed. He had a vision of good moral behavior and he understood the strategy for its implementation. "Honesty is the best policy" in the early days of this century as implemented by Penney was a good business decision, in the tradition of the classical businessperson. It implies that one should be honest because such a practice will lead to the most

successful results in your business endeavor. It was good business
to be honest. However, there were statements made again and
again by Penney that reflected something more than this. His
statements reflected the belief that there was an intrinsic value to
being honest. Penney stated many times that he could not remember a time when the Golden Rule was not his motto and
precept—the torch that guided his footsteps.

One manager stated in 1917:

> The J. C. Penney Company enjoys the reputation of being a char-
> acter and man builder as well as a builder of profits.
>
> It is because there always has been and always will be that ener-
> getic spirit of efficient honesty, directing and developing its affairs,
> not because honesty is the best policy, but because honesty is right
> and always has been and always will be until the end of time.

Penney, as reflected in his letters, his speeches, and his policies
for the developing company, believed there was a close relationship between honorable personal behavior and business success.

Penney was functioning in a world where the truths about
human behavior were stated in absolute terms. He was reared in
a religious home; he believed that one's behavior must reflect
honorable attributes. He saw his business as successful to the
extent that the partners worked hard, were careful with resources, and were honest in all their dealings. He saw personal
behavior as of the same source as business behavior. For example,
he felt that new partners should receive very little remuneration
initially. The new partners must exhibit basic concern for doing a
good job and at the same time disinterest in their own personal
welfare. The sacrifices one faced in getting a store underway were
deemed to be excellent training for one's character.

Penney wrote about ethical concerns; he spoke at meetings and
at annual conventions. One speech, illustrative of his presenta-
tions, was entitled, "The Four-Square Man". The "four squares"
were: purpose, integrity, service, and in tune with the infinite. In
his discussion of integrity, Penney said:

> An honest man is a whole man, not a fraction of a man. He is not
> one thing above the line and something else below the line; not one

thing at home and something else away from home, but a whole man.

I do not mean to apply this to the handling of money alone. Some men think so long as they can get by, or keep out of jail, that they are honest. A man of integrity is a man of sterling worth, a man of character, a man whose word is as good as his bond; a man who would not think of taking a minute of time that does not belong to him; a man honest with himself.

My father used to say that he never aspired to be rich; but he wished that when life was over, people in passing his grave might say, "Here lies an honest man." This statement of my father's has had a tremendous influence on my life.

The moral grandeur of independent integrity is the sublimest thing in nature; so, if a man is a man of integrity, a man of purpose, he is well on his way to the four-square man . . .

Throughout the years, first as an active leader in the company, and later as chairman of the board, Penney participated in very personal ways to communicate the basic business philosophy of the company. The implications of the code of the behavior were constantly being drawn in the publications and policies promulgated by the national headquarters.

On one occasion, Penney made the following statement:

By discipline a man subjects himself to rules of conduct and to habits of obedience in order that he may move directly toward the ideal that inspires him. As a man's character is, so will be his conduct. It is the individual morality which determines the character of this, our great organization, the J. C. Penney Company . . .

What Can Be Learned from J. C. Penney's Experience

. . . This is the basic lesson that can be learned from Penney: that the role of the top executive is paramount in establishing the culture within which business activity takes place. Penney had a set of principles that guided his behavior. Penney practiced what he believed. As the company leader in the early years, he established the culture of the company to be one where dishonest behavior would not be tolerated. The character of applicants was of primary importance. Penney had a clear vision of the behavior that he believed reflected good character. New managers participated in a ceremony that highlighted their commitment to high ethical behavior.

Penney and his colleagues in top management established policies and procedures that would support the ethical behavior reflected in the code of ethics. One critical component was giving partnership status to managers, who then would clearly share in the success of the business. Managers were expected to accept personal responsibility in carrying through the requirements of their jobs.

Penney lived in what now appears to have been a simple business world when compared with the contemporary business world. In fact, his statements may seem old-fashioned and inappropriate for today. For several decades, we have lived with the basic attitude that truth is relative. However, there appears to be emerging some discontent with this attitude. There is awareness developing that possibly some beliefs and attitudes are timeless and do indeed have relevance today. Also there is growing concern with the current level of moral behavior. Some are saying there is need for higher ethical behavior in the work environment. Evidence is being revealed that clearly shows that some people have gained large sums of money from their unethical behavior and others are hurt by such behavior. It was from such evidence, for example, that the National Commission on Fraudulent Financial Reporting (Treadway Commission) was established.

The recommendations of the Treadway Commission are being considered in companies throughout the United States. That task of implementation is not simple. And, the goals implied in the recommendations are not likely to be realized unless there is a genuine, wholehearted commitment to the substantive matters involved. Writing a code of ethics, establishing procedures for communicating the code to all employees, and setting aside time in the schedule of internal auditors to check compliance may give the aura of introducing a higher level of ethical behavior. However, even though such actions are necessary, they are not sufficient to assure success. There must be a constant, thorough, pervasive style of attention and assessment to ethical concerns if there is to be a difference in behavior throughout an entity. Penney's beliefs and actions may communicate something of value to today's business leaders and managers.